Teaching Tips
for College and
University Instructors

Related Titles of Interest

Teaching Tips for College and University Instructors

A Practical Guide

David Royse
University of Kentucky

Allyn and Bacon
Boston • London • Toronto • Sydney • Tokyo • Singapore

Executive editor: Stephen D. Dragin
Series editorial assistant: Barbara Strickland
Marketing manager: Stephen Smith
Manufacturing buyer: Chris Marson

Between the time Website information is gathered and then published, it is not
unusual for some sites to have been closed. Also, the transcription of URLs can
result in unintended typographical errors. The publisher would appreciate
notification where these occur so that they may be corrected in subsequent
editions. Thank you.

Many of the designations used by manufacturers and sellers to distinguish their
products are claimed as trademarks. Where those designations appear in this
book, and Allyn and Bacon was aware of a trademark claim, the designation has
been printed in caps or initial caps.

Library of Congress Cataloging-in-Publication Data

Royse, David D. (David Daniel)
    Teaching tips for college and university instructors : a practical guide / David Royse.
        p. cm.
    Includes bibliographical references and index.
    ISBN 0-205-29839-7
    1. College teaching--United States--Handbooks, manuals, etc. 2. College
teachers--United States--Handbooks, manuals, etc. I. Title.
LB2331 .R695 2001
378.1'2--dc21   00-038976

Printed in the United States of America
10 9 8 7 6 5 4 3 2 1   04 03 02 01 00

Contents

Preface

Robert Audi (1994) has written a sentence that I love: "Nearly everyone is sometimes a teacher and sometimes a student." What's intriguing about this line is that although we think of the roles of teacher and student as being very distinct, anyone who has ever stood in front of a class for the first time as a teacher is acutely aware of how uninformed one can feel, how much more there is to learn.

This book is offered to the reader as a guide—a handbook, if you will—because there are times when every new teacher needs a little practical advice. The graduate education we acquired in our specialized fields didn't prepare most of us for all of the situations and problems that can arise during an academic term. Once in the classroom, it is not unusual for new instructors (and sometimes very experienced ones, too) to wish that they knew quite a bit more about teaching.

Teaching is not a cakewalk. As Sawyer, Prichard, and Hostetler (1992) have noted, today's students are highly oriented to personal goals as well as sensitized to consumer issues (e.g., "My tuition pays your salary"), and there is an ethos of entitlement. If students feel defrauded in some way, they are quick to complain to administrative authorities. At the same time, cheating and plagiarism are widespread. "Students mean to succeed" (p. 209) one way or another. They are neither intimidated by authority nor embarrassed by their own lack of knowledge. Faculty are constantly challenged to master new technologies to keep from drowning in oceans of literature and new knowledge, as well as called to become teachers of distinction and world renowned researchers. The demands on the newest faculty members are even tougher than on those with tenure. Although the newcomer is "a specialist in a discipline and has been hired for expertise in a specialization, that very same newcomer is also a rank amateur on the new campus" (Menges & Associates, 1999, p. 3).

Teaching is a complex activity that is, in some ways, like a three-dimensional puzzle. In one dimension, the pieces we want to assemble are the core essentials, the knowledge that we hope to transmit or help students discover. On another level, there are the situational variables associated with every unique class—each one has its own temperament and personality. The group may be anxious or unfriendly; their interest and ability vary greatly from section to section. And on the third level are the individuals who compose the class—each with different life experiences, learning styles, deficits, and motivation. At times the instructor is a coach, at times a consultant, and not infrequently a catalyst and agitator.

Teaching is both an art and a science. The art of teaching refers to an almost intuitive knowing, such as when to provide a dash more structure to a class, when to "cook" a discussion just a bit longer, or when a particular student needs a word of encouragement. Seasoned educators learn to "read" a class—to recognize when students have not done their assignments, when a break is needed, or when to pay attention to this or that complaint.

In terms of the science, there is research on teaching that has investigated effective classroom procedures and that provides guidance to support certain teacher behaviors and favorite practices. New instructors can benefit from learning about the existence of this body of knowledge.

This book blends existing research with veteran educators' suggestions and tips. Its mission is to substitute for the missing mentor, the kindly colleague who doesn't mind answering yet another question about classroom management or test construction. *Teaching Tips for College and University Instructors* is not an exhaustive theoretical treatise; similarly, it does not delve into historical origins or roots of educational theory. Simply, it anticipates questions and problems common to all college and university educators and offers practical solutions and recommendations. Additional references and resources are available at the end of each chapter for those who want to do more in-depth reading on a topic.

Teaching Tips can be read cover to cover, serve as a textbook for graduate students preparing for teaching careers in higher education, or used as a reference—sitting ready on the shelf for the next time the reader needs a quick consultation.

Acknowledgments

My appreciation goes to the following reviewers for their helpful comments on the manuscript: Ann Austin, Michigan State University; Ken Bain, Northwestern University; and Jon Travis, Texas A & M University–Commerce.

I dedicate this book to Martha Tarry Simpson. As a gangly high school student, I had no appreciation of the formidable obstacles she faced in teaching English to the Class of '66 with all its attendant distractions of adolescence and Vietnam. There was, however, no mistaking her love of teaching, her ardor for literature, her passionate wish for each of us to do our best. Could there be a finer role model?

References

Audi, R. (1994). On the ethics of teaching and the ideals of learning. *Academe, 80* (5), 27–36.

Menges, R., & Associates. (1999). *Faculty in new jobs: A guide to settling in, becoming established, and building institutional support.* San Francisco: Jossey-Bass.

Sawyer, R. M., Prichard, K. W., & Hostetler, K. D. (1992). *The art and politics of college teaching.* New York: Peter Lang.

Contributors

Dinah Anderson is an assistant professor in the College of Social Work at the University of Kentucky. She is experienced in teaching via interactive television—broadcasting simultaneously to six sites and encouraging students' responses as if they were all in the same classroom. She has a keen appreciation for ethical dilemmas and issues.

Jonathan Golding is a social psychologist and an associate professor in the Department of Psychology at the University of Kentucky. He has won the Chancellor's Award for Teaching Excellence both in the tenured (1998) and nontenured (1994) categories and was a finalist on three other occasions. Golding is the coeditor of a book, *Intentional Forgetting* (1998), and the author of over 45 professional journal articles and book chapters. He enjoys teaching the large lecture course, Psychology 101, and consistently gets great evaluations from his students.

Cate Pearson is formerly a learning skills instructor at the University of Kentucky's Counseling and Testing Center. She has degrees in education and social work and is currently employed as a therapist working with adolescents.

David Royse is the associate dean and director of graduate studies in the College of Social Work at the University of Kentucky. He is the author of four other books—*Research Methods in Social Work* (1999), *Field Work: A Guide for Social Work Students* (1999), *Program Evaluation: An Introduction* (2000), as well as *How Do I*

Know It's Abuse? (1994)—and over 50 professional journal articles and book chapters.

Bradford W. Sheafor is a professor of social work at Colorado State University and is the associate dean for research in the College of Applied Human Science. Sheafor is the author of *Social Work: A Profession of Many Faces* (8th edition, 1998), *Techniques and Guidelines for Social Work Practice* (5th edition, 2000), *Practice-Sensitive Social Work Education* (1995), and numerous articles. He has been teaching at the university level since 1964 and is the former president of the Council on Social Work Education.

Brandon A. Sheafor is a relatively new (1997) assistant professor at Mt. Union College in Alliance, Ohio, and thus brings the perspective of a new instructor to this text. He was a teaching assistant for two years at Colorado College and won its Excellence in Teaching Award in the Department of Environmental, Population, and Organismic Biology in 1997.

Julie Vargas is a professor in the Department of Advanced Educational Studies at West Virginia University. She is author or coauthor of three books, numerous articles, and several computer-assisted instruction programs. Vargas is the former president of the Association for Behavior Analysis.

Linda Worley is an associate professor in the German Department at the University of Kentucky and a former director of the university's Teaching and Learning Center—a resource center and clearinghouse for teaching-related services, consultation, and programs. In 1991, she won the Chancellor's Award for Teaching Excellence.

1

The Mental Groundwork

Overview: You've received your first teaching appointment or teaching assistantship. Congratulations. Now, how do you start preparing for that first class?

Before selecting a text or creating a syllabus, before planning assignments or requesting audiovisual resources, it is imperative that the new instructor takes some time to thoughtfully consider the process of teaching—that is, to examine assumptions and beliefs about how students learn, how they differ, and what exactly the role of the educator is. Along this line, Brookfield (1995) has written:

> *We teach to change the world. The hope that undergirds our efforts to help students learn is that doing this will help them act toward each other, and toward their environment, with compassion, understanding, and fairness. But our attempts to increase the amount of love and justice in the world are never simple, never unambiguous. What we think are democratic, respectful ways of treating people can be experienced by them as oppressive and constraining. One of the hardest things teachers have to learn is that the sincerity of their intentions does not guarantee the purity of their practice. (p. 1)*

This chapter is designed to introduce the new educator to foundational considerations about the teaching enterprise before tackling the "nuts and bolts" typically associated with teaching.

How Do You View Yourself as an Educator?

A sociologist by the name of Austin L. Porterfield maintained that in every interaction with another person, a family of eight is created. There is, for example, the person I am, the person you are, the person I think I am, the person you think you are, the person you think I am, the person I think you are, the person I think you think I am, and the person you think I think you are. The point, of course, is that there are multiple ways of viewing ourselves. And not only that, but the image we think we project may be different from the one students perceive.

As an instructor in a classroom, you will convey a definite persona to the students. Back in their dorms, or walking across campus, or in the cafeteria, or as they drop coins into vending machines, students will discuss the character you portray before them. Unless you have exceptional students and are on a pinnacle by yourself, it is likely they won't be talking about your towering intellect or the frothy cerebral discussions you orchestrate three times a week. If you were to overhear their discussions, they would be likely conversing about how "hard" the last test was, perhaps how today's assignment was "a breeze," or how "nice" you were in giving them a take-home exam.

How do you want to be viewed by students? Almost all of us want to be liked. However, at times our notion of the educator's role may work against our winning any popularity contests on campus. How will your students view you?

To be sure, some faculty in every college diligently work to create a reputation not unlike that of a Marine Corps drill instructor. They assign 14 books to be read in a single semester, require 50-page term papers, and design final examinations that few can pass. These educators often love the power associated with being in charge and want to intimidate students. One such instructor introduced herself to every new class by bragging that she had been elected as a faculty trustee on the university's Board of Trustees—which is, she went on to explain, "a very important position, indeed." Students generally are afraid to challenge these instructors and may not ask questions in their classes or stop by their offices to ask for assistance.

On the other end of the spectrum, there are the popular faculty whose offices are almost student lounges. Whenever these faculty are in, the foot traffic in the hall is a steady stream to Mecca. All day long there is a procession of students waiting to share something personal, a story of mistreatment from a boyfriend or girlfriend, the death of a cat named Mephistopheles. At times laughter cascades from their offices, causing scholarly neighbors to shut their doors against the noise. These popular faculty complain a bit too happily about their work not getting done because of students dropping in to chat. "I'm going to set aside just a *few* hours every week to meet with students," they say disingenuously.

Besides these, there are other types you may have encountered in higher education: the serious researcher for whom teaching is not a high priority; the conscientious instructor who tries to encourage and empower students; the eager novice; and the burned-out, been-teaching-too-long academic. Each one has certain priorities and goals, and can be identified by distinguishing characteristics.

Whether we want to be viewed by students as "tough" or "easy" is often a conscious decision. We may, for instance, decide to be hard-nosed because we feel that the curriculum needs to be upgraded, or that our colleagues aren't asking enough of students. Sometimes when there are too many pupils in a course or enrolled in a given program, assignments and tests may be designed to weed out the weaker students. The opposite can happen, too. A faculty member going up for tenure may lighten course expectations to minimize the risk of student complaints and to help guarantee good course evaluations.

How do you want to be viewed by students? If the first thought that jumped into your mind was, "I want to be their friend," then you need to understand that students, being naturally perceptive, will realize this. And, there are two main drawbacks to having a friendship type of relationship with your students. First, students may attempt to use that relationship to their advantage, perhaps convincing you to cancel certain assignments or quizzes. When there is something akin to a equality of power in the classroom, students will find it easier to disagree with you about the educational value and importance of whatever you've planned.

Second, it is hard to be objective with our friends. You will find it difficult to give a low grade to a favorite student with whom you play tennis twice a week or to the one you meet for coffee every Friday morning. This is not to say that you shouldn't get to know your students—learning about them, their life experiences, and goals is one of the pleasures of teaching. However, just be aware that how students relate to you and perhaps even what they learn will be dependent on how you view yourself as an educator.

If you want to be considered as the "hardest instructor" in the philosophy or chemistry department, that's fine—just be clear in your own mind why you want that reputation. Particularly if you are new to a faculty, you need to think about what you gain and what you lose. Often, the more demands you make and the less flexible you are in accommodating students, the more problems you create for yourself. But you have to judge the climate at your institution. If you sense that the department is wanting you to go in with guns blazing, or if your mentor, dean, chief advocate, or best friend on campus is giving you advice to be less of a marshmallow—then you've got to toughen up. But all of this is a little premature. We don't need to worry about how tough we're going to be yet. Let's begin by thinking about what's important to us as educators.

Developing a Philosophy of Teaching

Imagine, for a moment, the best instructor you encountered during college or graduate school. How did that individual teach? What teaching style did he or she employ? If you were somehow able to interview your nominees for "The Best Teacher Ever," what would they reveal about their philosophies of teaching?

It almost goes without saying that excellent teachers, as well as poor ones, have influenced your thinking about what makes a good teacher. Specifically, they've furnished vivid examples of successful and not so successful ways to teach and treat students. Maybe you even decided on a teaching career yourself because of an exposure to a truly inspirational teacher or one who was so pathetic that you concluded that you could do better.

Do you see yourself (with apologies to Yeats) as "filling empty pails" or "lighting fires"? Do you view your mission as that of a dispenser of information or a facilitator who brings together resources and opportunities enabling students to make their own discoveries? Is teaching a process of mutual inquiry? Schoenfeld and Magnan (1992) have observed: "Faculty tend to teach as they themselves were taught; it's what they know and it has worked for them. But there are other approaches and techniques.... Approaches and techniques handed down from one generation of faculty to the next need to be examined and revised (p. 113). Similarly, Palmer (1998) has noted, "The way we diagnose our students' condition will determine the kind of remedy we offer" (p. 41).

What do you believe is important in teaching and what do you want to accomplish with your teaching? Indeed, what is the faculty member's role in the educational process? It might be helpful for you to jot down your thoughts. Do that now, and then we'll compare notes.

My Philosophy of Teaching: What I Believe Is Important

_____

_____

_____

_____

_____

_____

_____

_____

_____

_____

_____

Writing out your teaching philosophy is an exercise in making your unconscious assumptions explicit. Reviewing what you've written, you might discover that what emerged was a concern with imparting knowledge or skills. Or perhaps your philosophy centered on the importance of your students learning to become independent, creative thinkers. Maybe even a particular teaching approach (e.g., collaborative learning, problem-centered instruction) materialized. When I engaged in this exercise myself (it was required when I went up for promotion), these were some of the elements I identified as important to me as an educator:

Creating a Sense of a Community: *Students have a more enjoyable and more profitable learning experience when they feel connected to each other and to the faculty member.* To build a community of learners, students need to know something about each other. (An activity that I often do at the beginning of each semester is to have students introduce themselves—sometimes in a word or two. Often, it becomes great fun as students say unexpected and outrageous things, such as "pizza delivery boy," "chocoholic," or "married five times." In every class there are several who describe themselves as "quiet" or "shy." Sometimes it's appropriate to tell a quick anecdote about myself. It seems only fair to share something about myself if I ask students to reveal something about themselves.)

The use of ice-breakers assists the instructor in remembering students' names and also helps students to break down barriers and to get to know each other. On many occasions, students are surprised to find someone in the classroom from their hometowns or with similar interests. Especially when students move into a new city, not knowing anyone else, even a wobbly link to another person can be strangely gratifying and reduce one's anxiety. When there is no longer a sense that "we're all strangers," human resources within the classroom are made more available. Students who can draw on the support of others are less likely than those without comrades to fail or drop the class. Knowing a little about each of the students personalizes the experience and makes teaching far more gratifying. (Note: More discussion on ice-breakers is found in Chapter 3.)

Even after the first meeting, the instructor can continue to build a community within the classroom by such activities as dividing the class into pairs or small groups and creating opportunities for them to interact with each other. By the end of the term, students will not only know each other's names but they will also have become study partners and often friends as well.

Viewing Education as a Two-Way, Interactive Process: *I am not infallible, unerring, or The Authority On All Matters.* When I first began teaching, I erroneously believed that I had to be The Expert. My mission, I thought, was to transmit knowledge and it flowed only one way—from me to the students. The problem with that perspective is that occasionally I would be asked a question that I couldn't answer. It made me very uncomfortable, until I realized that I don't know everything. Now, almost 20 years later, I am comfortable saying, "I don't know. What do you think?"

Over that span of time, I've had students who have flown jet fighters, been professional tennis players, and worked for escort services. A few have been alcoholics and drug addicts. Even before coming into my classroom, some students have received degrees in law, nursing, or theology. One student left a lucrative job as a chemist when his best friend committed suicide. Another was an accomplished engineer who conducted state-of-the-art laser experiments before an airplane accident left him a paraplegic. Each student has life experiences and knowledge that I don't—and so I don't worry about being an authority on every issue. Sometimes someone in the class is more knowledgeable than I am on the topic being discussed. If the right atmosphere is created, the classroom is a forum where information can be shared openly and intelligently and issues discussed in a way that invites, not imposes, learning.

A major responsibility of the instructor is to ask good questions—not solely to disseminate information. As students tackle hard questions, they will respond with questions of their own, which will often stimulate new insights or learning—even on the educator's part.

Respect for the Individual: *Because I care about every one of my students, I take attendance at each class meeting.* Students are asked about extended absences if they don't volunteer an explanation. It's not in students' best interests to miss a lot of lectures. I try to respect each student—to realize that they may have jobs or family responsibilities that occasionally take priority over their assignments and tests.

I also try to show my respect by welcoming and completely listening to each question raised or comment spoken in class. The classroom is a laboratory, and each participant should feel free to speculate, to try new ideas out. I don't want anyone to leave the class feeling that he or she asked a stupid question. Usually, if one student raises a question, other less vocal students are probably wondering the same thing. Just about every remark or question provides the opportunity for a mini-lesson or a "teaching moment."

I want to hear my students' stories, to encourage their creativity, and to empower them to find their own solutions.

Accountability: *The instructor should be accountable to his or her students.* I have a responsibility to be prepared each and every class meeting. Being in the classroom well before time to start, starting class on time, stopping on time, specifying in the syllabus when readings will be discussed and when assignments are due communicates early on that there are expectations attached to *this* course. It is important to role-model accountability and so promptly returning all tests, assignments, and so forth—usually at the next class meeting—should be a goal. Being accountable also means that students have sufficient information to be able to compute their grades at any point during the course, because they know the points they received and the specific criteria used in evaluation. The syllabus should be regarded as a contract that is followed unless extenuating circumstances arise. Even then, the class is entitled to an explanation and the opportunity to discuss the necessity for making changes.

Accountability also means giving students the opportunity to evaluate the instructor, even when it's not required. Using this information for continued improvement of the educational process is valued, even though from time to time students' comments can be petty or barbed.

Humor: *Learning can be and probably should be fun.* It's not unprofessional to start a class with a joke or to project a comic strip or cartoon on an overhead transparency—particularly if it is relevant to the topic being discussed. In most lectures, I incorporate a little bit of "show and tell" to gently introduce the topic of the day. For instance, when I'm lecturing on questionnaires and survey design, I usually bring in examples I've received over the years. My favorite is a mailed poll from the Beer Drinkers of America, which included a wallet-sized plastic membership card, a decal of the American flag, and a request on their "opinion poll" that I contribute money to their organization. Sometimes I embellish these with hypothetical scenarios (e.g., having students think about being stopped by the police and instead of pulling out a driver's license, handing the officer their official membership card in the Beer Drinkers of America).

The point of any effort at humor is always to make the time together more enjoyable. If you have students' attention and interest, then you *can* teach them.

Timeliness: *Students hunger to see how the material they are learning applies to issues and problems today.* They want to know if it is relevant, to be shown how they can use this information. To be credible, the instructor should demonstrate current applications and uses of what is being taught. It's a good practice to scan the local newspaper and the campus paper everyday for articles that can provide vivid illustrations. Look for ways to connect students to the topics being discussed.

The opposite of this orientation was practiced by a professor I once encountered. This tall, dignified woman with a slow southern drawl wasted just about all of our time together. Close to retirement, this unimaginative faculty member brought to class the notes that she took as a graduate student some 40 years earlier and read to us from them. The class's boredom was so thick it could have been cut with a ruler. Students deserve much better than this.

Continuing My Own Education: *I have not learned all I need to know.* A philosophy of teaching should probably consider the importance of the educator's own learning and how much there always is yet to learn. Is it critical to stay current by reading journals, attending workshops, and examining new texts? To talk with faculty who teach in other disciplines to discover what teaching techniques they employ? Many excellent instructors feel that they are still evolving as teachers—that they are better each semester than they were the one before and that next year will find even more improvement. Good teachers read and consult with others in order to continuously improve.

What Research Says about Effective Teaching

Chickering and Gamson (1987) took on the task of boiling down 50 years of research "on the way teachers teach and learners learn" with a task force of scholars, and they identified seven broad principles of good teaching practice. Cross and Steadman (1996) have called these "the most succinct, comprehensive, and respected research-based conclusions about learning to be widely distributed to discipline-oriented college teachers" (p. 19). Sorcinelli (1991) has cited additional research findings that support and validate the seven principles. Included here is a brief summary. Good teaching practice involves:

1. *Frequent student-faculty contact:* Faculty who are concerned about their students and their progress, who are perceived as approachable and easy to talk to, serve to motivate and keep students involved. On another level, informal contacts where students have opportunities to talk with faculty members outside of their classrooms and to discuss such things as career choices seems to improve satisfaction with college and aids in retention of students.

Things you can do to apply this principle:[1]
a. Attend events sponsored by students.
b. Serve as a mentor or advisor to students.
c. Take students to professional meetings.
d. Learn students' names.
e. Keep "open" or "drop-in" office hours.
f. Arrive at class early and engage a different student in conversation every time.

2. *The encouragement of cooperation among students:* Chickering and Gamson (1987) noted: "Learning is enhanced when it is more like a team effort than a solo race. . . . Sharing one's own ideas and responding to others' reactions sharpens thinking and deepens understanding" (p. 3). As discussed later in Chapter 4, there is a wealth of research indicating that students benefit from the use of small group and peer learning instructional approaches.

Things you can do to apply this principle:
a. Have students share in class their interests and backgrounds.
b. Create small groups to work on projects together.
c. Invite students to share their ideas and views.
d. Encourage students to study together.

3. *Active learning techniques:* Again, Chickering and Gamson (1987) have written: "Learning is not a spectator sport. Students do not learn much just by sitting in classes listening. . . . They must talk about what they are learning, write about it, relate it to past experiences, apply it to their daily lives" (p. 5).

Things you can do to apply this principle:
a. *Encourage students to challenge ideas brought into class.*
b. *Encourage students to bring in newspaper articles, new readings, and ideas for new assignments.*
c. *Give students actual problems or situations to analyze.*
d. *Use role-playing, simulations, or hands-on experiments.*
e. *Require students to compare and contrast different theorists, authors, and so on.*

4. *Prompt feedback:* Learning theory research has consistently shown that the quicker the feedback, the greater the learning. Sorcinelli (1991) has observed, "Prompt feedback in college courses shows a clear and positive relation to student achievement and satisfaction" (p. 18).

Things you can do to apply this principle:
a. *Return quizzes and exams by the next class meeting.*
b. *Return homework within one week.*
c. *Provide students with detailed comments on their written papers.*

5. *Emphasize time on task:* This principle refers to the amount of actual involvement with the material being studied, and applies, obviously, to way the instructor uses classroom instructional time. Faculty need good time-management skills. This includes, but is not limited to, starting and stopping on time. Activities such as watching brief exerts from a film provide more academic learning time than having the class watch an entire two-hour movie.

Things you can do to apply this principle:
a. *Require students who miss classes to make up lost work.*
b. *Communicate the amount of time needed to prepare for particular assignments.*
c. *Require students to rehearse before making oral presentations.*
d. *Don't let class breaks stretch out too long.*

6. *Communicating high expectations:* "Expect more and you will get more" (Chickering & Gamson, 1987, p. 5). The key here is not to make the course impossibly difficult, but to have goals that can be attained as long as individual learners stretch and work hard, going beyond what they already know. Knowing where to set expectations that aren't too high or too low takes some practice, and you might not get it right the first time teaching a new class.

Things you can do to apply this principle:
a. *Communicate your expectations orally and in writing at the beginning of the course.*
b. *Explain the penalties for students who turn in late work.*
c. *Suggest supplemental reading.*
d. *Identify excellent work by students; display exemplars if possible.*
e. *Help students set high academic goals (e.g., publishing a piece of research or encouraging those who ought to consider graduate school).*

7. *Respecting diverse talents and ways of learning:* Not only do students differ in life experiences, skills/abilities, and personality but they also have sensory modality preferences (e.g., kinesthetic, visual, auditory) for learning and will vary in terms of how they process new information. Some students will come across as open and flexible; others will be closed and rigid. This principle suggests the necessity for the instructor to be sensitive to the various ways students acquire information. Within any classroom, there will be students who have latent talents and some with skills and abilities far beyond any that you might imagine. Understanding your students as individuals with their attendant idiosyncrasies and showing regard for their unique interests and talents is "likely to facilitate student growth and development in every sphere—academic, social, personal, and vocational" (Sorcinelli, 1991, p. 21).

Things you can do to apply this principle:
a. *Use diverse teaching approaches.*
b. *Allow students some choice of readings and in their assignments.*
c. *Try to find out about students' backgrounds and interests.*
d. *Provide extra material (readings or exercises) for students with gaps or deficits in their learning.*

Of course, you would do well to recognize that there is a formidable body of research literature on teaching. These seven principles are not all that you need to know or practice, but they will take you a long way.

In a related vein, Perlman and McCann (1998) surveyed undergraduate students (N = 671) enrolled in psychology courses at a public regional university one semester. All students were given index cards and asked to write down their pet peeves about faculty: 65 percent of the comments fell into the "teaching" category. In ranked order, what annoyed the students most were poor organization and planning, poor teaching mechanics (speaking too fast or softly, poor use of the board), lecture style and technique, testing procedures and exams, poor use of class time (coming late, stopping early), and monotone voice. All of these problems can be easily addressed when the faculty member really cares and wants to improve his or her teaching.

Quite honestly, you should expect to make many mistakes in your first year of teaching. Many, if not most, seasoned veterans of the classroom would be terribly embarrassed to watch videotapes (if they existed) of their first semesters. But once you have taught the same course three or four times and learned a bit about what works and what doesn't in managing a classroom, then you can begin to aspire to becoming a *great* teacher. This is what Moseley (1998) has said about the process:

> *A great teacher is a person who cares deeply about teaching, who wants to be teaching, and who wants to become a better teacher. Great teachers love their field of study intensely and have been working in that field long enough to know it almost unconsciously. They know the material and the ideas so intimately that they can focus on finding out where the students are, what they know, and how they learn, and then communicate in a way that students can respond to. Great teaching emerges from the passions of their lives. (p. 9)*

Respecting Differences: Diversity in the Classroom

It would indeed be an unusual classroom if all the students were completely homogeneous. Most of us, thank goodness, will never experience such a situation. Variety is good—whether we think about eating the same food (e.g., oatmeal) meal after meal, or whether we think about diverse points of views, environmental surroundings, or cultural experiences. In politics the different parties help provide a system of checks and balance. Often, we are attracted to those who are not like us but somehow very different—more extroverted, more athletic, more detail-oriented, whatever. So the problem is not diversity, per se, but distills down to (1) how to deal with differences of opinion and lifestyle and (2) how to help students (particularly those who have been raised in settings where tolerance was not practiced) identify and overcome their biases and prejudices.

Instructors who are not themselves members of any minority groups (e.g., those who have grown up with "white privilege") need to be alert to demonstrating subtle forms of discrimination. For instance, white instructors might unconsciously make less eye contact with minority students, call on them less often, or tend not to remember their names. The minority students will notice if you never refer to one of their comments, yet consistently praise and bring the class's attention to the remarks of a white student. It is also important to provide readings and assignments that involve authors who are not just "dead white guys" but inclusive of women, persons of color, and gays or lesbians.

Members of nondominant groups will also be attuned to phrases and expressions that can be experienced as *not* inclusive. For instance, if you are heterosexual, don't assume that everyone is. Don't use terms like *girlfriend* and *boyfriend*. Instead, use *partners* or *significant others*. Similarly, gays and lesbians have a particular *sexual orientation*, not a *sexual preference*. (Preference implies choice, but gays and lesbians do not choose their sexual orientation; there's as much deciding involved as with eye color or right- or left-handedness.) Asian American students don't like being referred to as *Orientals*. Women don't like the diminutives *gal* and *girl*. Also, don't assume that everyone celebrates Christmas and Easter.

Students can be invited to identify "triggers" (words or phrases that tap into their own anger or pain about false or stereotyped perceptions) as a way of educating each other about their differences. Examples of some prejudicial remarks are:

> *"People of color are blowing things way out of proportion."*
> *"If everyone just worked hard, they could achieve."*

"Men are better suited for leadership roles than women."
(Adams, Bell, & Griffin, 1997)

It is helpful to remember that no one wants to be called hurtful names or to be branded with inflammatory language. Do not permit your students to use "loaded" terms. For instance, even if a student joked about drinking too much on occasion, he or she would very likely become angry if called a "drunk" or an "alcoholic." Even a strong fundamentalist Christian might resist the label of "fanatic" or "zealot." No one wants to be a bigot, a prude, a fag, or a slut. Establish ground rules in your class that include no name calling or group labels.

Weinstein and Obear (1992) recommended implementing a ground rule that if anyone feels "triggered" by an oppressive attitude then he or she should identify it by saying "trigger" or "there is one for me" (p. 45). To help the class understand the notion of triggers, it is useful to have the students brainstorm their own individual triggers and to list these examples.

An exercise that can be employed to help make the point that everyone in the class is a unique individual and not just a member of some easily identified reference group is to ask the class to look around the room and to identify some of the ways students differ from each other. Jot these down on the board. Usually, the first 10 or so are easy: gender, skin color, hair color, height, weight, eye color, whether or not they wear glasses, right- or left-handedness, and so on. As the comments begin to slow down, you may note that the students have listed only observable characteristics. Ask again, "How else do the members of the class vary? Perhaps in terms of not directly observable traits?"

This time you'll typically get responses such as grade-point average, major, religion, income, martial status, political affiliation, sexual orientation, birth order, and so on. These suggestions also provide great opportunity for scoring points about diversity. For instance, you can ask, "You mean you can't tell I'm a Democrat by looking at me?" or "You can't tell I'm the first-born?" or "Don't you know what my father did for a living?"

At some point, the class begins to understand the broad diversity represented in any class of pupils. It's possible then to ask several more questions: "So how many different ways are there that we can be different? Want to guess?" Of course, this is a rhetorical question—there is no single correct answer. (It would depend on how many variables there were, the attributes of those variables, and whether we are interested simply in combinations or permutations.) If you want to be a little bit of a ham and drive the point home, you can walk up to a student who is physically different from you and ask, "Do we have to agree on everything? I mean, can we disagree on some things and still be friends?" What this does is to acknowledge that there are differences within the classroom but at the same time it sets the expectation that differences of opinion or point of view ought to be respected.

Minorities in the classroom may or may not speak up when there is an issue that you think they should weigh in on. Do not, however, single out minorities and ask Latonya, for instance, to represent the "African American" perspective. Don't ask, "Latonya, what do blacks think about...?" Latonya may feel very uncomfortable having to speak for all African Americans and resent your asking. Similarly, do not ask someone who you think *looks* gay/lesbian to speak pro or con on an issue dealing with sexual orientation. It is permissible, however, to ask open-ended questions that invite: "Does anyone else have another opinion?"

Try to create an open environment where even strong feelings can be expressed. Encourage students to give reasons or examples, to make logical arguments without personal attack. Sometimes in heated arguments students may be unable to explain rationally their beliefs or positions. At such times it may be helpful to ask the student how he or she arrived at that conclusion. The student may be able to relate a story from childhood that reveals a great deal about the social and environmental forces at work in that person's life. The class may be better able to accept even extreme views once it is known how they were shaped and influenced.

Diversity needs to be addressed on another level because faculty must also be sensitive to invisible disabilities (e.g., dyslexia) and the various ways in which students learn. For instance, the *concrete sequential learner* prefers step-by-step directions and touchable, hands-on materials; the *random concrete learner* does not want cut-and-dried procedures and does not respond well to teacher intervention; the *abstract sequential learner* desires extensive reading assignments and substantive lectures; and the *abstract random learner* has a predilection for movies, group discussions, short lectures, and multimedia sensory experiences (Kaplan & Kies, 1995). Students may not even be aware of their preferences and learning styles, and certainly you won't either until you get to know them as individuals. But what can happen when there is a mismatch between your teaching style and a student's learning style is that the student can become disgruntled and scapegoat you for his or her difficulties in the class.

In such situations, try to listen *nonjudgmentally* to the student's complaint. If possible, try to take the student's perspective. Misunderstandings can arise over differences of perception. A student who is assertive and a strong advocate for himself or herself in a particular disagreement (e.g., a grade on a written paper) can be experienced as threatening by the instructor. Sometimes there is a fine line between *intimidating* and making a spirited argument. Don't jump to the conclusion that you are being picked on because you are female or first-generation American, or whatever. Suspend the part of your mind that wants to rebut, to prove the student wrong. Instead, when all the information has been provided, think of it as a problem to be solved. Be flexible, particularly if several students are complaining about the same thing. Look for a middle ground, a compromise where there can be a win-win solution.

Suggestions for Inclusive Teaching

Inclusive teaching begins with the stance that differences (of opinion, ethnic cultures, lifestyle, and so on) are not only okay but, in fact, *necessary* for a vibrant and healthy society. How bland and uninteresting our classes would be if all the students looked, thought, and spoke the same way.

Here are a few suggestions to help you model the kind of open, accepting attitude within your classroom where students will feel it is safe to engage in give-and-take discussions:

- Don't assume that all, or even most, students in your class are Christian or heterosexual.
- View students as *individuals* instead of representatives of separate and distinct groups. Group classifications often serve as a basis for discrimination.

- Cultivate a climate that is accepting and respectful of diverse viewpoints and perspectives. Show students how to listen with an open mind; don't expect everyone to agree with you.
- Don't allow ridicule, defamatory, or hurtful remarks.
- Encourage everyone in the class to participate.
- Be constantly alert to showing favoritism. Don't show a preference in calling on mostly men or women, whites or nonwhites.
- Try to provide students with a variety of ways to learn; don't think one approach is going to reach every student.

Graduate versus Undergraduate Teaching

Faculty fresh from their own doctoral programs who are presented with undergraduates to teach for the first time often are disappointed that their new charges don't seem quite as highly motivated as one recalls being as an undergraduate. There's two points to remember here. First, those who have obtained doctorates are not representative of most undergraduate students. Persons with advanced degrees probably do have a greater capacity for self-discipline and concentration and are likely to be more conscientious about the details and fine points so necessary in academic discovery and writing. We probably *did* put in more hours and study more than did most of our peers. Hungry for learning, we ravenously consumed book after book and still were left eager for more. This is not true of all undergraduates.

Second, it is good to keep in mind what undergraduates are not. They are *not* graduate students. Many of them have not figured out what career path they will choose or what they want to do with the rest of their lives. They may know relatively little about your area of specialization. If your course is an elective, they may want to "try out" the subject matter to see if it will hold their interest. It is not uncommon for undergraduates to be in courses for all the wrong reasons: because it was offered at a convenient time or day and doesn't conflict with a job or sleeping late, because a friend is in the class, because Dad wants his son to follow his footsteps and become a CPA, or because the class meets in a building within a easy walk of the dorm. It almost goes without saying that some students enter college knowing that they may not succeed—and it doesn't bother them. They know ahead of time that if they don't make good grades, they'll return home to work in the family business. It shouldn't come as any surprise to discover undergraduates who come to college primarily to devote themselves to the pursuit of fun and social activities. And even if that group is relatively small, one recent survey found that 44 percent of all U.S. college students engage in binge drinking. Those who get most involved in drinking miss classes, get behind in their work, and do poorly in school.

Faculty who have the opportunity to teach graduate students after teaching undergraduates often marvel at the differences. Because of the amount of time and effort it takes to obtain a baccalaureate diploma (to say nothing of the expense), most of the lesser motivated students remove themselves or have been removed from the classroom; thus, faculty teaching graduate courses can usually assume that their students will be highly motivated. Graduate students are usually older, more mature, and self-directed. They generally read all of their assignments because they want to learn. This may or may not be true of undergraduates. Graduate students may be more eager to express their ideas and want to discuss intellectual questions. Undergraduates can be reticent to speak up in classes— especially beginning, first-year students who are often painfully aware that they are the "new kids on the block." Undergraduates tend to complain more about the amount of work you require and have a keen sense of injustice if they feel that another section of the same course is getting by with a lighter load. And finally, undergraduates generally don't have the same appreciation for theory as do graduate students. Although a good instructor should always be imaginative and constantly thinking about new ways to present material that may have lost its luster, it is probably more important to be creative with undergraduates than with graduates. Because of their interest in the topic, graduate students will often take responsibility for learning what they need to, with or without the assistance of the instructor.

Last, both undergraduates and graduate students differ in their stages of cognitive development. Some may be "stuck" in dualistic thinking and have difficulty appreciating the perspectives of others. If your students don't seem to be thinking on as complex a level as you think they should, it might be worthwhile to do some reading on the stages of cognitive development. See, for example, Perry (1970, 1981) or Baxter-Magolda (1992).

Common Anxieties of Beginning Instructors

Part of developing the right mindset prior to entering the classroom entails not becoming too anxious about our efforts. But it's easy to worry—every new instructor does. Almost all of us fear the unknown and each class (even for veteran teachers) is unfamiliar until the bell rings and we walk inside the classroom. The night before the start of a new term, we might not sleep well. The next morning, our stomachs might have too many "butterflies" to let us eat. That same logical, analytical mind that got us into graduate school poses question after unanswerable question about the students we've yet to meet: We wonder if they will "like" us, if they will talk when we are speaking, if they will be easy to control and manage? Will they sit there glassy-eyed and silent or will they smile and raise intelligent questions? And if they ask good questions, we worry that we might not have the right information to respond authoritatively.

Those unaccustomed to public speaking sometimes brood about the possibility of making misstatements—embarrassing ourselves by saying things like "orgasm" instead of "organism." And these things happen—most of us have made such mistakes or heard speakers make such blunders. Will it happen to us, too?

Worrying about negative evaluation is okay, to some extent. It's not good, however, when apprehension becomes so high that we are immobilized, unable to speak or think clearly, afraid to make eye contact, or deviate from a carefully prepared script of lecture. On the other hand, a little anxiety is quite natural and assists in getting us "pumped" for the preparation and presentations that we need to make. It's important not to appear too nervous to students, as at least one study found that students' estimates of instructor effectiveness were inversely correlated with the teacher's anxiety—the more anxious the instructors appeared, the less effective they were assumed to be (Erdle, Murray, & Ruston, 1985).

How do you reduce the first-day jitters? Here are some practical suggestions:

- Be prepared. Know what you want to accomplish, have your materials ready, make an outline or a "to do" list, and give yourself plenty of time to arrive early. Be familiar with the location of your class. If it is an early-morning class and you must drive, allow for the possibility of traffic jams or difficulty in finding a parking place. Have a back-up plan in case the bulb in the overhead projector burns out, or if you unexpectedly run out of lecture material with 35 minutes left in the hour. Always have on hand some discussion questions to toss out.

- If you arrive early, engage the students present in conversation. Find out something about them, introduce yourself. Shake hands. Smile a lot.
- Don't try to be perfect. Everyone makes mistakes, and you will, too. If you blunder, don't be terribly defensive and try to blame it on someone else. Laugh if possible. If you can't do that, admit that you goofed. Students are pretty forgiving if you're not arrogant and mean-spirited. It's hard to lecture for a whole semester without making a single misstatement—so don't even try.
- Talk with a friend, companion, mentor, or colleague whenever you need a "reality check." Those who know you well can sometimes say exactly the right thing to calm and reassure you. If your confidant makes you feel more nervous, then don't confide in that individual any more.
- Try not to get flustered, but take your time to consider a response before speaking. Don't rush yourself. If you are confused by a student's question, ask for additional information or explanation. It is okay to say, "I don't understand. . . . " If you are asked a question that is impossibly difficult, *deflect* it by opening it up to the class. Say, "I'd like to hear some different perspectives on this issue. What do some of you think?"
- Wear a watch so that you can pace yourself and not have to guess what time it is.
- Avoid unrealistic expectations. Not every one of your new pupils will have a scholar's curiosity or be highly motivated. Expect that students will come in late or not show at all during the first meeting. A minority of students may be uncooperative and indicate their disinterest by talking, sleeping, or reading something quite unrelated while you are talking. Don't take it personally.
- Visualize yourself doing a superlative job, being confident, poised, and in command.

Each time you master your fears and "survive" that first class, the better prepared you will be for the next time. As with most things, the more experience we acquire in performing a skill or behavior, the better we become. By the time you become a "seasoned veteran" and have taught four or five courses, you'll find that there's less first-day anxiety. But if you are conscientious and eager to do a good job, you'll probably always have a twinge of anxiety at the beginning of a new term.

This is what Palmer (1998), a teacher of "thousands of students" has observed about his own apprehensiveness:

> *After thirty years of teaching, my own fear remains close at hand. It is there when I enter a classroom and feel the undertow into which I have jumped. It is there when I ask a question—and my students keep a silence as stony as if I had asked them to betray their friends. It is there whenever it feels as if I have lost control: a mind-boggling question is asked, an irrational conflict emerges, or students get lost in my lecture because I myself am lost. When a class that has gone badly comes to a merciful end, I am fearful long after it is over—fearful that I am not just a bad teacher but a bad person, so closely is my sense of self tied to the work I do. (p. 36)*

Later on, Palmer adds:

> *As a young teacher, I yearned for the day when I would know my craft so well, be so competent, so experienced, and so powerful, that I could walk into any classroom without feeling afraid. But now, in my late fifties, I know that day will never come. I will always have fears, but I need not be my fears. . . . I need not teach from a fearful place: I can teach from curiosity or hope or empathy or honesty, places that are as real within me as are my fears. I can have fear, but I need not be fear—if I am willing to stand someplace else in my inner landscape. (p. 57)*

Being a new faculty member is stressful—there's no getting around it. You will feel pulled in 17 different directions at times. Besides the classroom issues, there's often pressure associated with your research and publication. Keep in mind, however, that you were hired because the faculty had faith in your abilities. You were not brought in with the expectation that you would fail. Quite the contrary—you were hand-picked by a very particular group of highly educated individuals. Your colleagues want you to do well because they will benefit almost as much as you from your success.

Everyone probably knows intuitively what helps in alleviating stress. For some, it is time away from the task—for instance, going to a movie, taking a long walk or a run, or conversation with a friend over mugs of steaming hot chocolate. Be kind to yourself: Take breaks and walks. Set a little time each day for fun or inspirational reading. Go to a conference or plan a short trip. Discover what works for you.

References and Resources

Adams, M., Bell, L. A., & Griffin, P. (1997). *Teaching for diversity and social justice. A sourcebook.* New York: Routledge.

Baxter-Magolda, M. (1992). *Knowing and reasoning in college: Gender-related patterns in students' intellectual development.* San Francisco: Jossey-Bass.

Boice, R. (1992). *The new faculty member: Supporting and fostering professional development.* San Francisco: Jossey-Bass.

Brookfield, S. D. (1995). *Becoming a critically reflective teacher.* San Francisco: Jossey-Bass.

Center for Teaching and Learning. (1997). *Teaching for inclusion: Diversity in the college classroom.* University of North Carolina at Chapel Hill.

Chickering, A. W., & Gamson, Z. F. (1987). Seven principles for good practice in undergraduate education. *AAHE Bulletin, 39,* 3–7.

Chickering, A. W., Gamson, Z. F., & Barsi, L. M. (1991). Inventories of good practice in undergraduate education. In A. W. Chickering & Z. Gamson (Eds.), *Applying the seven principles of good practice in undergraduate education.* New Directions for Teaching and Learning #47. San Francisco: Jossey-Bass.

Cross, K. P., & Steadman, M. H. (1996). *Classroom research: Implementing the scholarship of teaching.* San Francisco: Jossey-Bass.

Dams, M., Bell, L. A., & Griffin, P. (1997). *Teaching for diversity and social justice. A sourcebook.* New York: Routledge.

Eble, K. E. (1983). *The aims of college teaching.* San Francisco: Jossey-Bass.

Erdle, S., Murray, H. G., & Ruston, J. P. (1985). Personality, classroom behavior, and student ratings of college teaching effectiveness: A path analysis. *Journal of Educational Psychology, 77,* 394–407.

Gutek, G. L. (1988). *Philosophical and ideological perspectives on education*. Englewood Cliffs, NJ: Prentice-Hall.

Kaplan, E. J., & Kies, D. A. (1995). Teaching styles and learning styles: Which came first? *Journal of Instructional Psychology, 22,* 29–33.

Menges, R. J., & Associates. (1999). *Faculty in new jobs*. San Francisco: Jossey-Bass.

Moseley, J. G. (1998, Spring). What makes a great teacher? *Transy Today: The Magazine of Transylvania University,* p. 9.

Ozmon, H., & Craver, S. (1995). *Philosophical foundations of education*. San Francisco: Jossey-Bass.

Palmer, P. (1998). *The courage to teach: Exploring the inner landscape of a teacher's life*. San Francisco: Jossey-Bass.

Perlman, B., & McCann, L. I. (1998). Students' pet peeves about teaching. *Teaching of Psychology, 25,* 201–202.

Perry, W. G. (1970). *Forms of intellectual and ethical development in the college years*. New York: Holt, Rinehart and Winston.

Perry, W. G., Jr. (1981). Cognitive and ethical growth: The making of meaning. In A. W. Chickering and Associates (Eds.), *The modern American college*. San Francisco: Jossey-Bass.

Schoenfeld, A. C., & Magnan, R. (1992). *Mentor in a manual*. Madison, WI: Magna Publications.

Sorcinelli, M. D. (1991). Research findings on the seven principles. In A. W. Chickering & Z. Gamson (Eds.), *Applying the seven principles of good practice in undergraduate education*. New Directions for Teaching and Learning #47. San Francisco: Jossey-Bass.

Svinicki, M. D. (1990). *The changing face of college teaching*. New Directions for Teaching and Learning #42. San Francisco: Jossey-Bass.

Weinstein, G., & Obear, K. (1992). Bias issues in the classroom: Encounters with the teaching self. In M. Adams (Ed.), *Promoting diversity in college classrooms: Innovative responses for the curriculum, faculty, and institutions*. New Directions for Teaching and Learning #52. San Francisco: Jossey-Bass.

Endnote

1. These suggestions were largely derived from Chickering, Gamson, and Barsi (1991).

2

Basic Course Components

Overview: This chapter focuses on three of the four main essentials needed in a course of educational instruction (the syllabus, a text or body of readings, and assignments). Although it is not uncommon for instructors to go hunting for texts before drafting a syllabus, the entire course should not be centered on one book. Texts are resources, aids in accomplishing the educational objectives—not the prime reason a course exists. Developing a syllabus should, ideally, precede textbook selection. Writing a syllabus for the first time, even revising an old one, is a complex project—more difficult than simply allocating readings over an academic term and deciding on assignments.

The first portion of this chapter identifies the components that go into a well-constructed syllabus, and this is followed by a segment that discusses textbook selection. The next segment examines the purpose of assignments and their use as instructional devices. This is followed by several topics that relate to issues that arise whenever instructors require assignments and presentations.

Constructing the Syllabus

The compass that guides and keeps students and faculty on the right educational path in a particular course of instruction is the syllabus. The syllabus should clearly communicate course objectives, assignments, required readings, and grading policies. Every student should receive his or her own copy of the syllabus on the first meeting of the class—certainly no later than the second meeting.

Fewer misunderstandings and problems will occur if you take the time to be as specific as possible in writing the syllabus, exactly defining your expectations. Think of the syllabus as a stand-alone document. Those students who miss the first or second meeting of class should be able to learn most of what they need to know about the requirements of the course from reading the syllabus.

Start with collecting syllabi from colleagues who have recently taught the course you will be teaching. Particularly your first year, you may want to make only minor changes to the way the course has been taught over the past several years—unless you've been asked to make a major overhaul. Look for the common threads and themes if you gather syllabi from several instructors.

Creating a syllabus for a course you've never taught before is not the easiest of tasks. It forces you to plan three or four months ahead of time and to anticipate how the class will progress. You'll need to guess how much time will be spent on each topic, on in-class group projects, and on student debates. What topics will you treat superficially, which ones in-depth? The syllabus will reflect your philosophy of teaching and the pertinent educational objectives (e.g., knowledge, comprehension, application, analysis, synthesis, and evaluation; see the discussion on Bloom's Taxonomy later in this chapter) you hope to accomplish. Many curriculum specialists urge teachers to include a statement of intended learning outcomes. This makes perfect sense, both from the standpoint that students have the right to know what they are expected to learn and from the perspective that stating learning outcomes helps keep instructors from drifting too far afield. As much as possible, your objectives should indicate what students will be able to do once they have completed the course.

If your course is one in a series (e.g., the second calculus course), you will also need to consider what students should have mastered prior to the proposed course and how much they ought to accomplish to be fully prepared for the next one. If the course is being taught in the evening, or by Internet or television, or off campus, there may be special considerations in terms of the facilities or supporting resources available to students. In short, many "pieces" go into the construction of a syllabus.

The Basics: What Needs to Be in a Syllabus

These are the essential components of a well-designed syllabus:

Top of Syllabus

1. Course title and university course identifier (e.g., PSY 100: Introduction to Psychology)
2. Location of classroom as well as days and hours the class meets
3. Your name, office location, office hours, phone number, and e-mail address (Some faculty list their home phone numbers; however, there is no compelling reason for you to do this. If you choose to, you might want to include "No phone calls after 11 P.M.")
4. Course description (Usually this comes directly from the college bulletin; any prerequisites should be identified. You may want to identify how this course fits into the student's program of instruction—for example, the third of four required calculus courses.)
5. Course objectives or statement of intended learning outcomes (These are usually common to all sections of the class being taught within the department.)

Middle of Syllabus

6. Schedule of topics to be discussed (Check the school calendar and plan for holidays, spring break, etc. Identify any field trips or required activities outside of the class.)
7. Texts and/or equipment needed (Note required and supplementary titles, authors, publishers, and editions of any books the students are expected to read; full citations are necessary for any journal articles in a required reading list. If materials are placed on reserve, indicate where.)

8. Explanation of assignments and dates when they are due (Do not have "floating dates." Be specific, even if you have to make some adjustments later.)

Last Third of Syllabus

9. Scheduled tests (and locations if different from the regular classroom)
10. Policy on attendance, tardiness, and participation in class
11. Policy on work that is submitted late
12. Explanation of how overall grade will be computed (Provide students with specific information about the weighting of attendance, homework, major assignments, examinations, etc.)
13. Grading scale (e.g., 100 to 92 = A)
14. Miscellaneous information (This section may contain statements about plagiarism, the University's Honor Code, your policy on missed tests, class rules regarding such matters as talking or eating in class, computer and e-mail skills required, availability of instructional support services, course drop dates, etc.)

Do you need to put *everything* in writing? Probably not. In the first class, you might discuss, say, your philosophy of teaching and you shouldn't feel guilty about that material not being in the syllabus. Ideally, the syllabus should cover the basics about the course in 3 or 4 pages. Not too many students will read a 15 single-spaced course outline. Handouts of such things as lab safety procedures can be distributed separately from the syllabus.

Once you have composed a draft of your syllabus containing all of the essential items you want to convey, take a little more time to look at it from a student's perspective. If, for instance, you placed in heavy bold type that your office hours are available *only by appointment,* does this send the message that you don't want to be disturbed? On the other hand, if you orally mention your willingness to meet with students before or after class, or whenever they don't understand the material, then you have identified yourself as a student-friendly, concerned educator. Similarly, providing students with options regarding their assignments will set you apart from other educators who do not allow students to personalize their courses. Even the amount of time you choose to spend on the various points to be covered makes a statement about what you emphasize and value.

Often, syllabi are so concerned with stating requirements, policies, and penalties that little effort is made to stimulate student interest in the course. One way to create involvement is by posing a few challenging questions that the course will attempt to answer. Why should students be interested in your class? Whet their appetites by posing some questions that will be examined during the term.

No matter the length of your syllabus, be sure to use lots of headings to divide the various sections. Consider using a table of contents if the syllabus is extremely lengthy. Finally, keep a copy of the syllabus to make ongoing notes to yourself about needed revisions. These might be reminders to insert more detailed instruction on a particular assignment, that supplementary readings are outdated or have gone out of print, and so forth.

Example of a Syllabus

SW 650 RESEARCH METHODS IN THE SOCIAL SCIENCES
(3 Credit Hours)

Fall, 2000
MWF 3:00–4:15
17 Belding Classroom Building

George Gipper, Ph.D.
555-293-6645 or (gipper.@blt.edu)
641 Patterson Tower
Office Hours M,W, F noon to 4:00
(Other times by appointment)

I. Course Description

Introduction to systematic approaches to scientific thinking necessary for building basic knowledge as applied to problems in society. Issues addressed include conceptualization of research, measurement, ethical use of scientific inquiry, and appropriate analytical procedures. (The first of three required research courses.)

II. Course Objectives

A. To introduce the process of research as a sequence of rationally and systematically organized events. (What are the steps needed to conduct research in the social sciences?)

B. To acquaint students with the basic concepts necessary to understand written reports of research. (What terms, expressions, and statistics do I need to know in order to fully comprehend journal articles and reports?)

C. To teach students how to design research projects capable of making scientific contributions. (How do I craft a research design capable of providing objective, scientific information?)

III. Class Outline

Assignment for Class

III. Class Outline	Assignment for Class
9/2: Introduction to course and each other	None
9/9: The research process & operationalizing variables	Read Chapters 1 and 2. Write a hypothesis or research question that interests you, one that could be completed within one semester; (2) operationalize your dependent variable; (3) list three independent variables you will need.
9/16: Continuing discussion of Chapter 2	Find five references related to your topic from a computerized database. Write at least one page describing (1) the amount of material you found on your topic and (2) your experience in locating relevant material.
9/23: Single subject design	Read Chapter 3. Develop a single system design for some realistic problem that a client might have. Graph fictitious data for baseline and intervention. Write at least a paragraph describing (1) the client's presenting problem and (2) the intervention.
9/30: Group research designs	Read Chapter 4. Write a research design for an experiment. State (1) your hypothesis, (2) your operationalized dependent variable, (3) the intervention, (4) the type of design, and (5) how you will procure your research subjects. (1 to 2 pages, typewritten)
10/7: Measurement issues	Read Chapter 5. Find a scale or instrument that you could use in some research project. Address its reliability, validity, and how you might use it. Attach a copy of the scale to your paper.
10/14: Survey research	Read Chapter 6. Find an article in a professional journal that employed a survey, then, in 2–3 paragraphs, discuss (1) the confidence you have in it because of the sampling design, sample size, etc., and (2) Would you generalize from the finding? If so, how far? Alterna-

tively, find a survey in an issue of the *Gallup Poll Monthly* or the *Harris Poll* and explore the same issues. Attach the article to your paper.

10/21: Questionnaire design & review for exam

Prepare 5 items suitable for measuring self-esteem; bring questions for the review.

10/28: Midterm exam

11/4: Qualitative research

Read Chapter 11.
Propose a qualitative study that you would be interested in implementing (1.5 pages, typewritten).

11/11: Secondary data analysis & content analysis

Read Chapter 8.
Propose a realistic study that would draw on secondary data or rely on content analysis. State your hypothesis, your methodology (including how you operationalized your dependent variable), and the limitations of your research.

11/18: Program evaluation

Read Chapter 10.
Choose from 1, 2, 3, or 4: (1) find a journal article reporting a program evaluation and critique it in 250 words or so; (2) locate a program evaluation from a local agency and critique it; (3) propose a program evaluation that could or should be done; or (4) critique "Evaluation of a Residential Center for Emotionally Disturbed Teens."

11/25: Data analysis

Read Chapter 9.

11/27: THANKSGIVING!!!

12/2: Data analysis (cont.), application of research

Design a table showing fictitious data. Make at least one comparison that is statistically significant and indicate the appropriate statistical procedure.

12/9: Ethical issues & review

Read Chapter 12, skim Chapter 13; bring questions for the review.

12/16: Final exam

IV. Required Text

Gipper, G. (1997). *Research Methods for Knowledge Building* (2nd ed.). Chicago: Hall & Taylor.

V. Expectations and Student Evaluation

Students are expected to keep current with their reading of the text. If the instructor detects that the class as a whole is not reading the material, he reserves the right to conduct unannounced quizzes which will count as in-class assignments. Students are further expected to contribute to class discussions and to raise questions. All assignments are due at the *beginning* of class and unexcused *late* assignments will be penalized.

A. Exams: There will be a midterm exam plus a final exam which will be averaged together for **60%** of final grade. Missed exams will not be made up unless there is a valid excuse *and* the instructor is notified beforehand.

B. Assignments: **30%** of final grade

C. Attendance & Participation: These are required and will constitute **10%** of final grade. Participation in class discussion is highly desired. Class will start as scheduled. Please be present on time.

VI. Grading Scale

100 to 92 = A   82 to 74 = C
91 to 83 = B   73 to 65 = D

VII. Additional Scholarly Resources

Tabbie, E., and Talley, F. (1994). *Adventures in Social Research*. New York: Guru Publications.

Canebridge, E. S. (1989). *Survey Research: A Computer-Assisted Approach*. Wildflower, CA: Smart Books, Inc.

Loom, M., Wischer, J., and Arme, J. G. (1995). *Evaluating Your Practice: An Introduction*. Boston: Hamilton Books.

Korcoran, K., and Lister, J. (1994). *Measures for Social Research* (2nd ed.). New York: Knotty Books, Inc.

Judson, W. W., and Natters, P. S. (1994). *Controversial Issues in Research Methods*. Boston: Get-Reading Book Co.

Windle, Q. S., and Judson, W. W. (1993). *Research Methods in Human Services*. Pacific Grove, CA: Surfside Books.

Departing from the Syllabus

The syllabus is a contract between you as the university's represen-tative and the student. For this reason, it should be thoughtfully prepared and not changed for capricious reasons during the course of the academic term. It is almost always a bad idea to add additional requirements or to change the syllabus substantially once it has been distributed to students. With four weeks to go in the semester, don't surprise your students with an announcement that you've decided to make the 4-page minor assignment due next Monday an 18-page major term paper because the class did so poorly on the last quiz. That kind of thing will always generate a rash of complaints. Similarly, if you failed to state any expectations about attendance, don't announce half-way through the semester that because of your concern about high absenteeism, you are going to start grading students on their attendance. Learn from your mistakes and craft a better syllabus next time.

As a general rule, don't ask students to do *more* than the syllabus states; however, you probably won't have any trouble if you ask students to do a little less. For instance, suppose you underestimated the amount of work required for students to complete their assignments. Even though the syllabus stated that they had to turn in 12 of these, you might decide to require only 10. If you are going to cancel some assignments, make this decision early enough that students won't have already invested time working on the one you are thinking about canceling.

Even though you should think of the syllabus as a contract, there's no reason to be paranoid about it. Sometimes adjustments are necessary. If a blizzard blows in and no one can get to class on the date of a scheduled exam or when a major paper was due, accommodations must be made.

Note, too, that in preparing the syllabus you may discover a desire to establish certain "rules" to keep order and ensure that students perform to expectation, but at the same time you might experience a conflict because of the knowledge that too many rules smother creativity and interfere with learning. Finding one's place on the no rules/rules continuum is not always easy and is very much a personal decision. Experience suggests that unnecessary rules can be relaxed if they are not needed. And while, in theory, new rules can be promulgated at any time during the academic term, once a class has met together for several weeks, each class develops its own customs and traditions and the imposition of new standards is not always tolerated without much complaining and protest.

Selecting a Text

There are more options available to instructors today than in years past. First of all, you might opt not to require a textbook but to scan your lecture notes and other relevant materials into an Internet site that students can read on their computers. On campuses where most of the students have their own computers and easy access to the World Wide Web, this is becoming an increasingly popular way of providing instructional material. Note that it is necessary to secure copyright permission when electronically reproducing chapters from books, articles from journals, or graphs, charts, or illustrations appearing in commercially prepared publications.

Another possibility is to assemble a collection of readings that you like and to have them reproduced at your local photocopy center. These can be compiled in a number of different forms, from loose-leaf, three-hole punched for notebooks, to plastic spiral binding, to being bound like paperback books. This option allows you to finely tune the material your students will learn and to overcome the shortcomings of some texts. You get to choose the very best journal articles and to arrange the readings in a way that makes the most sense according to the way you teach the content.

The third choice, of course, is to adopt a text from one of many already on the market. There's a lot to be said for staying with a commercially produced text. For one thing, it provides continuity and, over time, standardizes content. Knowing what material students learned when they are transferring from or to another school is made a lot easier when a well-known text is used. Furthermore, texts often have features such as review questions and potential assignments or projects that will be lacking in collections of journal articles, unless you take the time to create them.

Choosing the right text to use with your class is an important decision—not only for you but for your students, too. After all, they will spend hundreds of dollars on these purchases each academic term. The textbook extends your instruction outside of the classroom; it is your representative outside of class. The text needs to be informative, current, and written on a level accessible to students. Students prefer that their books be inexpensive to purchase, not too densely packed with verbiage, and generously endowed with illustrations and graphics for visual interest.

Students are savvy consumers. About a third of the students in your classroom may not purchase their own copy of the text or texts you assign. Bookstores, of course, know this and often order substantially fewer books than there are students enrolled in courses. Students on tight budgets might borrow the assigned text from the library or from a friend, make their own photocopy of it, or go in with a classmate and jointly purchase the text. The bookstore managers also know that first-year students tend to buy proportionately more of their books than students in their third or fourth year. The student's decision to buy a text may hinge on what you say about it.

If, for instance, you suggest the book is only a supplement to the *required* text, or that the class will read portions of it—not the whole book—fewer students will make the purchase than if you clearly state that there will be weekly reading assignments from the book or that students should bring it to class with them at each meeting. All other factors being equal, students are more likely to buy books that are (1) not terribly expensive, (2) appear interesting and relevant, and (3) perceived as necessary in order to get a good grade.

As a new instructor, you may be faced with the decision of whether to adopt a new text or to stay with the one that has been popular with the other instructors in your department. If you stay with the current text, students will often be happier, because of the availability of used books—some students will have already purchased the old one from friends or roommates just completing the course. However, sometimes the very features of a book that were responsible for it being adopted change or get dropped in new editions and there is less reason to stick with it. Students will have to buy new books anyway when revised editions come out, so if you want to change texts, that might not be a bad time. Conversely, another time to go on the market for a new text is when the current one hasn't been revised for many years.

When you wish to consider a new text, what should you look for? Start with the preface. What does the author tell you about the book? Is it written for undergraduate or graduate students? Is it best suited for an introductory-level or an intermediate-level course? Next, browse the table of contents. Does the organization of the material make sense? Does there seem to be sufficient coverage of important topics and issues? Is it proportioned in a way that fits your teaching emphasis or academic term?

Read several chapters. Does the author have a writing style that is appropriate for your students? Is the content up to date? Is it presented in an interesting way? Would it stimulate thinking and class discussion? Is the content relevant? Are the ideas expressed clearly? Is the level of abstraction appropriate? Does the author make frequent use of headings and subheadings? When new terms are introduced, does the author highlight these? Is the index detailed?

There are also book features that especially benefit students— for instance, review questions or problems (with answers) at the end of each chapter. Recommendations of supplemental readings can also be helpful—particularly if they are current. In some disciplines, it might be important to have glossaries in the back of texts. You may also want to adopt a text that has an accompanying instructor's manual or test bank.

Although we know better than to "judge a book by its cover," we probably all do fall into that trap, at least occasionally. In fact, a colleague told me that he once chose one book over another because it looked more substantial. He chose a text of almost 800 pages over one about half that size. Although he usually was unable to get through the whole book, he thought that the smaller book suggested there wasn't as much for students to learn as there really was. Obviously, a smaller book that students are inclined to read and able to understand will do more to further their education than large, obtuse texts that they don't read.

Choosing texts always involves trade-offs. The book you choose may not be organized the way you like and it might be necessary to assign chapters out of order, or to assign additional readings for particularly weak chapters. However, students prefer to read chapters straight through rather than skip around. The best advice is: Choose the book with the most features you deem essential and the one with the fewest disadvantages.

If you make a mistake and choose a text that you later discover to be less than satisfactory, don't bemoan this all through the academic term. Students will wonder why you didn't give the decision more thought and may be troubled by the fact that your announcement of plans to change texts next term means they won't be able to sell their used copies back to the bookstore. Even a text with certain flaws will seldom cause students irreparable harm. The only problem will be that you will probably have to work a little harder to bring in material to cover its deficiencies. Doubtlessly, you will not choose any texts where there are factual errors or where the author's biases show too clearly.

Quick Checklist for Evaluating Texts

____ 1. Is the material pertinent to course objectives?
____ 2. Is the content up to date?
____ 3. Is the book organized and logical?
____ 4. Is it clearly written?
____ 5. Will students find the book interesting and accessible?
____ 6. Does it conform to general departmental or professional standards?
____ 7. Will students find its cost reasonable?
____ 8. Is this book well suited for the way I teach?
____ 9. Is this book/edition available in time for the start of class?
____ 10. Is there a test bank or instructor's manual available?

While you are reviewing texts, it is a good idea to keep on hand one or two that you like although you may not adopt. These will allow you to draw lecture material, examples, and so forth from texts other than the one you have chosen for the class. This is one way to provide variety to students and to keep them from knowing that you are "only one chapter ahead of them" (Sawyer, Prichard, & Hostetler, 1992, p. 188).

Problems to Avoid

Although there are many ways in which instructors may communicate less directly or clearly than they intend, one mistake commonly made by educators teaching a course for the first time is that they may have rich and intricate visions of how they want students to demonstrate comprehension and synthesis of the material, but they somehow fail to convey this information to those enrolled. Before you send the final version of your syllabus off to be duplicated, check to make sure your expectations have been fully articulated. Be very specific. Avoid vaguely worded instructions, as in the following instructions in the left-hand column:

Examples

Instruction	*Students May Interpret As:*
"Write a short paper."	Write a paragraph. Write a half a page. Type a two- to three-page paper.
"Keep a log of your experiences."	Make daily entries. Make weekly entries. Make an entry whenever the spirit moves me. At the end of the term, record what I recall. Record what interesting things I learned from the material, how I might be able to use it, questions that arose, how I reacted to the material on an emotional level.
"Obtain an article from a periodical in the library."	Any magazine article. An article from a professional journal. A *recent* journal article. A column from a newsletter. A journal article written in 1896. A journal article under three pages in length.

Is it important that all the papers be typed? If you leave the instructions open, some students will type and others will write in longhand. With no required word count (e.g., at least 500 words), one or two students will set their margins on 2 inches on all sides to make their skimpy papers seem longer. Others will handwrite in large, loopy letters to use as much space as possible. Similarly, if you expect that students should employ five references in their papers, then you need to include that in the instructions. And you might want to define what "counts" as a reference: Their textbook? Something they find on the Internet? Must it be from a professional journal?

With undergraduates, it is often useful to specify in the syllabus that assignments are due at the *beginning* of each class. Otherwise, there will always be a few students who forgot and who then proceed to do their homework while you are lecturing or attempting to involve the class in a discussion or group activity. Although it is possible to go overboard and to be *too detailed* in your instructions (I once heard of a 50-page syllabus), it is generally better to produce more guidelines than too few.

Weighting Tests, Assignments, and Participation/Attendance

Some otherwise intelligent students perform very badly on in-class tests. Other students with underdeveloped written communication skills do poorly on assignments that require composition and logical argument, but obtain the highest scores on multiple-choice tests. Putting too much weight on a single term paper without other controls can almost guarantee that students will get help (to say it nicely) or have someone else author their papers. And what professor hasn't experienced students who can't or won't attend class? Few individuals do all things well. So, how does one decide the best balance for assessing students?

The most fair way is to use a mixture of assessment approaches. Over the years, I've learned that I'm a soft-touch for students when it comes to grading their papers and assignments. Usually if they don't do well, I blame inadequate instructions and resolve to revise the syllabus. I tend to find some kernel of merit even in the vaguest of responses. Knowing this about myself, I almost always construct my syllabi so that the most weight comes from at least two objective (multiple-choice type) tests. With undergraduates, I frequently assess their performance with three objective tests. I prefer that 60 to 75 percent of a student's grade is based on such examinations. The weight given to everything else centers on that decision. However, in courses where there is less emphasis on content and more on creativity and original thinking, objective tests are not going to be the best method for assessment. These may need to be replaced with in-class writing assignments or projects that allow students to showcase their talents.

Assignments can also be structured so that subjectivity is minimized. However, homework where students are all working on the same problems makes it difficult for the instructor to know to what extent students shared information or helped each other. Of course, sometimes instructors want students to interact and collaborate on assignments. (See Chapter 4 for more discussion on the use of groups.) When collaboration is not wanted, one approach is to create assignments that produce individualized responses. These tend to be more enjoyable to read but require more time to grade. I tend to favor giving multiple (7 to 10) brief one- to two-page assignments that can be graded quickly. Even if a student doesn't do well on several of these, there are many other occasions when he or she should perform more successfully. These assignments can create opportunities for students to reflect on what they are learning and inform me whether the material is being understood. Short, 10-question quizzes could accomplish the second objective, but not the first.

Building in an expectation of attendance (e.g., 10 percent of their grade) conveys the message that it is important to attend class. This can also be communicated by including questions on every test that come from the lecture or class discussion and that would not be found in the text. Requiring attendance, however, is not a point of strong consensus among all faculty. Some adopt the position that if students learn (whether from the notes of comrades, reading independently, or even audiotaping)—that is the key issue, not whether students actually sit in a classroom during a given hour. Other faculty insist on attendance because they use Socratic dialogue or small group techniques or simply don't like lecturing to a bunch of tape recorders in a mostly empty room (a problem, I learned recently, that faculty in a medical school were experiencing).

Because I want to minimize subjectivity in grading, I usually do not distinguish between attendance and participation. If the two concepts are separated, the issue that arises involves judging the *quality* of a student's contributions versus their *quantity*. For instance, should participation be counted if a student regularly asks if the class can take its break? Is one astute question that generates stimulating class discussion better than three "staged" questions where the answers are obvious and possibly already known to the questioner?

However, over the years there have been times when I wished I had stated in the syllabus that attendance *and* participation were going to be evaluated separately. One semester I taught a class by interactive television (ITV) and the students were so hesitant to raise questions that the quality of the course was affected. I learned my lesson and vowed that if I taught that same class by ITV again, students *would be graded* on their participation.

Objective assessment may not be possible in every course. Creative writing is one example that comes to mind where objectivity in grading is not possible to the same extent as in the math or physics department. Great variation will also be found in how instructors develop their weights. The only caution is that basing too much of the final grade on attendance or a combination of attendance and participation can inflate a student's final grade. The following illustration shows how weighting can affect a mediocre student's grade:

Heavy Weighting of Attendance/Participation

	Average	*Weight*
Objective test scores	75	(40%)
Minor assignments	85	(30%)
Attendance and participation	95	(30%)
Final Grade	**84**	

Heavy Weighting of Objective Tests

	Average	*Weight*
Objective test scores	75	(70%)
Minor assignments	85	(20%)
Attendance and participation	95	(10%)
Final Grade	**79**	

All things being equal, giving more weight to attendance and participation can help weaker students earn higher grades than they might expect otherwise. Also, try to match the weighting of assignments and tests as much as possible to the course objectives. An assignment that covers two or three course objectives should be worth more than one peripherally related to a single or minor objective. Similarly, a comprehensive exam should count more than a test for a single unit.

Assignments as Pedagogical Tools

Most of us can recall, either from high school or our own college experiences, courses where the assignments could best be characterized as simply dreary, mind-numbing busywork. Instructors in high school who favored this legalized form of torture seemed to do so as a means of crowd control—students stayed occupied and quieter than they ordinarily would be. College instructors who engage in this behavior are just poor teachers.

In the best of all possible worlds, every assignment should be instructive—helping students make new discoveries while encouraging them to think independently and creatively. Now it's true, any one assignment that you think is strategic and essential might be viewed by students as a waste of time. If students complain more than you think they should, several factors may be at work: You may not have explained the importance of the assignment sufficiently, they may have already completed similar assignments recently for another instructor, or perhaps you are asking too much. What is it you want to accomplish with your assignments? Each one should have an objective and lend itself in some way to the overall plan of what students should be learning, but too much repetition kills interest.

Benjamin Bloom (1956) published a widely heralded set of educational objectives that may provide you with a useful starting place to begin thinking about the assignments you require.

Bloom's Cognitive Taxonomy

(Arranged from concrete to abstract and simple to complex levels)

Knowledge:	(Remembering factual materials)
	Students must remember, memorize, recognize, describe, and recall.
	Sample verbs that would be used: *define, describe, list, name, cite, recall, state, identify*
Comprehension:	(Grasping the meaning of materials)
	Students must interpret, describe, and explain knowledge.
	Sample verbs that would be used: *discuss, explain, interpret, extrapolate, arrange, sort, classify*
Application:	(Problem solving)
	Students must apply facts, rules, and principles to produce some result.

Analysis:

Sample verbs that would be used: *apply, illustrate, sketch, solve, demonstrate, use* (An understanding of the structure and components of knowledge)

Students must be able to break down knowledge and show relationships among the parts.

Sample verbs that would be used: *analyze, appraise, categorize, contrast, criticize, distinguish, examine, differentiate, compare*

Synthesis:

(Creating a unique, original product; combining ideas to form a new whole)

Students must bring together parts and components of knowledge to form a whole and build relationships for new situations.

Sample verbs that would be used: *compose, create, construct, formulate, propose, plan, design, organize, prescribe*

Evaluation:

(Making value decisions about issues; resolving controversies)

Students must make judgments about the value of material for given purposes.

Sample verbs that would be used: *appraise, argue, assess, attack, compare, evaluate, predict, support, defend, recommend*

In the lower-division courses, it is natural to expect students to commit new terms and vocabularies to memory, but few educators would be happy if that is all that students learned. Besides providing us with a structure to help us think about the assignments we create, Bloom's taxonomy is also useful for evaluating the types of questions we might employ when developing examinations.

Another consideration is the timing of the assignments. One or two opportunities to assess what students are learning before a major exam or project can be beneficial to all parties. Similarly, scheduling minor projects or quizzes through the academic term will encourage students to stay current and is preferable to a single, heavily weighted project or exam in the final week of the academic term. Many students will procrastinate and delay working until they absolutely have to, and the quality of classroom discussions will suffer when they are not reading and preparing for class.

Mastery learning is a concept proposing that students could, for example, be allowed to redo an assignment on multiple occasions—until they get it right. Many students like this idea because those who are willing to work hard and to put in the hours feel that they will eventually get a desirable grade. Pedagogically, the concept is sound. Students who receive feedback and revise and then get additional advice and revise have several (many?) opportunities to learn from their mistakes. Although only the most motivated of students will pursue this option, instructors who are considering adopting this teaching technique should realize that it also requires more of their own time for grading. Another point for consideration is whether students revising their assignments should get the same grade as students who got it correct on the first attempt. McKeachie (1999) recommended discounting the rewritten papers somewhat so that they are not counted as equivalent to those that have not been rewritten.

Critical Thinking

As we struggle to keep up with the latest developments in our field, most educators are well aware of how fast knowledge is multiplying. And, it is not just the amount of information that must be processed, but new ideas and research attack cherished theories and assumptions. What we learned only a handful of years ago may tomorrow become as outmoded as the manual typewriter. As a result, almost all college and university educators accept that the teaching of critical thinking should be a fundamental goal of education (Keeley et al., 1995). Unlike teaching in simpler eras, teaching in 2002 and beyond cannot consist solely of a one-way transfer of knowledge from the instructor to his or her students. Our pupils, the future leaders of this country and the world, must be taught how to find creative solutions to problems in an environment where the major feature is a constant barrage of new information. We cannot simply ladle out facts, theorems, or formulae and return to our offices. We must teach students how to think.

What is critical thinking? It is teaching students to analyze data and solve problems—to think—by examining, evaluating, and challenging the assumptions, premises, interpretations, and evidence that others have taken for granted. It is thinking "outside of the box." Critical thinking is sometimes known as developing *higher-order thinking* and is exemplified in the last three categories in Bloom's taxonomy (analysis, synthesis, and evaluation).

The Socratic method of teaching using probing questions instead of lectures is commonly cited as a model for helping students develop their reasoning skills. In this approach, the questions that are asked are not designed to test for acquisition of knowledge where there is a single correct answer, but to help the student examine alternative ways of viewing a problem and discover general principles or solutions. Critical thinking centers on the questions—lively, interesting, "deep" questions that stimulate self-reflection and debate within the class. Educators using this approach can ask questions regarding:[1]

- Interpretation (What underlying meanings or values are inherent?)
- Point of view (What other perspectives are possible?)
- Assumptions (What is being taken for granted?)
- Implications (What is the logical conclusion?)
- Relevance (Does the statement directly relate to the issue?)
- Accuracy (Is it true?)
- Logic (Do the parts fit together?)
- Evidence (Are the data reasonable?)

Teaching in this manner requires much skill in keeping the discussion focused. Each student's response must be carefully considered as implications and logical extensions are traced out. Students are not always comfortable with a Socratic style because they fear that they will give an "incorrect" answer and look stupid. Overholser (1997) recommended that if a student responds by stating, "I don't know," the instructor ought to rephrase the question or provide an example. "Simply repeating the question or dropping it entirely does nothing to facilitate the learning process. Inducing students to persist and attack the problem from several different vantage points can help them answer the question and can give them an important coping skill" (p. 15).

Instructors must model openness and integrity and be willing to explain their thinking—indeed, to expose it to public debate (Brookfield, 1987). You must create a climate in the classroom where most everyone feels comfortable to speculate and exchange ideas, where members can disagree with each other without feeling insulted or belittled. Brookfield has noted:

> *There is no point in . . . asking critically insightful questions and practicing a devastating critique of generally accepted assumptions, if people are insulted or intimidated in the process. The worst thing . . . is to suggest, by a verbal response or some kind of body language (smirk, sigh, quizzically raised eyebrow) that someone's comment, writing, or other form of contribution falls pitifully short of some desired critical standard. (p. 72)*

Students who volunteer information in the Socratic classroom very likely feel that they are taking huge risks. They are volunteering personal material, in some instances, that they may have never spoken aloud. Their thoughts may not be expressed eloquently; they may speak hesitantly with many false starts and stops. Because as instructors we have the decided advantage in having planned the questions ahead of time, reflected on them, and perhaps devoted considerable time to preparing with reading and discussion with colleagues, we must not intellectually bully our students. Once again, to quote Brookfield, "Humility is essential to teachers, lest they slip into the all-too-seductive (but appallingly arrogant) role of omniscient guru of critical thinking" (p. 81).

Techniques for Developing Critical Thinking

Here are a few ideas that you might be able to use in the classroom to help students develop higher-order thinking skills:[2]

- Have students develop flowcharts, models, concept maps, or decision trees.
- Schedule mock trials or debates.

- After a presentation or reading, have students write a critique, rebuttal, or rejoinder.
- Implement minute papers, reflection logs, student learning journals, or learning portfolios. Be creative: Ask for a 100-word analysis of the last class.
- Ask students to prepare abstracts of articles, reviews of books, or outlines with commentary of presentations.
- When there is a great deal of supplemental reading, request that students develop a taxonomy or categorization of the articles. Ask that they conceptualize three different ways the articles could be categorized.
- Practice brainstorming on some problem or issue.
- Involve the class in a nominal group decision-making process.
- Present a case that demonstrates a particular point. Ask students to analyze the case for factual errors, erroneous assumptions, or interpretations. Alternatively, ask them to write another case with the same basic information but to change it so that a different solution can be found.
- Around one central point, have students identify two different analogies to support the example and then two that contradict it. (Collaborative learning techniques are further discussed in Chapter 4.)

Assignments: How Much Is Too Much, Too Little?

In one class I heard about, the instructor assigned hundreds of pages of reading every week as well as a short reaction paper. The students complained vigorously but the instructor did little to reduce their workload. As the end of the semester approached, the students staged a mutiny and refused to do any additional reading because so much was expected of them that they hadn't been able to work on their end-of-the-term paper. When students en masse express their unhappiness about the amount of work required or the quantity of assignments, you need to listen. They often have talked with other students who have had the same course with different teachers and have a good sense of the amount of work being required by your colleagues. Sometimes we *do* get carried away. If you are hearing a lot of complaining, then talk with a more senior colleague about what you are having the students do. A different perspective is often helpful. It is also quite possible that other instructors are not demanding enough of their students and that the right thing to do is to expect your pupils to do more.

Pedagogically, there seems to be real value in requesting that students turn in some of their own handiwork at least once a week. These don't have to be long, complicated assignments requiring a great deal of research. Weekly assignments or quizzes communicate that you take the business of teaching seriously, that your course is the real McCoy, that students may not succeed if they don't give it a good effort. Weekly assignments provide a structure that many students need to keep them from procrastinating themselves into a deep hole at the end of the semester.

Many students will be delighted if their only assignment is a single paper due at the end of the term. Even though you know that in order to get a grade of A, they will need to be working on the paper each week, you shouldn't be surprised to find that some of your students will wait until the last minute before doing any work at all. If you don't require attendance (or if you do but you don't build in tests or assignments to be completed on a periodic basis), you may find that fewer students will attend and participate in class than if you expect more from them. Although a single end-of-the-term paper can require as much or more work than a series of weekly assignments, students who procrastinate until the last minute won't be as involved in the class and will contribute less to discussions.

In terms of the number of hours that students can be expected to work outside of class on their assignments, there are few hard and fast rules. However, there is some evidence that many instructors in the United States expect about two hours of involvement per week per credit hour; however, students *on average* actually spend less than one hour per week per credit hour (cited in McKeachie, 1999). Planning for students to spend *at least* three hours each week out of class in reading, studying, and involved with assignments for every three-hour course doesn't seem at all unreasonable—to the contrary, it may strike some instructors as much too little. Instructors concerned about the amount of time to require of students outside of class might want to estimate how much time is needed for their reading, library work, and so on, and then to approximate the amount of time required for the planned assignments. These estimates could then be checked with a more experienced colleague for reasonableness.

Another idea for arriving at the amount of time students spend out of class on course-related work would be to offer, at the beginning of the term, extra credit points to any students who keep *detailed* logs of the amount of time that they spend on the course outside of class. Alternatively, this could be a course requirement (an assignment). The instructor could then collect these logs periodically and adjust or fine-tune the amount of work levied on the students. A benefit of these logs could be that they might be diagnostically useful when students are not doing well in your class.

Do I Have to Read Every Sentence?

If you are requiring a lot (e.g., daily) of assignments from students and are hard-pressed to get them all graded, one option is to collect the papers and then pair each student with another for peer evaluation. Criteria can be prepared ahead of time to guide students in their grading. Sometimes the questions that emerge when students are asked to grade peers' papers serve as a review of points that may not have been well understood by the class.

Another option is to grade simply for completion of the assignment—students might get a check mark or a zero or four out of five possible points. There's also no reason why you can't take up homework on a more or less random basis. Grade the first four assignments but then don't take up the fifth assignment, grade the sixth assignment, skip the next one. As long as you don't make the announcement ahead of time, most students will do the assignments because you'll keep them guessing as to whether you'll be collecting the homework or not. But if students have invested a lot of time on an assignment, they will be miffed if you don't take up their work and give them the good grades they think they have earned.

When you are able to determine that the majority of students seem to have a good understanding of the material (e.g., by randomly calling on several students) one other option is to announce that you won't be grading that day's or that set of assignments, but that you will give feedback to any student who is concerned that he or she might not have done the assignment correctly. As a general rule, if you plan to *not* grade every daily or weekly assignment, tell the students this at the beginning of the academic term.

Should Spelling and Grammatical Errors Be Overlooked?

It can be very difficult to focus on the content of a student's paper and to give it any credibility if every other word is misspelled. Similarly, students who don't know when to capitalize or insert commas can distract and frustrate even the most tolerant of readers. Should instructors overlook grammatical and spelling errors? Not if your goal is to educate students. Oftentimes it is possible for student to go pretty far in college without knowing basics that should have been learned earlier. When you find yourself covering a student's paper with red correction marks on more than one occasion, this suggests that the student could benefit from a referral to a writing center.

Unless you are in the English department, students will probably think it unfair of you to grade down their papers because of spelling or grammatical errors. That doesn't mean you shouldn't maintain high standards. If you are a stickler for well-written papers, alert your students to this. Share with them the criteria you will use to grade their work. Encourage them to do more than one draft and to have someone else proof their rough drafts. Be specific. If you recommend in your syllabus that students spell-check all of their papers before turning them in, you will get a better-quality paper than if you don't emphasize the importance of good writing.

How much should you "punish" a student who has horrible written communication skills? This is a judgment call. Students seem comfortable with no more than 5 or 10 percent of their grades on assignments being affected by their own poor grammar or spelling. However, you could defend dropping the grade on a particular paper by a whole letter if you have stated the grading criteria in the syllabus. Suppose you are inclined to fail the student altogether just because of poor communication skills. Is that fair? Maybe, if you are in the English department, but it probably isn't if your discipline is geology. A wiser course of action might be to offer the student the chance to revise and resubmit the paper. This is one of those areas where you would be well advised to consult with your departmental colleagues first. What would they do in such a case? As a new instructor, you may not want to generate too many student complaints your first year.

What Student Presentations Could and Should Accomplish

Like a steady diet of chips and cookies, too much lecturing, even if you think of yourself as a skilled communicator, might not be as educationally "healthy" for students as allowing them to participate more actively. Variety is good. Using a mixture of approaches to convey material that students need to learn helps keep them interested and involved. One way to get out of the rut of lecturing every class meeting is to structure time for student presentations.

Educators usually incorporate student presentations for all of the following reasons:

- Presentations provide students with the opportunity to be creative and to demonstrate, often in an innovative way, what they have learned.
- Presentations help students learn organizational skills.
- Presentations provide students with the opportunity to hone their public speaking skills.
- Presentations (especially those coupled with discussion of the topic afterwards) encourage intellectual exchange and help students gain different perspectives and interpretations.
- Presentations give students a different motivation for learning class material and involve them actively in learning.
- Presentations reduce the amount of time or material that the instructor has to prepare.

This last reason is a terrible rationale for building in student presentations into the syllabus. However, realistically, many new faculty do rely on students to help shoulder some of the responsibility for their courses—for instance, the instructor might be scheduled to present a major paper at a conference in November and knows that he or she won't have the time to prepare a lecture in the week afterward. Also, many courses lend themselves to a format where students would naturally be expected to summarize and share with classmates their research projects at the end of the academic term.

When you decide to include student presentations in your course, be advised of the following problems you may encounter:

Problem	*Solution*
1. Many students will read their presentations word for word and make even the most attentive class slumberous.	Instruct students not to read, but to *tell* in their own words; encourage them to use transparencies or note cards.
2. Students may take too much time.	Explain how this might be a problem and you will therefore need to interrupt if they run over their allotment; bring a stopwatch or a kitchen timer to class; appoint a student to be the time-keeper.
3. Students (particularly group presentations) run well short of the time (i.e., a whole class period) allotted.	Clearly instruct the students to practice their group presentations—to hold "dress rehearsals" and to time themselves. Inform them that they will lose points if their presentation is too short.
4. Students who are not presenting don't pay enough attention or may not come to class.	Announce ahead of time that you will draw several test questions from the presentations; don't allow students or groups to show lengthy videos that may have been widely seen. Require and take attendance.

Above all else, student presentations should provide your class with another opportunity to learn. This means that students must wrestle with their material—integrating and organizing it differently than they would if just cramming for a test. When you hold the expectation that students will learn from these projects, they will be much more serious than when they suspect you don't value their presentations. If you create the right climate, students may relish the role of being educators, too. In order to make a good showing, they may put far more hours into preparation or into library research than they would if they weren't expected to make a presentation. However, you should be prepared to meet with students outside of class to give them ideas and resources, and, if necessary, to approve their plans.

References and Resources

Bloom, B. (1956). *Taxonomy of educational objectives. Vol 1: Cognitive domain.* New York: McKay.

Brookfield, S. D. (1987). Effective strategies for facilitating critical thinking. *Developing critical thinkers: Challenging adults to explore alternative ways of thinking and acting.* San Francisco: Jossey-Bass.

Diamond, R. M. (1989). *Designing and improving courses and curricula in higher education: A systematic approach.* San Francisco: Jossey-Bass.

Keeley, S. M., Shemberg, K. M., Cowell, B. S., & Zinnbauer, B. J. (1995). Coping with student resistance to critical thinking: What the psychotherapy literature can tell us. *College Teaching, 43,* 140–145.

McKeachie, W. J. (1999). *McKeachie's teaching tips: Strategies, research, and theory for college and university teachers.* Boston: Houghton Mifflin.

Overholser, J. C. (1997). Socrates in the classroom. *College Teaching, 40,* 14–19.

Sawyer, R. M., Prichard, K. W., & Hostetler, K. D. (1992). *The art and politics of college teaching.* New York: Peter Lang.

Endnotes

1. Many of these questions were drawn from the following website on "The Role of Questions in Thinking, Teaching, and Learning" at <www.sonoma.edu/cthink/>.

2. Most of these ideas were derived from a chapter entitled "Learner-Centered Web Instruction for Higher-Order Thinking, Teamwork, and

Apprenticeship" by C. J. Bonk and T. H. Reynolds (1997) in Badrul Khan (Ed.), *Web-based instruction*. Englewood Cliffs, NJ: Educational Technology Publications, pp. 167–178.

3

Classroom
Strategies

Overview: Knowing what you want to accomplish and deciding how best to go about achieving it requires advanced planning and preparation. To build a sense of community and lively discussion, you may want to employ ice-breakers and warm-up exercises. To continually keep students involved, active learning strategies may be useful. Lecturing, despite research that shows it is one of the least effective methods available to educators, remains a main staple in most classrooms. It stands to reason, then, that new faculty ought to know something about how to prepare lectures and how to help students to get the most from this teacher-centered learning approach.

The First Class Meeting

If you are a conscientious individual, you'll probably plan to do more than to merely hand out the syllabus on the first class meeting. Students are excited and enthusiastic at the beginning of a new academic term. They are curious about you, about how "hard" the course will be, about how many books they'll have to purchase, or about how many hours they'll be in the laboratory. Their exuberance may never be higher.

It is important to have a syllabus ready (and a few extra copies available) for the first class meeting. This shows students that you are prepared and conscientious. It also gives them the overview that they need. For instance, if you are teaching a literature course and expecting the class to read 10 paperbacks *and* write a 40-page research paper, a single working mother with young children at home may need to drop this course and take one less demanding. Inevitably, there will be students who've strayed into the wrong class or who haven't heard everything you've said—so the syllabus helps sort out students who need to be some place else.

Handing out and explaining the syllabus is a good way to begin your first class. As you explain, for instance, your attendance or grading policy, students get to know you as a person and what you consider to be essential for success. Something of your personality is revealed and they'll decide whether it is a good match with theirs. Even though you believe that the education of your young charges is weighty business, you are probably better off not to take yourself too seriously. Students feel a rapport with an instructor who can smile and perhaps tell them about the first time he inadvertently screwed up a lab assignment or got lost on campus.

After you've gone over the syllabus and answered any questions, then you might want to check the roll to see who is there and who isn't. There are two arguments for calling the roll the first several weeks: (1) it emphasizes the importance of attendance and (2) it allows the instructor to get to know his or her students—to associate names with faces. Starting the first class by calling the roll seems somewhat more formal than doing it later, after everyone has had a syllabus and heard you speak a bit about it.

Taking the time to go around the room (if you've got under 30 students or so) and to have everyone introduce themselves can create an atmosphere that indicates you want to know your students and to hear from them. If you plan to lecture from bell to bell and believe that any questions from students will be unnecessary, if not unwelcome, then you can skip having them make introductions.

What you do next is up to you. Since the first class meeting is regarded by most faculty as a "light" or no content day, you can begin to gently ease your students into thinking about your topic by posing several open-ended questions to get them thinking and at the same time to help you gauge their knowledge and awareness. For example, an instructor of an introductory statistics course might ask, "What good are numbers? What do they do for us?" Or the class could brainstorm the different ways that numerical values are used in our society. Brainstorming is a good technique to use. Since there is no single "correct" answer, most students feel free to make some kind of a response and it communicates to the class that you are open to hearing various points of view. Alternatively, the American Literature instructor could pose a hypothetical situation for class discussion: What would the world be like without any literature? This might be followed by telling the class how you became interested in the topic you are teaching—from the problem or circumstance that initially hooked your curiosity to the steps that led you to this particular college or university. Perhaps there's some question for which you have been seeking an answer? Maybe there's some research you hope to conduct? Students often aren't aware of the mysteries and unresolved questions in the various disciplines. Even a brief mention of a few of these questions can sustain students' interest in the course material to be covered.

The decision of whether to hold a "real" class during the first meeting and to actually lecture or present material that students need to know will likely be based on such considerations as the length of your class period and academic term. If you have been assigned to a class that meets once a week for two or three hours at a time, you probably will decide to present content at the first class meeting. This is usually a good decision. Some students actually do complain when they have driven some distance to get to class, fought for a parking place, arrived early with pens and fresh notebooks—only to be handled a syllabus and dismissed 15 minutes later. Also, it is logical that if you are feeling there is too much material and too few weeks to cover it all, you would not want to waste the first meeting. By the time you have finished drafting your syllabus, you'll have a good idea about whether the first meeting should be "light" or content-rich.

Just in case you need some further help, think about what message you want to send on the first day. Do you want to impress upon students how much work there will be? How many books they will have to read? How difficult it will be for them to get an A? Do you want to convince them that they will never be as smart as you? Or do you want to spark their curiosity in the topic and build a sense of community?

Judging How Much Material to Prepare

The rule here is simple: Always be ready with more material than you think you will use. Inevitably, whenever you prepare "just enough" for a 50-minute class, you'll run out of material 25 minutes after starting. You'll also be concerned and confused when a hand shoots up in front of you and some guy who has never paid much attention asks, "Do we have to take notes on this? Professor Smith covered it last semester—the same thing."

If you find yourself in this situation, ask for a show of hands to inform you of how many students got this content last term. You may decide to go ahead anyway and handle it as a review. If the majority of the class is insistent they've heard it all before and you don't need to go over the material again, then this is why you should always be prepared with more material than you think you'll use. Another situation is when you have planned for students to discuss some topic at length—let's say you set aside 20 minutes of the class period, but on that particular day the class just won't want talk, no matter what you do. This can happen when students are uncomfortable with a topic, such as diversity and ethnic differences, or where there are deeply held differences. When the larger group won't engage in discussion, another approach is to divide the class into small groups and ask them to deal with your questions. Then, after they've had some time, reconvene the class and have representatives from each of the groups summarize their discussion. So, if you can, always have additional material at the ready or some plans for what you might do if the class doesn't engage in discussion and you run short of material.

Ice-Breakers and Warm-Ups

If your goal is to create a community of learners where students can interact and learn from each other as well as from you, if you want your classes to feel comfortable debating and challenging each other, then you'll likely want to engage in some activities early in the academic term that will help them get to know each other. I have always thought of these as ice-breakers, but a colleague recently pointed out that teaching is a lot like performing (well, at least both are in front of an audience), and that entertainers often use warm-up acts to set the mood. So, if you want to set a climate that is conducive to students feeling comfortable raising questions and discussing with each other, you might want to use one or more of the following warm-up techniques:

For Class Introductions

Each student:

- Interviews a fellow student and prepares a 45-second introduction of the person on his or her right or left
- Informs the class of something very few people would know (e.g., once shook hands with the President)
- Describes the unique cultural experience or community in which he or she was raised
- Shares a wish, hope, or fear about the class
- Says, "To know me, you would have to be familiar with the book _____"
- Lists three adjectives that best describe him or her
- Jots down a pet peeve or myth
- Describes any relevant events or experiences that might make him or her an "expert" on some area (e.g., lived in Belize for two years in conjunction with Peace Corps assignment; spent last four years working midnight to dawn in a bakery)

When you ask students to reveal something about themselves that wouldn't normally come up in the classroom (one of my students once revealed that he actually *had* run away and joined the circus as a teen), you'll find a tremendous variety of rich experiences and diverse backgrounds that you can tap into when you want to make illustrations or examples. The class will also be more relaxed and willing to talk. You'll find yourself thinking of your students as a collection of interesting individuals (Marla went to a costume party as Medusa with papier mache snakes in her tresses!) rather than a dull and apathetic class that you dread to face.

Dynamic Lecturing

Most of us can easily recognize skilled lecturers. See if this description conforms to one that you have in mind: The lecturer approaches the podium with an air of confidence, pauses a moment or two, makes eye contact with the audience, and then proceeds to speak clearly about some subject or little known course of events that immediately captures your interest.

Contrast that image with this picture: The lecturer rushes in at the last minute or a few minutes late. Out of breath and with wind-blown hair, the lecturer fumbles with pages of text that appear to be shuffled out of order. His or her demeanor does not radiate confidence, but nervousness. He begins, "Uh, I'm here today, uh, because the chair of geography, um...Dr. What'shisname, asked me to speak to you people." Meanwhile, he is still trying to find page one of his notes but finally gives up and starts reading something that makes no sense because he didn't provide an introduction or context for the audience. He continues reading without looking up from his notes. As the lecture drones on, the microphone goes out or he loses volume and becomes almost inaudible but few care.

What do you want in a speaker? This would be my list of requirements for a successful lecturer: Someone who

- Makes frequent eye contact with the audience
- Knows the material so well that he or she can speak without reading the text and who, to be blunt, has something to say
- Incorporates humorous anecdotes or cartoons
- Provides an overview and summary
- Smiles occasionally
- Tells personal asides that illustrate points and provide a "break" from serious note-taking
- Has eliminated almost all redundancies and repetition from the lecture
- Emphasizes major points
- Knows how to tell a story
- Modulates his or her voice, speaking softly or more loudly at times
- Knows when to pause to let the audience reflect on a point
- Provides the audience with relevant examples or illustrations

- Has no distracting mannerisms or irritating verbal habits (e.g., saying "uh-h-h" after every complete thought)
- Is comfortable taking questions but who doesn't get sidetracked from the day's topic

Murray and Murray (1992) have suggested that four steps are required for lectures to become a "vibrant teaching method." The first step is *anticipation*. In this phase, the instructor considers the purpose of the lecture; the course itself; the resources available for drawing the lecture; the physical characteristics associated with the lecture hall or classroom; the specific content, including particular problems or concerns to be highlighted; and the students' demographics, level of motivation, and readiness. A major question is: What does the audience already know about the topic?

The second step is the *preparation* phase, where the instructor acquires needed resources, equipment, and examples; selects the content to be presented; prepares handouts; and composes the opening, the body, and the closing parts of the lecture.

Execution of the lecture is the third step. This involves conscious decisions about timing and pacing, demeanor, body language, and speech habits. For instance, never read to your audience, but speak to them. Work from an outline that makes it easy for the audience to follow while at the same time gives you the freedom to add a new example or illustration if it occurs spontaneously. Although many experts recommend driving your key points home by telling them once again (in summary fashion) what you've already told them, Brookfield (1990) has recommended concluding lectures with questions and unresolved issues. This, according to Brookfield, keeps the audience future oriented and in an inquiring state of mind.

The final step is *support*. By this, Murray and Murray mean that the lecturer engages in self-evaluation and examination in order to enhance his or her future presentations. Students can be asked to rate various aspects of the lecture and with this information the instructor can modify and revise the material for use the next time around. Run a videotape and watch yourself. If that is not possible, then bring a cassette recorder and make an audiotape.

Lecturers can also obtain rapid feedback from students after each class by using the "Minute Paper" (in which students are asked to jot down their thoughts at the end of class about a question such as, "What unanswered question do you have about the material presented today?" or "What was the most important thing you learned today?"). Another assessment technique is called the "The Muddiest Point," where students are asked to quickly write down a response on a half-sheet of paper or index card to the question, "What was the muddiest point in the lecture today?" (Angelo & Cross, 1993). Brookfield (1995) has described a "Critical Incident Questionnaire" that asks a few questions such as, "At what moment in the class did you feel most engaged with what was happening?" and "At what moment in the class did you feel most distanced from what was happening?" With any of these approaches it is not essential that students sign their names.

Lecturers have to contend with all kinds of distractions, from noisy heating/cooling ventilation systems to workers breaking up the sidewalk with jackhammers a few feet away. Be aware of your voice, and try to vary your pitch and volume at times. Don't speak in a monotone or so fast that students lose all hope of trying to take notes. If your voice doesn't project well, arrange for a microphone. Be careful not to use annoying words or verbal tics ("ah," "uh," or clearing your voice) too frequently.

Distribute outlines or write one on the board so that it's easy for students to follow your main points. Distinguish the key points and highlights from the falderal. When something is of significance, don't be afraid to say so. Always face your audience, don't lecture facing the chalkboard.

Brown (1978) has recommended that you start with a provocative question ("Have you ever thought, 'What if...'"), use task-oriented statements ("Now, let's look closely at ..."), signposts ("There are three main areas ..."), and linking/summarizing statements ("So far, we have looked at ..."). If you don't have a provocative question or dilemma, another technique is to start with an "alarming statistic," which can often be obtained from weekly news magazines or newspapers. Personal anecdotes work, too, as well as involving the audience by posing some question and asking for a show of hands.

When you've completed one major thought or section, pause momentarily before beginning a different topic. In a study by Ruhl, Hughes, and Schloss (1987), the instructor paused for two minutes on three occasions during lectures and allowed students to rework their notes or discuss the topic with another student with whom they were paired. At the end of each lecture, students were given three minutes to freely recall and write down the highlights of the lecture. A control group hearing the same lectures but without the pauses did significantly worse on the free recalls and the comprehensive test.

Take questions during pauses. Stop lecturing whenever you feel that your audience is not following you or whenever you notice raised eyebrows and feel that a portion of the class got lost on some point. Watch your audience as you speak; don't be so intent on your notes that you never make eye contact with your students.

Your posture and facial expression indicate your interest in lecturing to your audience. Try to be relaxed but slightly excited about what you have to present. Use gestures if they feel natural, but don't overdo it. Too much gesturing can be distracting. Most people enjoy humor, and lecturers should make use of it to keep the audience's interest. To paraphrase Noonan (1998), no one ever left a lecture saying, "I hated the way she made me laugh." If you make a mistake and the audience laughs, laugh, too. If humor is not easy for you, incorporate personal examples if they are relevant. Most audiences appreciate this kind of thing.

Finally, here's a wonderful quote that sums up rather nicely the lecturer's task. Follow this one bit of advice and you'll probably succeed as a lecturer: "Attitude is important. The teacher must consistently persuade that what is going on is important" (Kelly, Phillips, & Keaten, 1995, p. 158).

When finished preparing for a lecture, go over your notes a final time to make sure that your lecture passes the "so what?" test. Have you told them *what* is important and *why?* Have you been careful not to repeat the same content from their assigned readings? (Unless, of course, it is important to reiterate in order to emphasize points that students tend not to understand or to stress linkages that might not have been apparent.) Have you listed the key ideas and main points? Have you provided good examples? Have you summarized the main thoughts that you want them to remember? Have you told the class how you expect them to use the material?

Active Learning Strategies

The hardest classes to teach are those where students sit silently, seldom raising a question, staring at the top of their desks, avoiding your eyes. There's several possible explanations for this situation:

You have more shy students or fewer extroverts in your class for some inexplicable reason, you're teaching one of those required courses in which most students truly have no interest, or somehow you have convincingly conveyed the impression that *you* will be in *charge* and that *their* questions, comments, and concerns are *not important*. You didn't mean to kill their interest in raising questions. How could that have happened?

Well, have you been encouraging questions? Do you tend to dart into class at the last minute and bolt out of the room before any student can detain you? Have you attempted to learn their names? Have you shown them how the course is meaningful and relevant to the things in which they are interested? Have you been lecturing practically nonstop from bell to bell?

Regardless of the cause of students' lack of responsiveness, additional lecturing will not be the elixir that will make your students more dynamic and fun to teach. In fact, it will be counterproductive. To break any well-established notions of "Instructor talk, students listen," you'll need to stop being the center of attention and encourage students to interact more with the material and with each other.

Active learning is based on the following effective teaching principles (modified from Dearn, 1996):

- Students learn more when they are challenged to discuss, reflect, and problem solve.
- Creating opportunities for students to "try out" their ideas or understanding of the material and receive immediate feedback from peers increases participation and benefits learning.
- Students learn new knowledge easier if they can relate it to personal examples, life experiences, and knowledge they have already acquired.
- Learning styles within each classroom vary immensely, and not all students are well served by didactic lecturing.
- Students learn best with authentic tasks that build on and extend what they know.
- Students learn more when they have some control over what and how they learn.
- Prompt feedback is central to effective learning.

To employ active learning skills in the classroom usually involves such activities as role-playing, problem-solving tasks, case studies, simulations, debates, panel discussions, and the use of small groups in collaborative activities. It means, often, taking risks, allowing the classroom to get noisier (and students more excited), giving students the freedom to learn independent of you, allowing for the very likely possibility that some students will get off task, and realizing that these exercises will take longer and less material will be covered. In short, employing active learning techniques means that you will surrender some degree of control—learning in your classroom will be less authority based and more cooperative. However, the use of active learning doesn't have to be an all-or-nothing phenomenon—you can decide what is the best mix for your class. It could be that 80 percent didactic lecturing and 20 percent active learning is what you feel most comfortable with, or possibly a 70/30, 60/40, or even a 50/50 split.

Why Use Active Learning Techniques?

While it is true that lecturers can cover a great deal of material efficiently, the educator's task does not consist simply of broadcasting knowledge—if it did, we could stand on street corners with megaphones in our hands and shout at passers-by. Rather, our charge is to help students develop an understanding that allows them to apply their knowledge. So, while lecturing to a room of seated, silent pupils may be what we know best because that was what was perpetrated upon us, there are a few problems with the lecture-only model of instruction:

- *A lecture format relegates students to a secondary, passive role of absorbing knowledge. Depending on how long the lecturer lectures, there may be little or no opportunity to challenge or exchange ideas.*
- *Lectures themselves don't provide feedback about the amount of learning students have acquired.*
- *Students' interest wanes and ebbs, diminishes rapidly. Students are attending to what is being said about 40% of the time (Pollio cited in Meyers & Jones, 1993). Richard, Rogers, Ellis, & Beidleman (1988) found that four months after taking an introductory psychology course, students knew only 8% more than a control group who had never taken the course.*

- *Information obtained from lectures tends to be forgotten rapidly.*
- *Lecture-type classes require skilled oral communicators.*
- *Lectures don't assist students in developing the higher order thinking skills of analysis, synthesis, or evaluation.*
- *Teacher-talk type classes are based on the erroneous assumption that all students learn best by listening. (Bonwell, 1996)*

A frequently used rationale for active learning says, "Students retain 10% of what they read, 26% of what they hear, 30% of what they see, 50% of what they see and hear, 70% of what they say, and 90% of what they say as they do something" (Brock & Cameron, 1999).

In active learning classrooms, the instructor is more of a guide or facilitator. Consequently, students make discoveries that they can own and are motivated to apply this knowledge to new situations because it arrives at a rate they can absorb—unlike lectures flowing like a heavy downpour into a storm drain. Those who are a little squeamish about doing less lecturing would do well to read "The Case for Leaving Things Out" by Linc Fisch (1996). In that essay, Fisch draws on the analogy of directing a driver from one city to another. What's most useful in such situations is not a detailed description of every barn, place of business, or billboard that the driver might see along the way, but a schematic of the main roads and interstates that the driver must travel. Too much information confuses and distracts. Instead of trying to jam everything in, Fisch says, "When designing instruction, we might better ask ourselves: How much can I or should I leave out?" (p. 15). The more time we save from lecturing, the more time that is available for students to interact with us, the material, and each other.

Active Learning Techniques You Can Use

A number of different active learning techniques are available. Indeed, they can be thought of as a continuum running, on one end, from a position that minimally affects the traditional lecture-structured classroom, to the other end that makes use of peer teaching, learning tournaments, debates, "trials," and extensive use of informal small groups. The following section draws largely from Silberman (1996) and Bonwell (1996) in suggesting several techniques that involve active learning while still allowing instructors to rely heavily on a lecture format. Techniques that make greater use of small groups are discussed in the next chapter.

Active Learning Techniques That Minimally Affect the Lecture Format

Idea	*Instructions*
Starting with a Question	Start your lecture with an interesting question. Better yet, write it on the chalkboard so students can begin thinking about it even before class begins. Pose other questions during the lecture or even plant questions with students and cue them when you want the questions raised.
Guided Note Taking	List the major points of your lecture on a handout but make it incomplete (e.g., give students 3 of 5 points so that they have to capture the other 2 points on their own).
The Pause Procedure	Stop the lecture every 15 minutes or so to give students an opportunity to catch up on or rework their notes, to raise questions, or to consult with classmates.
One-Minute Paper	Provide students with a few minutes before the end of the class period to respond to no more than two questions, such as: "What was the most important thing you learned during this class?" and "What important unanswered questions do you have?" The value of this exercise is that students must evaluate and assess what they have learned. The

instructor can begin the next class with feedback relative to the unanswered questions and specifically target points that were not well understood. A variation of this idea is to ask students to jot down a quick response to "What was the muddiest point in the material today?" (Angelo & Cross, 1993).

Listening Teams

Before your lecture, divide the students into teams who will have such responsibilities as (1) raising questions about points they suspect most students didn't understand, (2) providing examples to demonstrate key concepts, and (3) playing the devil's advocate and identifying points that they disagree with or question. After the lecture, provide time for the groups to prepare and then share their thinking or questions with the larger class.

True or False

Prepare questions based on your subject matter that can be answered either true or false and write them on 3" × 5" index cards. Give each student a different question and have them find the answer to it. When everyone is finished, have the students read their cards and the correct answer. This can also be done as a team activity.

Journal Writing

Ask students to keep a journal and write at least twice a week about what they are learning. This can be done either in class or out of class; however, students should not be graded on grammar or punctuation. Emphasis should be on their personal reflections about what they are learning—providing them with an opportunity to see how the subject is relevant to their lives. These can be graded either by using standards such as "good insights, adequate, or inadequate" or "full credit, no credit" (Meyers & Jones, 1993).

Formative Quizzes   Prepare brief quizzes (i.e., 10 items) for students to use for self-assessment in class. These would not be graded, but the answers would be discussed after everyone has had time to finish.

"Growing" Classroom Discussion

When the class is stuporous and you are tempted to stop 30 minutes early, it's probably time to lecture less and attempt to get the class involved in exchanging ideas. But when you throw out a question and no one responds, you know in a sudden flash of revelation what no librarian can ever appreciate: Silence is *not* golden.

Most instructors come to recognize that each class has its own personality, but what is seldom noted is that each group of students develops its own history and traditions. For instance, even when students are not assigned seats, various individuals will "claim" certain seats and other students wouldn't consider sitting in Michelle's or Robert's seat. Similarly, when an instructor starts off lecturing from the first day and continues in this vein for the next seven or eight sessions, students quickly characterize the class as one where they are not expected to speak. Many will not read the assigned material before class because, after all, you will be telling them what they need to know in the lecture, right? And, since you won't be calling on them, they don't have to worry about embarrassing themselves by giving an "I don't know" in response to your question. In a short while, a tradition of "instructor talks–students listen" has been established. So, don't be surprised if no one takes the bait when you pause in the middle of your ninth lecture and ask the most stimulating and captivating question that has been raised in the last 10 years.

In order to have good classroom discussions, it is necessary to create a climate where the exchange of ideas is welcomed—where students get to speak, make comments, or ask questions frequently, not just in the last five minutes before the bell rings. This means that at the first class meeting, at the second class meeting, at the third class meeting, and at each subsequent gathering of the class, students are encouraged to pose questions and interact with one another and the instructor. The expectation that students should share their ideas and concerns needs to be stated orally in the first meeting and also placed in writing in the syllabus. Depending on the nature of the course, you may want to base part of their final grades on their class participation.

Students have to feel that their responses are wanted and that you enjoy hearing from them. Schoenfeld and Magnan (1992) have recommended thanking students for their questions as well as for their answers. Urge them to tell anecdotes and to connect their life experiences with the day's topic. As the group becomes "warmed up," present them with some tougher questions.

It's important not to dismiss students' ideas too quickly or to be overly judgmental. When a student says something that is wrong or partially correct, the instructor must fight the temptation to "smite this falsehood with the Sword of Truth" (Palmer, 1998). Instead of chopping the student in half, the instructor can open up the issue to the rest of the class (e.g., "Is there another view?" or "Does anyone else have a different opinion?"). Trust that someone in the group will tackle the false statement. Again, Palmer (1998) has observed:

> *How quickly do I need to do the smiting? Can it wait thirty seconds? A minute? To the end of the hour? Until the next class?*
>
> *As I consider my options, it becomes clearer that I need not smite immediately. Even with that untruth before us, we—and truth—will survive a few more minutes or hours or days. Then, as I step back from my sense of urgency, it becomes more and more likely that someone else in the group will step forward to challenge what has been said. (p. 134)*

Giving students adequate notice of the topics that you intend to discuss during the next class allows them time to think and prepare. Some syllabi are so minimal in the information they provide that students may not be able to tell what key questions will arise in the next class. State the questions you want to discuss well ahead of time. In the syllabus, beside the date of the class and the assigned readings, include a question to ponder: What constitutes good literature? What is acceptable as evidence? How do we know anything? What is meta-analysis?

You must save class time to discuss the questions you want to raise. If you fail to do this, then you have created a "tradition" of teasing the students and not following through by asking their thoughts about the questions. They'll soon tire of that game and put less energy into trying to ferret out answers on their own.

Pose questions that are interesting to consider. Don't be surprised if the class doesn't get excited about content-based questions that they may have already highlighted in their text (e.g., "What happened in 1492?"). Instead, challenge them with ideas that are progressive or avant garde—give them a controversy or a problem for which there is no best solution (e.g., "Should free needles be supplied to hard drug users to cut down on the spread of AIDS?"). Play the devil's advocate if you have to (although sometimes it is good to let the class know you're going to play this role ahead of time).

If you want the class to be in more of a recitation mode because the questions you want to ask are based on specific content, instruct the class to bring their readings or texts to class—particularly if you want everyone to dig in there and quickly find the right answer. Insist that everyone purchase or borrow the primary text. If it is important that they read the book; don't make it "optional."

When running a discussion in a large class, it may be necessary to repeat a student's question so that everyone can hear it. Remember, don't shame students for giving the wrong answer; instead, ask if anyone else can help out. Be warm and model acceptance when you can—even if students' ideas differ dramatically from your own. If there are multiple ways of viewing an issue, don't try to steer the questions so that the students are tricked into viewing it only from your perspective. If a student raises a question and you hear and respond to a different one, admit your mistake when it becomes obvious and invite the student to raise the question again.

If, despite your best efforts, the class does not seem to want to participate in a discussion session, there are a couple of other things you can try: Pose the issue or question in terms of pros and cons or some other dichotomy. Divide the class arbitrarily into equal halves and brainstorm the issue. Tell them you want every person to contribute some thought or idea, even if it seems a little silly. Alternatively, divide the students into small teams and allow them to debate questions. If the class is not too large, every student could be assigned to a debate team some time during the semester. Another discussion generator is to create a panel of students who are assigned to become "experts" on some topic and, after being given an opportunity to prepare, the class is invited to ask questions to stump the expert panel. You can also jazz things up by sealing answers to questions in envelopes and letting students draw the envelopes out of a hat. Each student selects one to read aloud and then the class must discuss what the question is. Or divide the students into groups and have them list questions they have about the lecture or topic.

Discussion sessions can be rich and profitable, but as with most things that you want to turn out right, a little prior thought and preparation is required.

Team Teaching

Team teaching is when two or more instructors collaborate together for the same course. Smith (1994) has identified the following benefits of team teaching:

- Provides stimulating multidisciplinary perspectives needed to make sense of complex problems
- Combats routinized teaching where instructors feel isolated and shop-worn
- Teaches new approaches—a "powerful vehicle for faculty members to learn from one other" (p. 134)
- Builds new collegial relationships
- Models diversity by bringing multiple perspectives into the classroom
- Useful for mentoring junior faculty

Ideally, team teachers would jointly plan the content to be covered as well as the assignments and exams. All of the educators would be in attendance at each meeting of the class and contribute valuable commentary at appropriate times—even if the other teacher had responsibility for that day's lecture or discussion. Each would bring a different set of life experiences, knowledge, skills, or expertise that would enrich the students' learning in a way seldom possible when a single instructor is the sole authority and assessor of students' performance. At least, that's the way it is supposed to work. (For an enlightening description of a survey course taught serially by virtually all the members of an English department, see Hussman, 1991.)

Much of team teaching is really "tag-team" or "relay" teaching, where a course has been divided into units with different persons responsible for the various components. Sometimes there are perfectly legitimate reasons for organizing the teaching in this way; other times it has to do with simple logistics. (Professor Wilkens is going to China after the first of November and won't be available for the rest of that semester.)

When they work well, team-taught courses can be intellectually stimulating for both students and faculty. But when this type of course is severely compartmentalized and the faculty don't attend each other's presentations or work conjointly, students can experience a sequential series of mini-courses more or less on the same topic. Multiple problems can arise. For instance, what happens if two faculty use different grading schemes and can't agree on a student's grade? If one faculty member requires more work than the other? If only one of them makes up the examination?

Sometimes junior faculty members in a team-taught course get stuck with selecting the text, making the tests, and computing final grades, while the senior member breezes by with a lighter load. This isn't fair, of course, and a word to the wise here would be to know something about your teaching partner before agreeing to co-teach a course. If that individual has such annoying habits as missing appointments and committee meetings, or is known to have lapses of undependability, you should expect to carry much more than your share of the workload.

Sometimes these arrangements can still work out. For instance, if you are compulsive about details (e.g., scheduling speakers, making arrangements with the audiovisual department, etc.), these duties will likely fall to you—and that will be okay, because you will see that they get done. You may even tolerate a team-teaching partner who does less than his or her share of the work overall because that person takes care of something that you don't enjoy doing. However, in most of these arrangements, compromises have to be made. If it were your sole responsibility it is likely that you would organize things differently, require another set of readings, or select a separate group of theorists to emphasize. But, since you are team teaching, you compromise, because—like in marriage—that's what's necessary for it to work.

From an administrative standpoint, team teaching might not be valued because it is not cost efficient (two instructors in one class). However, if this is something you want to try with a colleague, a possible strategy could be to volunteer to combine two sections of the same course into one large class so that the cost issue is neutralized.

Guest Lecturers

Occasionally scheduling a guest lecturer can be a good pedagogical technique for three reasons. First, students like variety; they like to hear other perspectives. Second, guest lecturers are usually chosen because they are especially knowledgeable about a particular topic and can supplement textbooks or readings where coverage is less than adequate. Third, guest lecturers are role models—generally they are individuals who have become successful and are recognized for their accomplishments. Their very presence indicates that there is a life after college, and helps to suggest not only that the course content can be mastered but that one can actually be reimbursed for knowing this material well.

Well-chosen guest lecturers can validate the importance of knowing the very items you have been struggling to get across. Often, guest lecturers are the stimulus for good class discussions and can challenge a class in a fresh, nonthreatening way. And if you are skilled in your planning, you might find that a guest lecturer frees up some valuable time (because you would need to do less class preparation)—a gift of a few extra hours to apply to your own writing or to catch up with grading papers.

Don't overdo it with guest lecturers or use them as a way to avoid teaching. Even though students like the variety guest lecturers bring, they prefer not to have a steady diet of "outside" experts continually coming into the classroom. Students want to know what to expect, who is in charge, how they will be graded, and what they need to know. "Too many cooks spoil the broth."

The other piece of advice here is to be prepared with questions or material in case the speaker becomes ill, gets lost, forgets, or turns out to be absolutely the worst presenter in the world. If the speaker puts your class to sleep inside of 15 minutes with the driest, dullest, monotone imaginable, don't hesitate to interrupt the speaker with some questions of your own. If you need to, gently interrupt and elaborate on points the speaker did not make well. After all, it is your class and your responsibility that students learn something from this course you have orchestrated. Even if the presenter was a total disaster, sending a brief note of appreciation is the courteous thing to do.

References and Resources

Angelo, T. A., & Cross, K. P. (1993). *Classroom assessment techniques: A handbook for college teachers.* San Francisco: Jossey-Bass.

Bonwell, C. C. (1996). Enhancing the lecture: Revitalizing a traditional format. In T. Sutherland & C. C. Bonwell (Eds.), *Using active learning in college classes: A range of options for faculty.* New Directions for Teaching and Learning #67. San Francisco: Jossey-Bass.

Brock, K. L., & Cameron, B. J. (1999). Enlivening political science courses with Kolb's learning preference model. *PS: Political Science & Politics, 32,* 251–256.

Brookfield, S. D. (1990). Lecturing creatively. *The skillful teacher: On technique, trust, and responsiveness in the classroom.* San Francisco: Jossey-Bass.

Brookfield, S. D. (1995). *Becoming a critically reflective teacher.* San Francisco: Jossey-Bass.

Brown, G. (1978). *Lecturing and explaining.* London: Methuen.

Dearn, J. M. (1996). Facilitating active learning in introductory science classes. *Research and Development in Higher Education, 19,* 158–163.

Fisch, L. (1996). The case for leaving things out. *The chalk dust collection: Thoughts and reflections on teaching in college and universities.* Stillwater, OK: New Forums Press.

Hussman, L. (1991). The faculty's forte: "Team teaching" the literature survey. *ADE Bulletin, 99,* 29–33.

Kelly, L., Phillips, G. M., & Keaten, J. A. (1995). *Teaching people to speak well: Training and remediation of communication reticence.* Cresskill, NJ: Hampton Press.

Meyers, C., & Jones, T. B. (1993). *Promoting active learning: Strategies for the college classroom.* San Francisco: Jossey-Bass.

Murray, J. P., & Murray, J. I. (1992). How do I lecture thee. *College Teaching, 40* (3), 109–113.

Noonan, P. (1998). *Simply speaking: How to communicate your ideas with style, substance, and clarity.* New York: Regan Books.

Palmer, P. J. (1998). *The courage to teach: Exploring the inner landscape of a teacher's life.* San Francisco: Jossey-Bass.

Rickard, H., Rogers, R., Ellis, N., & Beidleman, W. (1988). Some retention, but not enough. *Teaching of Psychology, 15,* 151–152.

Ruhl, K. L., Hughes, C. A., & Schloss, P. J. (1987). Using the pause procedure to enhance lecture recall. *Teacher Education and Special Education, 10,* 14–18.

Schoenfeld, A. C., & Magnan, R. (1992). *Mentor in a manual: Climbing the academic ladder to tenure.* Madison, WI: Magna Publications.

Silberman, M. (1996). *Active learning: 101 strategies to teach any subject.* Boston: Allyn and Bacon.

Smith, B. L. (1994). Team-teaching methods. In K. W. Prichard & R. M. Sawyer (Eds.), *Handbook of college teaching.* Westport, CT: Greenwood Press.

4

*Small Groups,
Peer Learning,
and Role-Playing*

Overview: In recent years, educators have discovered that a great deal of learning can occur when the instructor steps down from the lectern and allows students to teach each other. Although the noise level within the classroom may increase considerably and instructors may fear losing control, courses can be infused with an exciting vitality when a conscious decision is made to do less lecturing and to rely more on student-centered teaching strategies.

There are numerous ways that students might be actively involved in teaching or learning from each other. This chapter starts with a discussion of small groups in the classroom and then moves on to examine more current conceptualizations and approaches that are based on students "push-pulling" each other. Finally, mention is made of role-playing. Although it is not strictly a student-centered teaching strategy (because the role-plays could be performed by faculty, professional actors, community members, etc.), nonetheless, role-plays usually occur within group settings and often involve students playing the roles and discussing with each other what ensued.

The Pedagogical Value of Small Groups

There are several arguments for using small group activities in the classroom. First, it affords greater opportunity for students to actively participate. Individuals who are loathe to speak before a class of 30 are usually comfortable in sharing their ideas within a small group composed of two or three other students. Also, there's more chances to respond. Meyers and Jones (1993) stated that small group activities can incorporate all the key elements of active learning: talking, listening, reading, writing, and reflecting.

Second, small group activities teach students how to work together collectively. Even students with poor social skills can observe positive role models and learn how to disagree without getting angry or upset. In small groups, students learn to cooperate in common tasks, to give and receive constructive feedback, to support opinions or notions with evidence, and to tolerate, if not respect, diverse points of view. These are all skills needed to succeed in future employment and in life.

Third, small group instructional activities provide a nice change of pace, a stimulating way to augment student interest and break the monotony that can occur when the instructor lectures every class meeting. Fourth, small groups can increase the occasions students have for receiving individual help and encouragement (Greenwood et al., 1995, as cited in Topping & Ehly, 1998). Last, students may be motivated to expend greater effort if they know their work is going to be scrutinized by peers and if they are involved in helping teach the material to their peers (Astin, 1993). In addition to peer tutoring, here are some other specific ways small groups can be used by educators:

- *To brainstorm applications of examples or theories*
- *To solve problems*
- *To compare and contrast theories, issues, or models*
- *To provide evaluative feedback to the instructor or other presenters*
- *To provide constructive feedback to peers for improving assignments*

- *To review for exams or quizzes*
- *To summarize main points and process learning outcomes (Meyers & Jones, 1993)*

Small group activities can range from a quick pairing or grouping of students for discussion of some point in the last 15 minutes of class to carefully planned cooperative student projects that span an entire quarter or semester. Scholars in this area usually view small group activities as existing on a continuum, with collaborative learning projects on one end and cooperative learning at the opposite, most structured end (Millis & Cottell, 1998). Cooperative learning teams are not one-shot activities but relatively permanent (at least for the academic term) groups designed to harness the dynamic forces of peer pressure and group cohesiveness to evoke both individual and group learning.

Cooperative Learning

Since the 1980s, the term *cooperative learning* has been used to describe the use of small groups for educational purposes where individual's grades are in part determined by group accomplishments. We've all had the experience where "two heads are better than one" and small group work builds on this idea. Studies indicate there are beneficial effects of cooperative learning in the mastery and retention of material being studied, the quality of reasoning strategies used, the generation of new ideas and solutions, and the transfer of what is learned (Johnson & Johnson, 1992). Johnson, Johnson, and Smith (1991) noted that cooperative learning, in hundreds of studies conducted by a wide variety of researchers in different subject areas, has repeatedly produced generally positive results. Slavin (1995) has observed that "cooperative learning is one of the most extensively evaluated of all instructional innovations" (p. 19). In a meta-analysis of 90 studies, Slavin found that 64 percent of the experimental-control comparisons significantly favored cooperative learning and only 5 percent favored the control group. Bossert (1988) also concluded that cooperative learning benefited students of all ages in various content areas. Using samples from

159 baccalaureate-granting institutions, Astin (1993) claimed that cooperative-learning approaches produce outcomes that are superior to those obtained through traditional competitive approaches. Besides benefiting problem-solving skills, there is also evidence that self-esteem and self-confidence of the learner improve as well as the development of social skills and the ability to take the perspective of another person. The most powerful achievement effects seem to occur when there is a combination of group goals and individual accountability (Davidson & Worsham, 1992).

By fostering discussion within the groups, cooperative learning promotes oral summarizing, explaining, and elaboration—all of which aid long-term retention. Further, learning material sufficiently well to explain or teach improves one's own understanding and retrieval of it. Indeed, vocalizing what is being learned is more strongly correlated to achievement than is listening (Johnson & Johnson, 1992).

Collaborative Learning

Collaborative learning and cooperative learning are similar in that they both agree that it is "the social experience that educates" (Bruffee, 1999, p. 84). However, they are slightly different concepts—somewhat like the difference between fraternal and identical twins. Cooperative learning emerged from a view that students competing with each other for grades was unsound, if not unhealthy. Groups, however, could be held accountable for individuals learning within the collective. Collaborative learning theorists, however, viewed the traditional classroom hierarchical structure as an obstruction and sought to replace the one-way conveyance of knowledge from teacher to student with a social process that valued spirited inquiry, conversation, and the exchange of ideas.

Bruffee (1999) has further identified these differences: The cooperative learning teacher assigns classroom roles and demonstrates vigilance in supervising students' group work. The teacher is still very involved in establishing and maintaining his or her locus of authority. Collaborative learning teachers do not assign classroom roles; leave group governance in the students' hands;

tend not to intervene within groups, allowing groups to solve their own problems; and shift the focus from individual competition to competition among groups.

Collaborative learning may take many forms: classroom consensus group work, peer tutoring, collaborative project work, writing peer review, or consensual responding to lecture material. An instructor using a consensus groups approach would typically:

- Divide students into small groups.
- Provide students with a task or problem and instructions on how to proceed. (These are not tasks for which there is only one correct solution but problems designed to stimulate discussion and differences of opinion.)
- Ask the groups to decide on one member to be a recorder.
- Allow the groups to discuss freely without close monitoring of activities.
- Bring the groups together again when their tasks are finished so that the recorders can report their findings and explain how they arrived at decisions.
- Act to help the class arrive at a consensus while serving as a representative of the larger academic or professional community. The instructor compares the class's consensus with current knowledge or thinking on the problem and shares with the class any incompatibilities or contradictions.

Common Fears about Small Groups

Instructors resistant to the idea of using small instructional groups in their classrooms may have some of the following concerns, as identified by Millis and Cottell (1998):

The Fear	*The Rebuttal*
1. Group work is less rigorous.	It doesn't have to be. Research indicates that student achievement might actually be raised. Assessment of student progress is conducted more frequently than might normally occur in lecture-only classes.

2. Lectures are a more efficient means of imparting knowledge.

Cooperative learning is built on the assumption that students learn the bulk of course material outside of class. Lectures that rehash textbook readings are not needed. Cooperative learning approaches may save time in the long run.

3. Breaking the class into small groups results in a loss of classroom control.

Allowing groups of students to talk, even to argue among themselves, does increase the noise level in a class. However, the increased activity level makes it more difficult for students with low motivational levels to sleep or otherwise "tune out."

4. Colleagues may think my class is out of control.

That's a remote but actual possibility. Explain what you are doing to a few key colleagues before the semester begins. Instruct the class to observe a prearranged "now-it's-time-to-get quiet" signal.

5. Students don't want to learn from peers, but from the authority.

When the course is properly structured, there is little doubt about who is the authority. There are still many opportunities for the professor to demonstrate his or her knowledge (e.g., preparing the tests, reviewing the correct answers, troubleshooting the groups' questions and problems, and designing projects that both challenge and teach students the content they need to learn).

6. Small groups allow some students to slide by and "hitchhike" on the efforts of others.

In a properly designed cooperative learning course, only a portion of students' grades are determined by the group project—individual effort is still monitored. Groups work best when each member's tasks are essential for the group's success.

Employing Small Groups Effectively

A variety of cooperative learning methods have developed in the last 30 or so years for use with primary and middle school students. Slavin (1995), for example, has identified some of the better known student team learning approaches based on team rewards, individual accountability, and equal opportunities for success. Many of these techniques can be and have been used at the college level without committing an instructor or class to a full-fledged cooperative learning approach. To give you a brief glimpse of several of these, the following descriptions are provided:

- *Student Teams-Achievement Divisions (STAD):* Four-member teams work to ensure all members have mastered the lesson, then they take individual quizzes on the material. Points are awarded to each team based on the degree to which team members meet or exceed their own earlier performances. Students are motivated to help each other in order to earn team rewards.
- *Teams-Games-Tournaments (TGT):* Weekly tournaments are substituted for quizzes. The top scorer for each team brings a bonus of points to all team members.
- *Jigsaw:* Each member of the team is randomly assigned material to master and on which to become an "expert." Each expert briefs team members on that portion of the common topic.

There are many other approaches, carrying such names as Group Investigation, Learning Together, and pair learning strategies. The point here is that there are a host of group learning techniques that can be applied in college classrooms. The next section will look at one of these in-depth.

Team Learning

Small group instructional methods go by different names, but one that seems to be gaining increasing popularity in industry and on college campuses is known as *team learning*. The essential features of this approach, developed originally for use in large college classrooms, are (1) relatively permanent heterogeneous task groups; (2)

grading based on a combination of individual performance, group performance, and peer evaluation; (3) organization of the course so that the majority of class time is spent on small group activities (there is practically no formal lecturing); and (4) a six-step instructional process similar to the following model:

Team Learning Instructional Sequence

1. Individual study of material outside of class is assigned.
2. Individual testing is used (quizzes of 15 to 20 multiple-choice items over readings or homework at the beginning of each class).
3. Groups discuss/debate their answers and then are given a group test of the same items. When finished, they get immediate feedback (answers). (Groups typically get 90 percent or better of their answers correct.)
4. Groups (but not individuals) may prepare written appeals of items.
5. Feedback is given from the instructor.
6. An application-oriented activity is assigned (e.g., a problem to be solved requiring input from all the group members) (Michaelsen, 1994).

It is important to note that casual, informal, or occasional use of groups is not considered cooperative learning or team building. Team learning approaches stress application of concepts being learned. Slavin (1995) has observed that when small instructional groups are used without specific group rewards based on the learning of all group members, the results are no more effective in increasing achievement than traditional methods.

Tips for Using Team Learning Approaches

Although you are strongly urged to go beyond this brief overview and to read Michaelsen (1993, 1994), for instance, still there are a few observations that may prove helpful whenever an instructor desires to emphasize the importance of small groups for instructional purposes:

- Announce at the beginning of the term and inform students in the syllabus that group learning techniques will be employed.
- Inform students about the benefits of group learning.
- Do not allow students to form their own groups but constitute them yourself in order to ensure maximum heterogeneity and inclusion.
- To foster group cohesion, allow groups to sit together and to create "identities" (names, slogans, or logos for their groups).
- Don't expect that teams will magically coalesce without structure, supervision, and devoting a significant amount of class time to group projects.
- Group projects must result in a tangible product—don't assign "busywork" projects. Projects should be interesting and involve creative thinking, give-and-take discussions, and realistic problems.
- Group projects must be difficult enough that the effort of all group members is needed; projects should not be tasks that one or two persons could do on behalf of the group. In a group of four, tasks should be structured so that each member's contribution is 25 percent of the project. Each group member's unique contribution should be identifiable.
- Group projects must build on the newly acquired learning.
- Competition among groups can have advantageous effects within the class.
- Serial presentations one right after another at the end of the term are often boring. Spread out presentations over the term or have the groups videotape themselves—choose the best of these to show the entire class.
- Peer evaluations are gathered on a project-by-project basis.
- Impress on the class the necessity for fairly evaluating the effort expended by team members. Give them criteria by which they can assess contributions; do not allow them to give everyone in the group the highest grade or points allowed.

Regarding this last point, it may make sense to spend the time to allow the class to brainstorm the criteria by which peers should be evaluated (e.g., attendance, participation, timeliness of performance of assigned responsibilities, quality of work, etc.) so that each member understands how this portion of the course grade will be determined. Students usually are much more charitable in their grading than faculty would be, and the instructor needs to be proactive to keep this tendency from contaminating the peer evaluation process. Certainly, groups should not be asked to evaluate the performance of their members while they are sitting in those groups in class. A better procedure would be to instruct group members to carefully consider the grades they would award in the privacy of their own homes and then to seal these ratings in an envelope that the instructor would collect.

Because of the potential for problems with peer evaluations, a great deal of thought must accompany the instructions to the class about the specific criteria to accompany peer evaluations. Even before that, the instructor must think through the weighting of individual achievement (e.g., from quizzes and tests), group achievement (e.g., projects or assignments), as well as peer and student self-evaluation in order to state these proportions in the syllabus.

The first couple of times that small group instruction is being pilot tested by an instructor, the individual achievement portion of the grade ought to be the greatest (e.g., 60 to 70 percent) portion of the grade. However, one shouldn't have the portion of group work counting for the total course grade to be too low (e.g., 10 percent). Fiechtner and Davis (1992) have reported on a survey in which they found that students said that their *best* group experience came in those classes in which more than 20 percent of their course grade was determined by group work. There is less incentive to work together as teams or within groups if almost all of the course grade comes from individual effort.

Once you have developed guidelines, policies, and criteria that will hopefully result in honest assessments of team contributions by team members, the percentage of the grade associated with group achievement and peer evaluation can be increased. Until you become comfortable with your and the class's ability to tease out individual contribution to group effort, the temptation will be great to give undifferentiated group grades for group projects (e.g., assigning the same grade to everyone in the group). However, this is not recommended (Millis & Cottell, 1998).

Additionally, Meyers and Jones (1993) have suggested that any time an activity is given to a group, a written handout should be prepared, describing what the group is expected to do and how the group should go about it. Further, since students do not come into most classes with a wealth of experience working in small groups,

Meyers and Jones have recommended providing each group with working rules, such as respect the contributions of others, do not interrupt a classmate who is speaking, and do not dominate discussions. Students can also be prepared to think about ways to solve problems within their groups by posing a question (e.g., "What would you do if someone in your group didn't do his or her share of the work?") and brainstorming possible responses before these problems even present themselves in the classroom. The more input students have into the small group instruction process, the greater will be their ownership and support of it.

According to Michaelsen (1994), the most difficult aspect of using a team learning approach is in designing group activities that develop students' abilities to use the concepts that they have just learned. But what makes small group instructional activities work best is when group members have a positive interdependence and must rely on each other to get the job done. Further, they must hold each other personally accountable for performing a fair share of the work. Karl Smith (1996) has said it well:

> *Cooperation is not having students sit side-by-side at the same table to talk with one another as they do their individual assignments. Cooperation is not assigning a report to a group of students, on which one student does all the work and the others put their names. Cooperation is not having students do a task individually and then having the ones who finish first help the slower students. Cooperation is much more than being physically near other students, discussing material with other students, helping other students, or sharing material among students, although each of these is important in cooperative learning. (p. 74)*

Grading Cooperative Learning Projects

Although most instructors applying a cooperative learning framework don't base students' entire course grades on group performance but also consider individual achievement, the issue of how to grade individuals working within a group poses a quandary at times. Basically, however, there are three options you have for grading students placed in cooperative or team learning groups:

1. All group members get the same grade for that portion of their grade associated with the group project.
2. Group members are graded for their individual contributions to the group project. (Contribution to the group can be determined by the instructor, group members, self-ratings, or a combination of these three.)
3. Group members are graded individually for their contributions to the group effort but members receive "bonus" points when their group performs well on tests (e.g., 90 percent or better). This fosters even greater group cohesiveness and cooperative learning as peers work to ensure that they will get the bonus points by coaching and tutoring group members. Alternatively, instead of bonus points, students can be given two sets of grades: one for their individual achievement and another for the performance of their group (Johnson, Johnson, & Holubec, 1994).

As an instructor, you will know that the cooperative or team learning approach is working when you come into the classroom early and find most of the class already assembled in their groups and working on their group tasks or tutoring each other. It may also be commonplace to overhear student conversations in which they discuss plans to meet outside of class for some course-related activity. This approach requires some rethinking and planning about the role of the instructor and how class time should be spent, but it offers some exciting possibilities for teaching and learning.

Peer-Assisted Learning

In addition to the use of small groups of three or four students, the instructor might want to consider pairing students for peer tutoring, mentoring, monitoring, or assessment. Peer tutoring is a well-documented technique that produces academic gains and the benefit of one-to-one instruction without the prohibitive cost. Studies with students from kindergarten through high school since the early 1980s have shown that students have learned more in the areas of reading, spelling, vocabulary, and math in less time using ClassWide Peer Tutoring (CWPT) than conventional forms of teacher-directed instruction (Arreaga-Mayer, Terry, & Greenwood, 1998).

Although the literature on peer tutoring in higher education is less abundant than that in the primary and secondary systems, there is still sufficient evidence to commend this approach. For instance, in a study of the effects of reciprocal peer tutoring (RPT), Fantuzzo and colleagues (1989) found that psychology students who created tests for each other, administered and scored them, discussed the outcomes, and coached their partners showed greater achievement, greater satisfaction, and less stress than students in two other comparison groups.

Peer tutoring is "learning by teaching" and is a deliberate development on the notion that "to teach is to learn twice." Preparing to teach requires that the tutor not only pays greater attention but also obtains mastery of the curriculum. In the process of attempting to simplify, clarify, and develop examples, existing knowledge is organized and integrated in a way that seems to facilitate storing and applying the information (Topping, 1998). Additionally, being paired with another student provides social support and alleviates feelings of social isolation. It is a more democratic, less authoritarian approach to learning.

Greenwood, Carta, and Kamps (1990) have noted these advantages of peer tutoring: a reduced pupil-teacher ratio that results in quicker feedback and prompting, more active learning with greater student ownership of the learning process, and better application of knowledge and skills to new situations. Greater self-disclosure and opportunities to respond may also result in less anxiety and fear of making errors.

On the other hand, preparing a class for peer tutoring does require organizational time from the total available for instruction. Another potential problem is that not every peer tutor may be motivated or willing to engage in the task of teaching another student. It may be difficult to ensure an evenness of quality of tutors across all pairs. Some students will not like or be able to get along with matched partners, or may not accept peer feedback as valid. Additionally, instructors need to be alert for the potential that unequal power relationships and abusive treatment of some partners could occur. Finally, if pairs are expected to meet outside of class, then problems might arise around schedule conflicts, work hours, and so on.

Using the CWPT approach, students are paired either intentionally (e.g., by ability level) or randomly. (Larson and colleagues [1984] found that students with low verbal ability performed best when paired with students having high verbal ability. However, the latter were not adversely affected by these pairings.) Each pair consists of a student in the teacher role (tutor) and one in the student role. Roles are switched periodically in order for both students to have responsibility for teaching, assessing the tutee's progress, and providing feedback. Pairs are also changed on a weekly basis if one is closely following the CWPT model. Tutoring occurs simultaneously for all pairs during the scheduled class time. This provides the instructor with ample opportunities to monitor and supervise the peer tutor pairs. Weekly assessments are conducted of material mastered.

Training students about the purpose of peer tutoring is recommended. Topping and colleagues (1997) expressed the intent this way to students about to use reciprocal peer tutoring to learn undergraduate economics: "Peer tutoring is not like 'working with your friends'—it is about learning to work in a team with people you don't already know, staying on task, systematically managing and being responsible for your own learning, and developing other 'transferable skills'" (p. 99).

Participants also receive full written instructions as well as checklists for their activities and grading. Pairs are told that peer tutoring sessions should not be used to work alone, copy lecture notes, or read the textbook. If anyone is unable to attend a peer session, they are asked to notify the department office. "Spare" partners are to form another pair or to join another grouping whenever circumstances prevent them from working with their regular partners.

Riggio, Whatley, and Neale (1994) paired students on the basis of academic ability and required the following of psychology undergraduates engaged in an RPT study:

- Pairs made outlines of "important points" they believed would be covered on the unit test and held discussions using these outlines.
- Prior to every unit exam, each partner created a short test consisting of at least 10 multiple-choice questions based on the assigned readings and lecture materials. The correct answers, along with brief written rationales, were placed on a separate sheet.

- During the tutoring session, pairs met and administered tests to each other under test-like conditions.
- Upon finishing their own tests, members of each pair scored each others' exams.
- Discussions were held about questions answered incorrectly and any material from their outlines that they were having difficulty understanding.
- Corrected tests, answer sheets, and outlines were turned in on the day of each unit exam.
- This material was scored by the instructor and returned to students along with comments suggesting ways they could improve.

As Topping and colleagues (1997) noted, peer tutoring is not a universal, undifferentiated, or instant panacea. It is, however, another technique in the instructor's repertoire. One thing to keep in mind is that a theme emerging from the literature on peer tutoring is the need for structure when using this approach. Fantuzzo and colleagues (1989) found that a higher degree of structure was associated with desired outcomes and concluded that it was not mere pairing but the structured exchange that was effective. Similarly, Riggio and colleagues (1991) found that more structure produced better scores on stress inventories. Topping and colleagues (1997) recommended against offering a wide choice of activities or materials if the pairs cannot be closely supervised. Clearly, preterm planning and detailed preparation are critical to the successful implementation of peer tutoring.

Role-Playing

Role-playing and dramatization are commonly used in disciplines such as psychology and social work to prepare students for counseling with actual clients. The instructor might appoint one student to be a "therapist" and another to be, for instance, an angry 16-year-old who is doing poorly in high school. In 10 minutes or so, the "therapist" might attempt to draw the "client" out or to evaluate any underlying problems, such as alcohol or drug use. Or the "therapist" might be instructed to help the "adolescent" make plans or goals to stay out of trouble. Because there's usually no rehearsing or scripts, the role-play often has unexpected twists—just like real life. Students learn to think on their feet, and sometimes discover that despite their knowledge of a given topic or problem (e.g., adolescents or drug use), they will make mistakes, fail to see opportunities for success, and be completely thwarted at times (e.g., the "client" might refuse to talk). In language classes, students can be given a situation (e.g., being lost in a foreign country or ordering from a menu) that forces the role-players to apply their vocabularies in something like a true-to-life problem. Similarly, students in counseling, psychology, and social work and can learn interviewing skills when a classmate or the instructor poses as a client in a hypothetical "clinical setting."

Role-playing is a form of active learning that allows students to test what they've been learning in the safety of a classroom where they won't be exposing real clients to any potential harm or bad practice. Except for the shy students who fear being called on to perform in front of the class, most students are entertained by and enjoy role-playing because it is often a welcome relief to lectures and note-taking.

The main disadvantage to the use of role-playing is that it can consume a lot of class time. If you decide to use this approach, vary the situations, scenarios, and problems assigned to the students so that the audience's attention doesn't wander because they've heard essentially the same dialogue or solutions before.

To enrich this experience even more, arrange for a videotape to be made of the role-play so that participants can see themselves. Also, give the students the opportunity to evaluate themselves in writing. Additionally, you can ask members of the class to provide feedback for the students engaged in the role-play. Typically, impromptu role-plays are not graded, although they could be if these were out-of-class assignments where students had time to be creative and do such things as writing scripts, rehearsing, and making use of visual props. Out-of-class role-play projects could also be videotaped and brought into class for viewing.

References and Resources

Arreaga-Mayer, C., Terry, B. J., & Greenwood, C. R. (1998). Classwide peer tutoring. In K. Topping & S. Ehly (Eds.), *Peer-assisted learning*. Mahwah, NJ: Lawrence Erlbaum.

Astin, A. W. (1993). *What matters in college: Four critical years revisited.* San Francisco: Jossey-Bass.

Barlow, C. A., Blythe, J. A., & Edmonds, M. (1999). *A handbook of interactive exercises for groups.* Boston: Allyn and Bacon.

Bossert, S. T. (1988). Cooperative activities in the classroom. *Review of Educational Research, 15,* 225–250.

Bruffee, K. A. (1999). *Collaborative learning: Higher education, interdependence, and the authority of knowledge.* Baltimore, MD: Johns Hopkins University Press.

Davidson, N., & Worsham, T. (1992). Introduction. In *Enhancing thinking through cooperative learning.* New York: Teachers College Press.

Fantuzzo, J. W., Riggio, R. W., Connelly, S., & Dimeff, L. (1989). Effects of reciprocal peer tutoring on academic achievement and psychological adjustment: A component analysis. *Journal of Educational Psychology, 81* (2), 173–177.

Fiechtner, S. B., & Davis, E. A. (1992). Why some groups fail: A survey of students' experiences with learning groups. In A. Goodsell, M. Maher, & V. Tinto (Eds.), *Collaborative learning: A sourcebook for higher education.* University Park, PA: National Center on Postsecondary Teaching, Learning & Assessment.

Greenwood, C. R., Carta, J. J., & Kamps, D. (1990). Teacher-mediated versus peer-mediated instruction: A review of educational advantages and disadvantages. In H. C. Folot, J. J. Morgan, & R. H. Shute (Eds.), *Children helping children.* Chichester, England: Wiley.

Greenwood, C. R., Terry, B., Delquadri, J., Elliott, M., & Arreaga-Mayer, C. (1995). *ClassWide Peer Tutoring (CWPT): Effective teaching and research review.* Kansas City: Juniper Gardens Children's Project, University of Kansas.

Johnson, D., & Johnson, R. (1992). Encouraging thinking through constructive controversy. In N. Davidson & T. Worsham (Eds.), *Enhancing thinking through cooperative learning.* New York: Teachers College Press.

Johnson, D., Johnson, R., & Holubec, E. (1994). Myths about cooperative learning. In D. Johnson, R. Johnson, & E. Holubec (Eds.), *Cooperative learning in the classroom.* Madison, WI: Magna Publications.

Johnson, D. W., Johnson, R. T., & Smith, K. A. (1991). *Cooperative learning: Increasing college faculty instructional productivity.* ASHE-ERIC Higher Education Report No. 4. Washington, DC: George Washington University School of Education and Human Development.

Larson, C. O., Dansereau, D. F., O'Donnell, A. M., Hythecker, V. I., Labiotte, J. G., & Rocklin, T. R. (1984). Verbal ability and cooperative learning: Transfer of effects. *Journal of Reading Behavior, 16,* 289–295.

Meyers, C., & Jones, T. B. (1993). *Promoting active learning: Strategies for the college classroom*. San Francisco: Jossey-Bass.

Michaelsen, L. K. (1994). Team learning: Making a case for the small-group option. In K. W. Prichard & R. M. Sawyer (Eds.), *Handbook of college teaching*. Westport, CT: Greenwood Press.

Michaelsen, L. K., Jones, C. F., & Watson, W. W. (1993). Beyond groups and cooperation: Building high performance learning teams. *To improve the academy: Resources for faculty, instructional, and organization development* (pp. 127–145). Stillwater, OK: New Forums Press.

Millis, B. J., & Cottell, P. G. (1998). *Cooperative learning for higher education faculty*. Phoenix: American Council on Education.

Riggio, R. E., Fantuzzo, J. W., Connelly, S., & Dimeff, L. A. (1991). Reciprocal peer tutoring: A classroom strategy for promoting academic and social integration in undergraduate students. *Journal of Social Behavior and Personality, 6* (2), 387–396.

Riggio, R. E., Whatley, M. A., & Neale, P. (1994). Effects of student academic ability on cognitive gains using reciprocal peer tutoring. *Journal of Social Behavior and Personality, 9,* 529–542.

Slavin, R. E. (1995). *Cooperative learning: Theory, research and practice*. Boston: Allyn and Bacon.

Smith, K. (1996). Cooperative learning: Making "groupwork" work. In T. E. Sutherland & C. C. Bonwell (Eds.), *Using active learning in college classes: A range of options for faculty*. San Francisco: Jossey-Bass.

Topping, E., Hill, S., McKaig, A., Rogers, C., Rushi, N., & Young, D. (1997). Paired reciprocal peer tutoring in undergraduate economics. *Innovations in Education and Training International, 34* (2), 96–111.

Topping, K. (1998). The effectiveness of peer tutoring in further and higher education: A typology and review of the literature. In S. Goodlad (Ed.), *Mentoring and tutoring students*. London: Kogan Page.

Topping, K., & Ehly, S. (1998). *Peer-assisted learning*. Mahwah, NJ: Lawrence Erlbaum.

5

Teaching the Large Lecture Class

JONATHAN GOLDING

Overview: Nearly all faculty expect to lecture to "typical" classes of 15 to 40 or so students, but a few are called on to teach sections of 200, 300, or even more. These large classes require special preparation and management as well as present a different set of problems than those faced by instructors of smaller classes.

There is no way around it: Lecturing to a large class demands that you have your "head together." Walking into that auditorium with all those students for the first time requires you to swallow your fear, ignore the butterflies, and be ready to teach. Despite the initial anxiety, there are two important things to keep in mind. First, it is likely that most of the initial anxiety will subside, even before your next class. Second, there is a good chance that you will find teaching a large class can be a rewarding and fun experience.

Let's start by discussing what constitutes a large class. The definition is open to some debate, but typically a large class is described as one with at least 100 students. Although most would agree with the 100 student cut-off, there is another way to think about large classes. Poole (1993) has noted that it is not the number of students per se, but rather that a large class is one in which the size of the class inhibits certain teaching techniques, most notably discussion or question-and-answer interchanges. By Poole's definition, a large class may also depend on factors such as the instructor's experience. That is, if you typically teach a class of 15 students, doubling that number to 30 students likely would be perceived as large, because you might be unable to teach in your normal fashion. The point is that, regardless of the number of students, whenever you feel a class is large, you must be prepared to deal with it in ways that are different from your usual teaching methods. Keep in mind, though, that it is not as if everything you have ever thought about teaching or actually done in the classroom will have to change, but there are specific aspects of your teaching that likely will need to be modified.

Before discussing specific methods of teaching large classes, perhaps you are wondering why colleges and universities allow or encourage large classes. There are several reasons for having large classes (see also Knapper, 1987). First, at many institutions, there are simply too many students and not enough qualified faculty to teach students in small sections. One could argue that it would be better simply to let the students take other classes, but in a time of tight budgets, it is unlikely that any department would lose the chance to bolster its student-to-faculty ratio by not accepting students into specific classes. Moreover, some large classes are required courses; students simply must take the courses. Second, large sections are sometimes taught in an attempt to offer additional courses in a department. For example, a department may decide to have one faculty member teach a large section of a course instead of having eight faculty members teach smaller sections. This strategy allows the latter faculty to teach other needed courses. Third, if the goal of a department is didactic and achievement is measured in conventional ways, large classes are the ideal way to accomplish this goal (Jenkins, 1991). Fourth, Lewis (1994) has noted that for large introductory courses, because the courses assume little prior knowledge of the subject, the course can work to socialize students into the conventions of the topic. "The common background obtained in these large classes can provide a basis for engaging in subsequent discussions because the students have had the same introduction to the topic and 'speak the same language'" (p. 319).

Regardless of the reasons for offering large sections, there have always been (and will continue to be) critics of such courses. For some, teaching large classes is an emotional issue, because these courses are perceived as ineffective, immoral, or both. For example, McKeachie (1999) stated that, in general, large classes are simply not as effective as small classes for retention of knowledge, critical thinking, and attitude change. Moreover, he has asserted that students feel less personal responsibility, which can damage morale and diminish motivation, and that large classes make it less likely to know students as individuals.

Jenkins (1991), however, has argued that the research on class size indicates that the perspective just described may be unwarranted. He stated that in the past 20 years, very little research has shown a definitive effect of class size on achievement or student attitudes. Why is there the lack of an effect? According to Jenkins, a search of the literature prior to 20 years earlier reveals the probable reason: The old literature indicates that class size is rarely an important variable with respect to any of the measured outcomes of instruction. For example, he cited a meta-analysis by Glass and Smith (1979; cited in Jenkins, 1991) on class size (heavily weighted with elementary and secondary school studies). They found that the results of studies vary as the conditions of each experiment change and as the circumstances of the studies differ (i.e., complex interactions). Glass and Smith did find that a class size of one person (i.e., a tutorial) raised achievement by about a half a standard deviation over the mean of all class sizes. However, the increment in achievement due to class size then diminished in a negatively accelerated fashion as the class size increased to 20, after which class size had essentially no effect on achievement. It should be noted that another study by Gilmore, Swerdlik, and Beehr (1980) actually found that students rated general teaching effectiveness highest in very large classes (211 to 350 students).

Based on the results of the prior studies, Jenkins (1991) concluded that, "the implication of these data is that faculty must frankly consider their goals for the course. If their interest is in the students' first familiarization with basic principles and terms, then large classes can be recommended." In fact, Jenkins stated that large classes are as effective as small classes when the goals involve learning factual information and comprehending that information;

when traditional tests are used to measure learning, large classes compare well with smaller classes. If, however, the instructional goals involve higher cognitive skills—such as application, analysis, and synthesis—then smaller classes are recommended.

Given that large classes are going to be taught, and the research on class size does not preclude students learning in such a context, there are a number of questions that must be addressed with regard to large classes:

Who Should Teach a Large Lecture Course?

Given the demands of teaching a large class, the person who actually does the teaching needs to be the right person. The importance of this statement is reflected in a survey at University of California, Santa Barbara, in which over 80 percent of students felt that the instructor affected the quality of their classes more than class size (Jenkins, 1991). Thus, the success of a large class is greatly improved if the person teaching a large class has three important characteristics. First, the person should want to teach the course. Forcing someone to deal with a large class is a recipe for disaster. Second, the person who teaches the large class should have the personality to handle this endeavor. Defining the "right" personality may be difficult, but it is clear that the instructor must be enthusiastic about teaching, especially with regard to being in the large class, and must be comfortable dealing with large groups of people. Finally, having a voice that projects well in the large classroom is a benefit for an instructor in a large class.

How Do You Plan for a Large Course?

Answering this question requires a clear understanding that there are unique issues (some would say problems) associated with the large class. Most important, because of its size, everything done in a large class is usually exaggerated to some degree. The issue of exaggeration cannot be overemphasized, especially if you are teaching a large class for the first time. It is important to step back and think about what is in store for you throughout the semester. Remember, however, that you cannot think just about issues. You need to be active; go out and determine what it is going to take to make teaching a large class a success. This is a whole new ball game, and the more planning that goes into the course, the greater the probability that everything will run smoothly. Related to this, keep in mind that planning takes a great deal of time and energy. Therefore, set up weekly schedules for yourself (especially around exams and the end of semester) and cut back on other obligations (Davis, 1993).

The issue of exaggeration works in paradoxical ways. On the one hand, a large class often requires more work to be done. Put another way, tasks that seemed trivial in a typical class gain much more importance. Imagine, for instance, that you have a handout you want to distribute to all students; how will students get this handout? One way would be simply to hand out the sheets in class. Of course, this will take time, and Gillespie (1996–1997), and Lewis (1994) have advised against such a practice. Instead, you might want to put the material in specific location in the lecture room so that students can take the handouts as they enter, or put the materials in a course packet that students purchase prior to class. Gillespie (1996–1997) has suggested that you can place the handouts as part of a campus computer resource from which students can download materials as needed.

On the other hand, being in a large class requires the instructor to be more precise than with smaller classes; there are simply more chances for confusion. This latter point is especially true with regard to the actual lecture. Lapses in the flow of the lecture may not seem like a big deal in a small class, but lapses seem like hours in a large class. Thus, there is little room to collect one's thoughts or locate instructional material, because it can quickly result in a loss of attention from students. Given that the attention span of students is only about 10 to 20 minutes (Penner, 1984), making students wait until you have regained your place in the lecture will only lead to problems.

There are other issues that must be considered. To start, you should be clear about who will be taking the course. Will students be enrolled because it is a survey course that satisfies a general education requirement or is it a course only for majors? A related question is whether the course includes mostly first-year students or those further along in school. Answering these questions will be important as you think about how you are going to teach the students. For example, if the class includes first-year students of all intellectual levels, will you teach at a lower level so that no student is lost during lecture, or will you teach sometimes to the highest level and sometimes to the lowest level?

Another issue of concern is how you want to structure the course. In this realm, questions dealing with the specific course material to be treated must be addressed. It is difficult in a single semester to cover everything relevant to a particular course. Thus, you will probably need to select a subset of material. As for how the number of topics that can be easily handled, Davis (1993) has a rule of thumb: Make a list of topics you want to cover, estimate the time required to address the topics, and then increase your time estimate by 50 percent to allow for questions and the "inevitable slippage" of a large class. As for the course content, you need to consider the balance between discussing new advances in your field with covering the basic, perennial problems of your field that change very slowly (see Jenkins, 1991). Also, you must determine how you will evaluate students and how they might evaluate you. The former includes the number and type of exams that you will give, as well as any other means for determining grades (e.g., in-class writing assignments, homework, etc.). You may want to include evaluations at different points in the semester (especially around midterms) that let you know how students are thinking about your teaching style and effectiveness. Try to anticipate problems. For instance, you will need to plan well in advance if you are going to require your large lecture class to use books or materials placed on reserve in the library. Multiple copies will be needed and the library will need time to prepare for the onslaught of students.

Next, you must think about exactly how you are going to present information. You can write on a board or on overheads, use computer displays, or present preprinted outlines on overheads. Whatever you decide, you must be sure that the material is clear and that students are not too dependent on the overheads. That is, students should not simply be copying everything down without any thought to what is being presented. Students should use the presented material as a catalyst to other notes, so that the active process of taking notes helps the students to learn. Besides, if students were only in class to write down what was on an overhead, why not simply sell the overheads to students and not have them come to class?

The presentation of information will likely require you to develop teaching aids not used in smaller classes (see Jenkins, 1991). For example, the use of overheads may be something you never considered with a small class, but they are often essential with a large class (even for announcements). If you use overheads, I always tell colleagues to get a pointer to help with lectures. I have a pointer that looks like a hand (that gets me many laughs). You may prefer a laser pointer that will allow you to be at different locations in the room, and still be able to point on the screen. Likewise, the use of videos may be just what you need to help provide concrete examples as well as fight off monotony. If you use the preceding tools, you should probably consider having your personal class notes reflect the various teaching techniques you decide to use. You might use different colored sheets of paper, one color to denote lecture material and another to denote a video to help you keep your lecture flowing smoothly (see Davis, 1993). Remember, it is almost impossible to plan too much!

An interesting question arises with regard to the presentation of material: Should you videotape or audiotape your lectures for students who missed class? Also, you may want to have your class notes on reserve at the library or at a local copy center for this same reason (see Felder, 1997). Of course, this could inadvertently encourage students to skip class more often, because they know your notes are readily available.

Finally, before the beginning of the semester, take a trip to the lecture hall where you have been scheduled. The first thing you will discover is that there really are a lot of seats! When you are in the auditorium, check out the status of audiovisual equipment:

Will you need a microphone?
Is the print size in your overhead transparency large enough?
Can you show videos or use PowerPoint?
How does sound travel in the room?
Where are the entrances and exits?
How do you control the lights?

All of these questions (and others) must be answered prior to the start of the class, and arrangements must be made for having the appropriate equipment available during the semester. Then, you should practice in the room. Make sure everything works properly and that you have a plan if something should malfunction. For example, what are you going to do if a lightbulb burns out on the overhead? Will you have an extra bulb, or is there a technical person close by to quickly replace the bulb? Also, it is probably worthwhile to check the audiovisual equipment while you sit in various locations in the classroom. This will enable you to determine how well students will be able to see you at the front of the room as well as to see overheads and see and hear videos presented (Lewis, 1994).

Day-to-Day Management

Thinking about the course on a day-to-day basis requires you to think about what you want to occur each day you step foot in the class. Thus, it is best to think about how you plan to set the tone for the class. This is achieved in two places: your syllabus and the first day of class.

Your syllabus should reflect the rules in a clear and concise manner. Avoid any possibility for ambiguity. Some helpful additions to your syllabus include stating what will be your required text(s), goals for the course, weekly schedule, cheating and plagiarism policy, and make-up exam policy. Erickson and Strommer (1991) showed the importance of the syllabus in their research. When students were asked at the end of their freshman year what instructors might have done to help them, one of the three most frequent responses was "provide a better syllabus."

Although your syllabus is important to the daily flow of the class, the first day of class is perhaps the most important day of the entire semester with regard to day-to-day functioning. It is on this day that you not only give out the syllabus but you also set the tone for the entire semester. What you say and how you act on that first day may be irretrievable, so plan accordingly. I have found that giving a short autobiography is useful to the students to get a feel for what I am like as a person. That is, most of the time students will see me in class and may get a very distorted picture of me as an individual. By letting students hear about my history and my likes and dislikes, they have a better understanding about me, and it opens up the possibility for future conversations with students.

After talking a little about yourself, it is time to discuss your thoughts on other important issues. You should let students know what you do like (e.g., questions, comments) and what you do not like (e.g., sleeping in class, coming in late, leaving early, reading the newspaper) in class. Although the latter may seem to students as a bit rigid, setting the standards on the first day is the surest way to avoid any complications later on in the semester. (The issue of class rules will be discussed in more detail later.)

Once you actually start lecturing on course material, there are several points that you should keep in mind. First, you should have a clear plan for every class. It's not a bad idea to plan out the entire semester before the first class, knowing for each class exactly what material is covered and what overheads and videos to bring to class. You might, however, feel too constrained by this type of semester-long planning. Regardless of what you do, it is advisable to have classes planned out for some amount of time, even if it is for a week. In planning for each class, Davis (1993) stated that instructors of large classes should vary the type of lecture that is presented.

Among the different types of lectures (see Frederick, 1986) that could be used would be a traditional lecture (hierarchical organization of major and minor points) or a case study method (following a realistic situation step by step to illustrate a general principle or problem-solving strategy). Also, keep in mind that you should probably reserve 30 minutes prior to each class to get ready to lecture. That is, review your lecture, make sure you have everything you need, and get your energy level up to what is needed for a lengthy presentation as you get ready for each class (University of Illinois Instructional and Management Services, 1986).

Second, fashion your lecture so it will work to the students' advantage. This includes being aware of basic principles of memory that can help students learn better. Therefore, make sure to organize your lectures each day in a way that allows students to easily determine the structure of the material. A great deal of research has shown that information that is organized is learned better than unorganized information (Bower et al., 1969). In this regard, Davis (1993) has noted that you should present the main points of each lecture so that they come at the beginning or end of class. This strategy takes advantage of research on the serial position curve (serial position effect), which shows that material in the middle of a list is not learned as well as that at the beginning or end (Rundus, 1971). Consider, also, not lecturing the entire class period (see Davis, 1993). As noted earlier, given that the average student's attention span is between 10 and 20 minutes, it is worth changing the pace every 15 minutes or so to relieve monotony and recapture interest. Finally, to make sure students understand each point, take your time. If you are using overheads, give students a chance to write down what is on the overhead as well as think about what they have written (University of Illinois Instructional and Management Services, 1986).

Third, try to create a supportive environment during each lecture so students can be involved in the lecture. If you plan to talk the entire lecture, you are heading for a group of bored and restless students who may not learn very much.

> *If you're teaching a small class and you're good, you may be able to prod many of your students into activity—get them asking and answering questions, discussing issues, challenging conclusions, laughing at your jokes, whatever. No matter how good you are, though, you probably won't be able to persuade most students to open their mouths in front of 120 classmates—it feels too risky for them. (Felder, 1997, p. 1)*

Therefore, you must work hard to make your students active in the classroom. There are many types of activities that can turn your class from a passive into an active learning experience (see also Ebert-May, Brewer, & Allred, 1997). One way this can be done is by having students ask questions or offer comments (see also Frederick, 1987). These questions or comments can be given to you at the beginning or end of class, put in a "Question Box" (Lewis, 1994), or simply asked as you lecture. You can choose to answer the questions at any time, including putting the answers in a class newsletter or webpage. If you answer questions during lecture, repeat the question when it is asked, since the size of the room may preclude everyone from hearing it. Also, remember that encouraging a lot of questions and comments can consume a great deal of lecture time (Geske, 1992). Thus, plan accordingly and anticipate how much time you can allow for questions and comments. Finally, if a question is asked for which you do not know the answer, try to find the answer and report it back to the class; students will really appreciate your effort.

The value of answering questions and responding to comments is twofold. First, it lets students think more actively about the course material. For example, a student may make a comment that runs counter to something stated in lecture. Do not use this comment to have a slugfest with the student. Instead, use this situation to your advantage by bringing up the idea of how students need to think for themselves which side of a controversial position they are going to take. Have the students comment on connections between the class material and their own life experiences—this assists them in becoming actively involved.

Second, according to Lewis (1994), answering questions (and responding to comments) lets students know that you are interested in helping them learn the course material. If you do not take questions or respond to comments, you run the risk of students perceiving you as uncaring.

Another way to keep students involved is through the use of demonstrations in which students actively participate (see Erickson & Strommer, 1991). There are different types of demonstrations you can use in class. These include conducting experiments that divide the class into different groups, bringing students up to the front of class to help, or presenting material on an overhead for which students then offer a response. Sometimes, you do not even need a formal response from anyone in the class. For example, during a lecture on perception, my colleagues and I present different ambiguous stimuli on the overhead. I then simply watch and listen to the class figure out the different pictures that can be perceived. It may seem like this demonstration would lead to mass confusion, but the students work hard and quietly to disambiguate the pictures.

You can aid in your professional development by learning new skills to use in class demonstrations. These might include doing magic or juggling as a way to introduce new topics. (Both of these I use in class to demonstrate specific topics: magic and perception, juggling and attention.) One criticism is that such demonstrations are just a way to make a class a "show." My response to this is that a class is a show, but it is a show whose goal is learning. If students can understand issues by having a concrete example demonstrated to them, then it is a valuable learning activity. Moreover, sometimes it is the combination of the lecture and the demonstration that leads to learning.

There are other active learning strategies that can keep the ball rolling in lecture (see also Geske, 1992). Felder (1997) has commented extensively on the use of in-class exercises. Typically, these involve providing the students with a problem. The students can work individually, in pairs, or even in larger groups to come up with the response. Other strategies include the "minute paper," where students either summarize the main points made so far, ask a question, or apply what they have heard (see Wilson, 1986). After the minute is up, the instructor collects the papers or breaks the class into small groups to review and discuss one another's papers. One key aspect of these papers is that they do not necessarily have to be graded. This can help with getting students to think and write without being so concerned about a grade. Another strategy is to use a "half-sheet response," where a student tears out half a sheet of paper and responds to a question such as: "What do you think about a particular concept?" or "Can you give an example of the concept being discussed?" Still another strategy is to invite a guest for the class to debate or interview on a controversial issue.

There is one issue to keep in mind with regard to class involvement: Do you call on students or have students volunteer to participate? This is a tough decision, and there probably is no clear answer as to what works best. One can argue that calling on a student keeps everyone alert and ready to answer. Still, there is a certain risk in singling out a student who would prefer not to speak up in such a large class. Calling on only students who volunteer avoids the problem of making a student feel uncomfortable, but this strategy may lead to just a few students sharing their thoughts during class.

Keeping Order in a Large Class

Faculty interested in teaching large classes almost always ask a question about how to keep the class under control throughout the course of the lecture. Some note that this control seems to fly in the face of recent articles about insubordination and incivility in classrooms, especially large lecture classes (Schneider, 1998). The uncivil behavior that has been discussed includes students arriving late and leaving early, sleeping in class, talking to classmates, reading newspapers, and even bringing portable televisions into class.

Dealing with uncivil behaviors, in the sense of making sure they do not occur, requires a great deal of thought and preparation. First, you must decide exactly what you are willing to put up with in class. For example, some instructors do not view a student sleeping in class as a problem. To these instructors, such behavior can easily be ignored without affecting the class as a whole. For others, this behavior is unacceptable and must not be allowed under any circumstances.

Second, after determining how you feel about certain behaviors, you must decide what will be the most effective way to deal with your students. McKeachie (1994) has described two ways to achieve order in the classroom. You can insist on strict attention, set up stringent rules on the point, and enforce them. However, McKeachie has warned that a problem of this approach is that when order is achieved, it has been dictated. Thus, there is perpetual conflict with students, and students try to "beat the game." Also, according to McKeachie, this approach dampens enthusiasm, leading to fewer questions asked by students. McKeachie has suggested that order also can be achieved by having students understand that the accomplishment of course objectives is partly under their control. Accordingly, students are informed that they have certain responsibilities and, at the same time, certain rights. Thus, students learn that you are willing to entertain reasonable suggestions, objections, and questions in connection with course material. It should be clear that the two ways of thinking are really endpoints, and what you adopt in class may be anywhere along this continuum.

Whatever your thinking about keeping order, it is most important that you communicate it to your students. Be clear about the rules of the class, and why you have made them. The latter may include an explanation of how certain types of behavior (e.g., coming to class late, leaving early) can disrupt the flow of the class. This disruption can make learning more difficult, which in turn can affect exam grades. Once the issue of grades gets introduced, you will be amazed at how students become much more receptive to what is being discussed.

The rules themselves should be in your syllabus and/or explicitly mentioned in class (preferably on the first day of class). You may decide to include rules dealing with issues of civility (e.g., not falling asleep in class) in your syllabus (see Schneider, 1998). There is the danger, however, that the inclusion of these rules may be perceived as extremely rigid by students (see McKeachie's stringent rule viewpoint described earlier). Nonetheless, remember that it is easier to start with rigid rules and become more flexible than it is to do the opposite. Also, if you formulate a rule, stick by it! Although there may be some wiggle room for any particular rule, students will see right through you if you have a rule and then do not enforce it.

Some specific pointers as to how to maintain order in class are noteworthy: First, get serious about how you begin each class. The start of each session is critical for determining how smoothly the rest of class will proceed. Taking time at the beginning to quiet down the students is simply wasted time; you need to get the class ready to pay attention immediately. Therefore, develop techniques that can help you start class in an efficient manner. There are two ways to do this, both of which may be used in combination. One way is to play music before class. You can choose music you like, or have students contribute to your play list. (The latter can really help to encourage student-faculty interaction.) The music may even be used as a tie-in to the topic of a particular lecture. The music gives students some time to unwind right before class, to get rid of any excess energy before all attention is focused on you and the lecture. As soon as you are ready to begin the lecture, shut off the music. The change in sound is quite startling, and is a signal to students that class is now beginning. Thus, instead of having to "shush" the class countless times until everyone is quiet, the cessation of the music serves this function.

Another way to help with the start of class is to use a common phrase to start class, such as, "OK class, let's get ready to begin." After a few times, this phrase will serve as a signal to students to quiet down and get ready for the lecture (Poole, 1993).

With regard to the beginning of class, keep in mind that with a large class, there are bound to be stragglers. Students probably are coming from all different locations on campus to your class. You can decide to be rigid about these latecomers, or you can simply request that latecomers should enter quietly and sit in the back of the auditorium so they do not disturb anyone. Another possibility is to take a few minutes at the beginning of class to review the previous class—this will assist stragglers and those who were absent. Of course, this latter technique generally means that valuable time is lost from your lecture.

The second recommendation for maintaining order concerns classroom behavior by students. It is critical that during the course of lecture, students remain attentive. To achieve this is usually quite simple: Let students know from Day 1 that all exams will include lecture material. This alone typically serves to keep the class under control. You may, however, include quizzes or in-class papers on lecture material as additional control strategies. Students will learn quickly that if they are going to do well on exams and assignments, they had better sit quietly and pay attention.

The issue of class attendance should be raised here. The methods just described will not only lead to order in class but will also likely increase attendance. Still, you might feel that the only way to increase attendance is to make it mandatory. If you decide to have a mandatory attendance policy (but see Gillespie, 1996–1997), you will need to figure out how to take roll. You can use attendance sheets, given at the end of class to avoid a student writing his or her name and leaving. These sheets, however, do not preclude a student from writing in the name of his or her absent friend. Another possibility is using a seating chart. Given the hassles and time expenditures of such methods, it might be best to avoid an attendance policy, and to discover ways of making the presentation interesting enough to get students to come to class and actively participate.

If you should have a student who is continually talking or is disruptive in other ways, you must make a decision (stated earlier) about whether the behavior is severe enough to warrant a reaction on your part. If you decide to address the behavior, you can ask the student to stop his or her behavior immediately. This will likely stop the behavior, but at the same time it will also break the flow of your lecture. Still, the cost of the latter may be outweighed by the benefit of putting an end to the disruptive behavior. If the student does not stop the disruptive behavior, you should ask the individual to leave class and meet with you later. Another option is to confront the student when class is over. If you decide to confront a student, make sure that you never let that student intimidate you (see Aronson, 1987). Once you become intimidated, you will likely lose control of the class very quickly.

A final suggestion for class order concerns the ending of class. There are at least three strategies that you could adopt. I refer to one of these as the "closure/lead-in" strategy. This involves summarizing the main points for the day and discussing what will be covered in the next class. Although there is value to this approach, there are some problems with this strategy, including students leaving early or starting to collect their books and papers (in a noisy manner) as soon as you begin summarizing. Another strategy is designed to make sure students do not leave or prepare to leave early. This involves giving a question at the end of class that is assigned for credit. As you can imagine, this will keep students in their seats. The final strategy is to finish discussing a topic and simply end class, thereby avoiding students leaving early or preparing to leave. The problem of this approach is that you lose the advantages of a summary and a tie-in to the next lecture.

How Do You Get to Know Your Students?

As you can imagine, getting to know your students in a large class will be difficult. Nonetheless, there are a number of activities and behaviors that facilitate interacting with the students. Remember, however, that getting to know your students better in a large class is going to require work on your part; in the end, however, it will make the large class a more positive experience for you and your students.

To begin, it is important in a large class to appear approachable. There are various ways to do this. One way is simply not to appear too stuffy. This can involve the use of humor in class, jokes before exams to calm everyone down, or funny asides during lecture. Also, starting on the first day of class, you should get to class a little early (and stay a little later after class) and talk to students as they arrive. You will likely not meet everyone, but the contact you have with this subset of students will have an enormous impact on how they think about you and the class. Moreover, the students you meet will talk to their friends who will talk to their friends, and before you know it, everyone in the class will know how nice you can be in a one-on-one situation. The way I think about it is like this: If I was a student in a class of 500 and the instructor happened to walk up to me and ask me how I was doing or what new movies I had seen recently, I would be blown away. That is, I would be highly impressed that the instructor took the time to speak to me, and I would want my friends to know this occurred.

Other ways you can meet students have been noted by McKeachie (1999), such as (1) extending invitations for coffee or lunch; (2) passing out brief observation forms to several students at the start of class, and asking them to meet with you to discuss their observations of class; (3) circulating among lab sections; (4) teaching the lab section; (5) using a seating chart to learn students' names; (6) arranging an out-of-class review session at night or on the weekend; and (7) having students fill out information cards that indicate career plans, hometowns, and special skills and interests. If you are compelled to try and learn the names of students, you can take photos of the students or videotape the class and then note the names to help you remember (Felder, 1997).

Next, make it clear to your students that you want to meet with them in your office. You should always have office hours set up (and note these hours in your syllabus), but you should also be flexible in allowing students to stop by at any time to talk to you. It might even be worth having "office hours" not in your office but maybe in a small classroom or centrally located room on campus if it facilitates students stopping by (see Lewis, 1994). I often joke with students how I love to have them come by to talk to me, because it keeps me from having to do other work. I also let them know that meeting with me in my office will be very low key and that I will not talk as loud as when I lecture. Be clear that your students know that they can come by to talk about a variety of subjects; it does not just have to be about your specific class. Also, let your students know that they can contact you via e-mail. For some students, this mode of communication is just the right ticket to interacting with faculty, especially if a student is just too intimated to stop by to see you. It may not be nearly as effective as a one-on-one conversation in your office, but at least the student has contacted you, and it may lead to an office meeting. Regardless of how you do it, the key is making students understand that you are interested in them and their academic careers.

The manner in which you lecture can also work toward getting to know your students. In this regard, it is important to deal with the large size of the auditorium. The problem with the auditorium is that it promotes an impersonal feeling for students. Along this line, Hall (1966) studied the distances at which people interact in the United States and found that the upper limit of comfortable social distance is 12 feet. In an auditorium, however, the distance between instructor and student is well beyond this distance. Therefore, you must communicate to students that the space need not intimidate or prevent interaction (Gleason, 1986). Moreover, you must actively use as much space in the room as possible in order to make the room seem smaller to students and to help reduce anonymity (see Poole, 1993; Gillespie, 1996–1997). In fact, research by Gibb (1961) showed that moving to different sections of the class and making eye contact helped students feel that their presence is noted and encouraged participation and a feeling of involvement.

Another key issue is how you speak to the class. For example, it is best if you do not read your lecture. If you do, students will likely feel disengaged, partly because you cannot keep eye contact, and it casts your voice down instead of out toward the students. Also, reading your lecture may lead to a monotonous pitch and tone of your voice. Both of these issues have been cited as important when lecturing before a large class (Poole, 1993; University of Illinois Instructional and Management Services, 1986). If you are reading your lecture because you are concerned about the lecture running smoothly, take the time to practice your lecture so that you will not have to read it and you will be able to present the material in a more effective manner (see Davis, 1993).

Finally, let students see you as more than their instructor. Of course, you are not going to become their best friend, but there is no reason why a student cannot appreciate you beyond how you lecture. Thus, I feel that you can let students know about yourself (as described earlier) and that you can share your personal experiences with them. Being a bit more open with your students may be the catalyst for the students to open up themselves, especially during class (i.e., asking questions, making comments). Two ways I have found this can work is that I let students know about my favorite television shows and movies and my interest in collecting and trading postcards. I find that students are always willing to talk about what they watch on television and see in the movies, and I never miss the opportunity to discuss what happened on the latest *Ally McBeal* episode. As for the postcards, when students go somewhere, I ask them to bring me back a postcard with a message on the back. In return, I give them a postcard from my collection, also with a message. Over the years, I have found this allows me to interact informally with numerous students—besides allowing me to collect a lot of postcards!

How Does Testing Change in a Large Lecture Class?

I have heard colleagues argue that teaching would be much more fun if they did not have to worry about giving exams. (By exams, I am referring to questions that evaluate a student's knowledge of material that is given over more than a week of lectures.) Of course, this is a pipe dream, because whether we like it or not, exams are the most efficient method for evaluating students in a large class.

As with other topics I have discussed, giving an exam in a large class is not a simple matter. To start, you must decide what kind of exam you are going to give. Typically, large classes receive multiple-choice tests. The use of these exams primarily occurs because of the relative ease in administering and grading them, compared to essay exams. Despite the anti–multiple-choice exam sentiment among some colleagues, remember that it is possible to write multiple-choice questions that evaluate depth and understanding of a topic. These exams, however, do take quite a bit of time to construct, so plan accordingly. In your planning time, do not forget to include time to have the exam proofread by at least two of your teaching assistants (TAs).

You can always decide to give essay exams or to include an essay question on your exam, but either of these options will lead to taking much longer to grade than a multiple-choice exam. If you decide to use an essay exam, you might consider having all responses to one question marked by the same TA. You might also consider a suggestion by McKeachie (1999) to include an essay question on the final exam, with the stipulation that it would be graded only if it might make a difference and change the student's letter grade. Keep in mind that regardless of the type of exam, you will probably need to work out some arrangements with the departmental staff (or TAs) to be sure that sufficient copies of your exam are produced in time. Also, make sure the exam copies are reproduced in time for any additional preparation of the exam, such as collating different exam forms (see Felder, 1997).

In preparing for the exam, make sure you meet with your TAs. They need to be clear on what needs to be done prior to exam day. For example, the TAs may have to help with checking IDs (if you choose this option) and may need instruction on the proper way to proctor an exam, what to do if someone is suspected of cheating, how to deal with latecomers, and procedures for collecting the exam.

You also have some decisions to make about the exam itself, long before it is constructed. You must decide if you are going to use a single exam form or multiple versions; the latter will help to discourage cheating. Also, you must decide if students will be able to keep the exam itself. I typically do not let students keep the exam, because it is not easy to construct a set of new questions each semester. That is, although I change the exams each semester in significant ways, I recycle a number of old questions. Thus, I would not like to see some students have an unfair advantage because they were able to see one of my old exams.

A final bit of advice is to remind students of your guidelines about taking tests. These should include going over your institution's cheating policy. You do not want to have a student get away with cheating, because you did or said something that may be used against you in any disciplinary hearing. These rules are typically listed in both the students' book of rights and responsibilities as well as in a university/college bulletin. Also, if you have not done so in your syllabus, be clear about your views on cheating and your policy on make-up exams. Even if these are in your syllabus, repeat the policies anyway. On the issue of make-ups, some have argued (e.g., Geske, 1992; Felder, 1997) that instructors of large classes should have only a single comprehensive make-up near the end of the semester as a way to discourage absences on exam days. Still, it can be argued that such a policy is too rigid, simply because you cannot stop students from getting sick or having personal problems arise.

In preparing your students for exams, it seems only fair to let them know what to expect on the exams. For example, if you are using multiple-choice exams, students will appreciate seeing some examples of the type of questions you will ask. This includes letting students know whether your questions include alternatives that include more than one answer (i.e., "a and b," "all of the above") or "none of the above" answers. These examples can easily be displayed on overheads. I should add that I always take some time to let my students understand how multiple-choice exams are constructed. For example, I explain how I try to make questions that require students to really think about the material, and how very few questions are straight from the overheads or book (i.e., exam questions often involve application of content). Also, I discuss how I come up with distracter choices. Students often think this is a simple process, but my discussion lets them understand that coming up with distracters can be a lengthy endeavor. By taking the time to discuss how you construct the exam, you can avoid many of the questions that arise during the course of the test, such as, "Can a question really have a 'none of the above' answer?"

When exam day finally rolls around, be ready. To me, exam days raise my anxiety more than any other day of the semester. Everything must run perfectly, from handing out the exam to collecting all of the exams. Part of the problem in this regard is that the length of time available for giving the exam is typically short. Thus, everything must be done relatively quickly. To improve your chances of successfully administering the test, make sure that the students in large classes know exactly what to do on exam days. The following is an example of a handout I give to all of my students:

What You Should Do on Exam Days

1. Bring your student ID.
2. Bring (at least) one number 2 pencil.
3. Come to class on time. The exam will begin at exactly 11:00 A.M.
4. You will be given an answer sheet (called a "bubble sheet") when you enter the auditorium.
5. When you enter the auditorium, take a seat immediately. You will sit in the rows closest to the stage. DO NOT skip seats. It is important that there are no empty seats.
6. NO ONE can wear a hat of any kind during the exam.
7. Using PENCIL ONLY, print your NAME and STUDENT NUMBER in the appropriate places on your bubble sheet. Also, in the place that says SPECIAL CODES, put your section number (example: 000033). You should then fill in the circles for your NAME, STUDENT NUMBER, and SPECIAL CODES. It is critical that you fill in your section number. DO NOT come to class without knowing your section number.
8. If you come to class after the exam has started, you will receive your exam after those students who arrived on time.
9. When exams are handed out, write your name, student number, and section number on the top of the exam itself. In addition, fill in the place on your bubble sheet that says TEST FORM. In this place, fill in the circle for the exam form letter at the top of your exam booklet.
10. Begin when you are ready. Make sure you fill in the circles for your answer. If you make a mistake, completely erase the answer you feel is wrong. Answer each question. Try not to lose your place when filling in circles on your bubble sheet.
11. The exam will end at exactly 11:45 A.M. At that time, the exams and the bubble sheets will be collected. NO ONE CAN LEAVE THE ROOM WITH AN EXAM!

12. Class will be dismissed when everything has been collected. NO ONE WILL BE ALLOWED TO LEAVE CLASS EARLY! That is, even if you finish early, you are free to check over your exam, daydream, sleep, etc. Do not pick up your books, listen to your Walkman, or start talking. Be considerate of your classmates.

13. Good Luck!

For the administering of the exam, there are a few things to keep in mind. First, decide how you want the class to sit in the auditorium. For example, if your class has multiple sections, you may want to have the class sit by section (University of Illinois Instructional and Management Services, 1986). This can help your TAs determine who was at the exam. Second, it is important to proctor at all times. This involves walking down the aisles and keeping an eye out for students cheating. Keep in mind that there is a low likelihood that you will ever catch someone cheating, but students must believe that you are constantly on the lookout for cheaters. This is what keeps cheating to a minimum; students are scared of getting caught. Third, make sure that you post the time in some way (I use an overhead) so students are clear about how much time is left for the exam. Fourth, be careful when you answer student questions, especially on multiple-choice exams. For example, students will ask, "This one can't be correct, can it?" You do not want to answer "You're right," because this then eliminates an alternative. Try to answer questions in a way that helps the students better understand the question, but avoid taking the exam for them.

After the exam is over, there are still a number of things for you to do. If you give a multiple-choice exam, you might consider putting a copy of the exam with the correct answers in a glass case so that students can look over the exam. If you do not do this, make sure there is some opportunity for students to go over the exam. For many large classes, this opportunity will be in a lab section. It is in this context that students should also receive some hard copy of their test performance. If you can, you might want to write a quick note (e.g., "Excellent") with your signature on a student's answer sheet (see Lewis, 1994).

Make sure you go over the questions and determine which were most frequently answered wrong; the computer program that scored the exam should permit you look at this. This information will allow you to determine if there was a question that should be thrown out. You should discuss the results of the exam soon after it was scheduled, making sure to emphasize the problem questions you have identified. In my large classes, I make overheads of the problem questions, so that I can discuss any comments from the class about why these questions led to so many incorrect answers. This process has sometimes led to me giving credit for a question. You might even consider selecting a student committee whose charge is to identify problem exam questions and suggest remedies (see Davis, 1993).

In most large classes, it will be necessary to post the exam grades beside students' identifiers or student numbers. You should do this outside of your office or the auditorium. Post grades as soon as you can after the exam (even if it is before you discuss the exam in class), and make sure there is no way to identify a particular student from the information posted. For example, never post a student's entire social security number. Finally, make sure your TAs record the grades. This is done most efficiently in computer files that you can then easily access, and that can be used to calculate descriptive statistics for the class (see Felder, 1997).

Should Quizzes and Homework Be Given?

This is another difficult question when you teach a large class. Some will argue that the amount of work (e.g., collecting papers, grading) required for quizzes and homework preclude their use. Others will argue that one or both of these are important for getting the most out of a large class. Moreover, the latter group will argue that the use of quizzes and homework allow students to get important feedback about their learning.

There are various types of questions that can be asked for quizzes and homework. For example, you can include multiple-choice questions or even short essay questions. These do not necessarily have to be graded. You might simply present the correct answer to a question or read what is a good answer to an essay question. Alternatively, you can have students exchange papers or read their own and then supply the correct information. Either way, students will receive feedback about what they have learned. Moreover, this feedback will let students gauge what they might need to cover as they study for an exam.

If you do decide to grade quizzes and homework (hopefully with the help of TAs), you might want to cut down the amount of grading by scoring only samples for each quiz or assignment (Davis, 1993). Also, it might be best to use a relatively simple scoring system that notes (for quizzes) whether a student was not in class, was in class but gave the wrong answer, or was in class and gave the correct answer. For homework assignments, you might also want to decrease your work for a particular day by staggering due dates. Finally, with regard to handing back quizzes or homework assignments that were collected, you should probably give them back in sections.

How Should Teaching Assistants Be Used?

If you are provided with one or two teaching assistants, use them to your advantage. TAs are critical to the success of any large class, and should be used in all facets of the course. This involvement should start prior to the beginning of the semester. Meet with your TAs and explain how you perceive their role in the course. Take the time to think about what you are going to say at this meeting, for you will want everything to run smoothly from the beginning. This initial meeting should emphasize how important it is for the TAs to be invested in the course. In addition, you should lay out (possibly in a handout) what your expectations are for them during the semester with regard to issues such as class attendance, meetings during the semester, getting in touch with you, dealing with exams, grading (quizzes, homework, and/or exams), record keeping, teaching lab sections, office hours, and so on. In addition, TAs need to be reminded of university and departmental policies (e.g., cheating).

In thinking about the use of TAs, remember that they are not just there to relieve your burden. Although there is no doubt that TAs can serve in this capacity, you must be more to the TAs. As Lewis (1994) noted, you must serve as manager, role model, and mentor. The issues related to being a manager were described earlier. With regard to being a role model and mentor, keep in mind that TAs are learning the ropes. You may be the first instructor the TAs have gotten a chance to observe dealing with a large class in such a detailed manner. Show them by your words and actions how dedicated and enthusiastic you are about teaching. Let them know you are there for them if any difficult situation arises. Finally, offer them unsolicited advice so that they can benefit from your teaching wisdom.

Is It All Worth It?

You bet! After talking to many of my colleagues who teach large classes, we would not trade the experience of teaching a large class for anything. Sure, it has its disadvantages at times (so does teaching a small class), but the positive aspects of teaching to so many students can be exhilarating. Moreover, it is clear that students can learn in large classes and enjoy doing so. So, grab your transparencies and handouts, and have fun!

References and Resources

Aronson, J. R. (1987). Six keys to effective instruction in large classes: Advice from a practitioner. In M. G. Weimer (Ed.), *Teaching large classes well* (pp. 31–37). San Francisco: Jossey-Bass.

Bower, G. H., Clark, M. C., Lesgold, A. M., & Winzenz, D. (1969). Hierarchical retrieval schemes in recall of categorized word lists. *Journal of Verbal Learning and Verbal Behavior, 8,* 323–343.

Davis, B. G. (1993). *Tools for teaching.* San Francisco: Jossey-Bass.

Ebert-May, D., Brewer, C., & Allred, S. (1997). Innovation in large lectures—Teaching for active learning. *BioScience, 47,* 601–607.

Erickson, B. L., & Strommer, D. W. (1991). *Teaching college freshmen.* San Francisco: Jossey-Bass.

Felder, R. M. (1997, June). *Beating the numbers game: Effective teaching in large classes.* Presented at ASEE Annual Conference, Milwaukee, WI.

Frederick, P. J. (1986). The lively lecture—8 variations. *College Teaching, 34,* 43–50.

Frederick, P. J. (1987). Student involvement: Active learning in large classes. In M. G. Weimer (Ed.), *Teaching large classes well* (pp. 45–56). San Francisco: Jossey-Bass.

Geske, J. (1992). Overcoming the drawbacks of the large lecture class. *College Teaching, 40,* 151–154.

Gibb, J. R. (1961). Defensive communication. *Journal of Communication, 11* (3), 141–148.

Gillespie, F. (1996–1997). The phenomenon of large classes and practical suggestions for teaching them. *Teaching Excellence (University of Georgia), 8,* 1–2.

Gilmore, D. C., Swerdlik, M. E., & Beehr, T. A. (1980). Effects of class size and college major on student ratings of psychology courses. *Teaching of Psychology, 7,* 210–214.

Gleason, M. (1986). Better communication in large classes. *College Teaching, 34,* 20–24.

Hall, E. (1966). *The hidden dimension.* New York: Anchor Books, Doubleday.

Jenkins, J. J. (1991). Teaching psychology in large classes: Research and personal experience. *Teaching of Psychology, 18,* 74–80.

Knapper, C. (1987). Large classes and learning. In M. G. Weimer (Ed.), *Teaching large classes well* (pp. 5–15). San Francisco: Jossey-Bass.

Lewis, K. G. (1994). Teaching large classes (how to do it well and remain sane). In K. W. Pritchard & R. McLaran (Eds.), *Handbook of college teaching* (pp. 319–343). Westport, CT: Greenwood Press.

McKeachie, W. J. (1994). *Teaching tips* (9th ed.). Lexington, MA: Heath.

McKeachie, W. J. (1999). *Teaching tips* (10th ed.). New York: Houghton Mifflin.

Penner, J. G. (1984). *Why many college teachers cannot lecture.* Springfield, IL: Thomas.

Poole, G. (1993). *Instructor's resource guide for Plotnick's Introduction to Psychology* (3rd ed.). Pacific Grove, CA: Brooks-Cole.

Rundus, D. (1971). Analysis of rehearsal processes in free recall. *Journal of Experimental Psychology, 89,* 63–77.

Schneider, A. (1998, March 27). Insubordination and intimidation signal the end of decorum in many classrooms. *The Chronicle of Higher Education,* pp. A12–A14.

University of Illinois Instructional and Management Services. (1986). Teaching large classes. *Illini Instructional Series,* pp. 1–4.

Wilson, R. C. (1986). Improving faculty teaching: Effective use of student evaluations and consultation. *Journal of Higher Education, 57,* 196–211.

6

Teaching Students How to Learn

CATE PEARSON
DAVID ROYSE

Overview: Each year, a new crop of students enters your college or university. Are they well prepared for the rigors of academe? Until otherwise demonstrated, most instructors probably hold the assumption that each student comes to the university with all of the skills and knowledge necessary to survive and possibly even thrive in a new learning environment. Unfortunately, this is not always the case. Unless your school recruits only the crème de la crème, you may encounter some very bright students who don't have even the most rudimentary knowledge of how to prosper in the classroom. If they are not well prepared, how do they develop into competent students? This chapter highlights several techniques that faculty can use to assist their students in making the transition to the college classroom.

High schools in the United States have a very uneven quality. Some take the notion of academic excellence very seriously; others are poor charades where few demands are made and good grades are obtained without students having to apply themselves. Many college-bound students did not find their high school learning experiences to be particularly challenging and, in fact, would tell you that they never had to study in high school. Some did, of course, "hit the books" the night before an exam and managed to get acceptable grades. Others will tell you that the extent of their reading is quite limited. Most importantly, a large percentage would probably tell you that no one ever spent any time teaching them how to learn.

The nation's elementary and secondary educational systems are often so bogged down by trying to produce a learning experience aimed at the "least common denominator" that they tend to neglect students needing a greater challenge (U.S. Department of Education, 1993). Educators in these systems seem to take for granted that students who are naturally bright or who are performing well in their classes know how to learn. Although raw intelligence is a necessary ingredient in the making of a scholar, it alone is not sufficient. Even students with high intelligence can bobble and stumble once they hit the university if they don't have good study skills. The suggestions in this chapter are aimed at helping instructors to help students acquire the skills they need to succeed in a postsecondary educational environment.

Engaging the Would-Be Learner

Research from educational psychology suggests that an individual not only has a basic temperament but also a preferred learning style that can be identified at an early age and remains relatively consistent. Helping students identify their preferred learning styles, teaching them how to develop flexibility in learning preferences, and offering a wide variety of presentations of course material can enhance the learning process (Ellis, 1997).

Several learning styles inventories are available for use with college students and offer self-scoring for immediate interpretation of results. David Kolb's theory of experiential learning suggests that students tend to have preferences for one or two of four learning stages: concrete experience, reflective observation, abstract conceptualization, or active experimentation. Opportunities can be provided within the classroom so that students can use their preferred styles while also developing in the other stages (Brock & Cameron, 1999).

In-class demonstrations, simulations, storytelling, newspaper articles, and films are examples of teaching techniques that provide students with *concrete experiences*. Students who want concrete experiences also appreciate such techniques as role-play and peer feedback. Students who, instead, learn primarily through perception most enjoy *reflective observation.* Techniques that engage the reflective observers are discussion and brainstorming sessions, answering questions on assigned readings, and keeping journals of their learning experiences. They need plenty of time to consider what they are learning as they watch others as a means of better understanding what they are learning. *Abstract conceptualizers* benefit from model-building assignments and writing critiques of theories or models. Instructors can ask students to point out the assumptions within a model of analysis or to analyze a model using a different set of assumptions. Abstract conceptualizers prefer to study alone so that they can organize, structure, and logically analyze ideas and theories. In contrast, students whose preferred stage is doing, which Kolb terms *active experimentation,* want to participate by immediate application of the material or practice of the concept. Active experimentation activities include labs, field work, projects, assignments, case studies, individualized learning activities, and model testing (Brock & Cameron, 1999; Ellis, 1997; Anderson & Adams, 1992).

Richard Felder (Felder, 1993, 1996; Felder & Henriques, 1995) and his associates have developed another model based on the Myers-Briggs Type Indicator that is getting a lot of attention. This scheme describes different types of learners along four dimensions: One separates learners into those who understand information best by doing *(active learners),* whereas their counterparts are *reflective learners. Sensing learners* like to learn facts and solve problems by well-established methods (they like details), while *intuitive learners* like innovation and dislike repetition. *Visual learners* remember best what they see in the way of charts, films, pictures, and diagrams, whereas *verbal learners* pay more attention to words, both written and spoken, than they do to pictures. Finally, *sequential learners* prefer to have linear steps that follow logically, while *global learners* quickly grasp concepts and complex problems but may not be able to explain how they solve problems. For those who are interested in this model, a 44-item assessment instrument developed by Soloman and Felder (the Index of Learning Styles) can be found on the Internet at <www2ncsu.edu/unity/lockers/users/f/felder/public/ILSdir/ilsweb.html>.

It will not be possible to teach to every student's favorite learning style; however, once students recognize their preferences, then they can be given suggestions for how they might use activities that will benefit them. For instance, active learners who find themselves in classes where they can't participate much may want to form a study group where they can discuss and explain class material to fellow students. Reflective learners, on the other hand, need time to themselves and may benefit from writing out summaries of what they have learned. Sensing learners need specific examples and must ask for these if the instructor does not supply them. Intuitors are urged to try to make connections to the facts or theories that must be mastered. Persons who realize they are sequential learners need to make sure their instructors don't skip steps and may want to outline their material. Global learners may want to make a practice of previewing their material before reading it. Because of the different learning preferences in the classroom, instructors should strive for a balance and diversity in their approaches and not teach exclusively in a way that would always disadvantage certain students. Instructors need to be aware that their choices of instructional activities are very likely to represent *their own* preferred style of learning. Students need stimulation in each dimension, not only to engage them by using their learning preference but also to encourage them to develop other learning strategies.

If issues about learning style arise within your classroom, it may be beneficial to discuss these matters more thoroughly with a colleague in educational psychology, to consult your university's learning skills center for further information, or do some additional reading on your own.

Teaching Note-Taking Skills

Although you can't prevent a student from day-dreaming now and then, you can teach students how to take notes. To start with, many students attempt to write down practically every word uttered by the instructor. They don't have any notion of what they ought to be recording. Fortunately, however, there are in-class exercises that teach students what to listen for in a lecture.

Some lecturers find it productive to provide (at least initially) students with an outline of the day's material at the beginning of the class, leaving ample white space for students to write in definitions, examples, comments, and notes. This approach requires the instructor to be organized ahead of time and to know exactly what major and minor items will be covered. Students can "coast" once they have grasped the concept or point currently being made but are brought to active involvement again once the instructor says something like, "The next point, number 5, is...." If you don't have enough time to create outlines of your lectures before each class meeting, you might want to start off this way the first several classes or so to help students begin to think about key points and the structure of a lecture as opposed to trying to capture everything that is said. Similarly, students will capture more of the major points if you list them on the board as you make them. Also, when speaking, try to use language that indicates what theorists, dates, formulas, and so forth are more important than others.

Another technique for teaching note-taking skills encourages students to take notes for 20 minutes and then requires that they exchange what they have recorded with someone else and compare what they each listed. The instructor can then highlight the points considered important for another comparison. This exercise can be conducted until you feel the class has acquired the necessary note-taking skills.

In reviewing how others take notes, students may pick up more efficient ways of taking notes. For instance, a few students may find a modified outline style beneficial. Others may write in a more narrative or paragraph form and draw arrows to connect related material. Still others make lists of points to remember. In any case, it is crucial that students develop their own version of shorthand, abbreviations, and other shortcuts. You might want to demonstrate the ones you commonly use. To illustrate this point, consider that one's rate of writing is approximately 50 words per minute (wpm), yet one can easily talk at the rate of 150 wpm. Simple math shows that the literal note-taker who tries to capture a professor's every word misses 5,000 words in a typical 50-minute lecture.

Some experts recommend the Cornell note-taking system over others. The Cornell system is a dual-column method requiring that students draw vertical lines 2½ inches from the left side of their paper. This space is known as the *recall column*. Class notes are taken in the larger, right-hand portion. Students are instructed to capture general ideas and to write in paragraph form. After the lecture, students should read through and review their notes, adding any comments or clarifications. The left-hand column is used for reviewing and preparing for a test. Students can identify key ideas or terms from their notes on the right and list them on the left prior to beginning reviewing for an exam. A sheet of paper can be used to cover up the material on the right and the student can self-test knowledge (i.e., when reviewing for an exam) by using only the stimulus of the key words.

A variation of the Cornell system that some students like is to use the left column for listing any important dates, theorists, or concepts that are judged to be important enough to become test questions. The right margin, then, would contain the explanation of the key terms or dates.

Whatever form of note-taking that your students use, urge them to review their notes and, when they do so, to indicate in some fashion the key concepts (e.g., use of a highlighter, underlining, or separate column) that they think are important to learn. This will help them to anticipate test questions well before they actually have to begin preparing for exams.

Encourage students to review their lecture notes while the notes are still fresh. If they have a free period or lunch immediately after your class, students can use that time to skim over their notes and fill in any gaps or examples that they did not have time to record earlier. Urge them to write down any questions at the end of their notes that they could raise at the beginning of class the next time.

Here are a few additional helpful hints about note-taking to share with students:

- *Don't use too small a notebook—give yourself space to write and outline.*
- *Leave blank lines or space when moving to a new topic. (This might be filled if there is a related point later in the lecture.)*
- *Try to differentiate major points from minor points by listening to cues from the lecturer.*
- *Ask questions when you are not sure.*
- *Sit close to the front of the class where it is easier to hear. (From Virginia Polytechnic Institute and State University's webpage <www.ucc.vt.edu/stdysk/notetake.html>)*

Teaching Reading Skills

Although every student knows how to read, many have never learned good reading skills. Teach students to preview a chapter before beginning to read it in order to assist with advance organizing the information that they will be acquiring. Encourage students to read headings, introductions, and so forth for clues to understanding a chapter. Point out summaries and bold text and stress the importance of these devices. If a student is hopelessly behind in reading, he or she might benefit from knowing that often there is no necessity to read every sentence and paragraph. Instruct all students to read for *understanding*. It's not the number of pages that one's eyes have moved across that really matter—it's the information gleaned that becomes available for use and application.

As they read their material, challenge students to ask themselves such questions as "Why is this topic important?" and "How does this topic relate to the previous one?" and to make personal associations with the material (i.e., "This sounds like the same theory we discussed last semester in sociology"). If they have questions that are not answered during their reading, then these questions ought to be raised during class discussion.

Reading should not be a passive activity. Instruct students to highlight key concepts and passages they read. Even better, encourage them to highlight *and* take notes over the material. Because everyone forgets a great deal of what they've read shortly after reading it, detailed notes will aid students' recall and improve retention.

When you make reading assignments, avoid saying, "Read Chapters 9 and 10." Instead, briefly discuss the content of these chapters and prepare students for the kinds of questions they should be able to answer after doing this reading. Say, "Read Chapter 9 on the early years of psychoanalysis and Chapter 10 on Jung's Analytical Psychology. We want to be able to compare Freud and Jung—to look for similarities and differences in their conceptualization of therapy." Whenever possible, briefly preview the material and indicate the major themes or controversies—what students should be attempting to extract from the reading.

Some required texts are denser and more difficult to read than others. You may find that students benefit from a recommendation of at least one or possibly two other texts that they can consult. Every text has its own set of strengths and weaknesses. A "back-up" text might have superior examples in a chapter that is made overly complex in the text you adopted.

The act of reviewing material already read is an often neglected but invaluable aspect of the reading process. Without reviewing, students are likely to be able to recall merely 50 percent of what they've read 24 hours later. This drops to a mere 20 percent within two weeks. By simply reviewing, students can increase their retention to 80 percent, a figure that remains constant over time (Miller, 1980).

Teaching Students How to Prepare for Tests

Unless first-year college students attended high schools where they were required to develop good test preparation and test-taking skills, they may not know how to get ready for your first major exam. Many resort to "all-nighters" and "cramming"—hoping, wildly, that such efforts will have a beneficial result. Although it may be impossible for educators to discourage students from cramming, it is possible to provide students with another alternative—one that is a lot less stressful and may help them perform better on tests.

Primarily, students need to be advised to review frequently and regularly. Ellis (1997) has suggested that there are three different types of review strategies. Ideally, each student would make the effort to review *daily* such information as one's lecture notes, starting each time with the first class. Students who feel that's excessive might consider reviewing their relevant materials weekly. Suggest to them that although they should conduct a major review of all their notes immediately before an exam, such a strategy is not going to be as effective as reviewing more frequently.

It is your choice and decision whether to furnish students with a review or study sheet, to allow class discussion regarding potential test questions, or to encourage them to contribute test items. Some instructors hate to "waste" class time for reviewing, but if they do conduct such a session, they inevitably discover a contingent of students who lack understanding about key concepts. Naturally, students would prefer that you summarize and boil down to the absolute minimum what they "should know" for an exam. Some professors have no problem with this; others refuse. Another aid to students is to conduct a review session or sessions. These can be done either during class time or separate from scheduled class meetings.

Encouraging students to pair up with other students can be helpful. "Study buddies" can prepare mock exams for each other so that students can more objectively identify what they know and where they need additional work. Other review tools they might want to collaborate on could include flash cards, checklists, and outlines. Studying with a friend, if done far enough ahead of time, is not as tiring as cramming and it can allow the student to get a good night's sleep and have a clear head for the test. Even without a "study buddy," students can orally rehearse information and write essays on their own to anticipated questions.

Finally, encourage students to use mnemonic devices to assist with the recall of their notes. You probably can recall a host of these from your own childhood, "I before E, except after C," "Thirty days has September, April, June . . . ," and so on. Mnemonic devices may be rhymes, phrases, formulas, or acronyms (such as "Roy G. Biv" for the colors of the rainbow and "George Eats Old Gray Rats And Paints Houses Yellow" to remember how to spell geography).

More advanced systems, such as peg or loci systems, require some additional effort to learn but can be particularly useful for courses requiring the need to recall numerous details in a particular order. The peg system links visual images to numbers (e.g., one = bun, two = shoe, three = tree, four = door, five = hive, six = sticks). A student trying to remember that water boils at 212 degrees Fahrenheit might create the mental image of a baby shoe (2) stuffed with a hot dog bun (1) being dropped into a large, oversized shoe (2) full of boiling water. A colleague who teaches study skills used the peg system to successfully memorize key details of the first 100 pages of a text and could recall the information with amazing accuracy.

The loci system is similar but it is based on visual associations that are well worn into memory. For instance, a college student trying to recall details of the Civil War for an essay question might picture his or her residence hall room. Abraham Lincoln's long legs could be hanging over the bed's end. Facts regarding Confederate forces could be placed in each of the drawers of the clothing chest. The desk could contain information on Union forces (Ellis, 1997).

Although some students find that it takes more time to create the device, others enjoy the creativity and absurdity of the techniques. One selling point to students about memory recall is that this is the one time that dwelling on sex and violence could actually boost academic performance, particularly due to the link between strong emotion and memory recall. Additionally, the more senses employed to recall encoded information, the more likely the chances for effective recall (McWhorter, 1992).

The basic memory rule is that anything can be remembered if it is associated with something already known. Linkages are important and that's why images, rhymes, and so forth work. Ridiculous associations tend to be easy to remember. However, practice is critical in memorization. The most success comes with time on task and practice.

A strategy that students may find useful when reviewing for a test is the mind map summary method. The mind or concept mapping technique involves the construction of a visual image or images similar to a flowchart (see Figure 6.1). Mind maps are often hierarchical in structure and may contain key words as well as shorthand symbols, images, or abbreviations to represent clusters of ideas and to assist in organizing knowledge.

There is some evidence that concept mapping may be more useful in helping students answer essay questions requiring "deep thinking" rather than memorization of facts (Hadwin & Winne, 1996). In a comprehensive review, Romance and Vitale (1999) stated that "the research literature supports the effectiveness of concept mapping" (p. 75).

Unlike Roman numeral outlines, which standardize and organize information in a linear fashion, mind maps created by different students over the same material may not closely resemble each other. This is because each mind map is individually fashioned to portray associations that make sense to the student. Using one's own diagram or scheme for linking facts and concepts seems to give the brain an increased ability to recall pertinent information.

Concept mapping may also be used to promote cooperative learning where a small number of students work together and produce a group concept map (Dorough & Rye, 1997). They can be supplied with large sheets of white butcher paper, colored pens and pencils, and "sticky" notes so that concepts can be moved and placed in different positions. These can even become class assignments, and scoring rubrics can be constructed based on such criteria as the number of relevant concepts shown to be associated with the overarching topic concept, the number of valid propositions, the number of specific concepts, and so forth (Dorough & Rye, 1997).

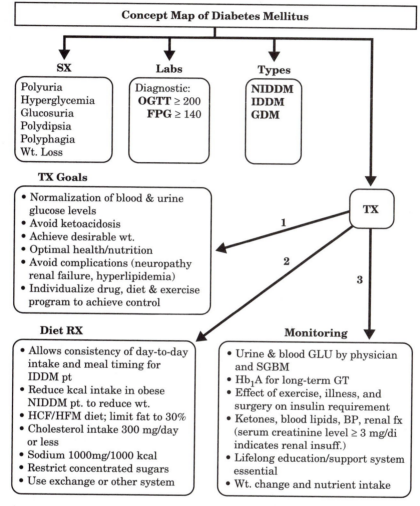

FIGURE 6.1 Sample of a student-generated concept map of diabetes mellitus. The completed map provides the instructor with a view of the student's ability to analyze, synthesize, evaluate, and communicate information. In this example, Hb_1A for HbA_{1c} reflects the student's misunderstanding and prompts corrective feedback from the instructor.

Key: **GDM = gestational diabetes mellitus, IDDM = insulin-dependent diabetes mellitus, NIDDM = non-insulin-dependent diabetes mellitus, wt = weight, OGTT = oral glucose tolerance test, FPG = fasting plasma glucose, HCF/HFM = high carbohydrate-high fiber/high fiber maintenance, GLU = glucose, SGBN = self blood glucose monitoring, pt = patient, SX = symptoms, TX = treatment, RX = prescription, GT = glucose tolerance, BP = blood pressure.**

Source: C. M. Roberts, K. Sucher, D. G. Perrin, & S. Rodriguez, Concept mapping: An effective instructional strategy for diet therapy. Reprinted by permission from *Journal of the American Dietetic Association,* 95 (8) (1995): 908–911.

Possibly the most valuable piece of advice that you can share with students getting ready for tests is that they must schedule enough time to prepare thoroughly. They shouldn't wait until the weekend just before and then take Saturday or Sunday to cram. Urge students to make study schedules—to look for free hours and not to fall victim to the thought that since there isn't an uninterrupted block of four hours at a time that it's pointless to begin studying. Even those with jobs or other responsibilities can usually make better use of unscheduled time during the day, finding an hour here or there when they could go to the library or some other quiet place to begin reviewing. Reviewing can begin anytime during the semester and ideally should occur *regularly* and *well in advance* of the exam. Good preparation means that not only has all of the assigned material been read but it has also been reviewed and understood. Students' textbooks often provide review questions and exercises that provide a good place to begin reviewing.

Teaching Students How to Take Tests

Instruct students to look over their tests when they first receive them so that they will know what to expect and how best to use their time. You may also want to announce the time periodically; this is particularly important when there is only 5 or 10 minutes remaining.

When you plan on developing an objective-type test, encourage your students to leave the difficult questions for last—going on and completing the easier questions first. Often, reading other questions will refresh associations that may produce the right answer. Test scores also improve when definitely incorrect response choices can be eliminated.

Students will appreciate your sharing with them sample test questions or examples from previous tests. This is especially important if you've not given them any kind of a quiz or exam, and they will know little or nothing about your test-writing style. Sample questions will give students a good idea of the extent to which they must memorize names, dates, facts, or other particulars. Or the sample questions will show that they must be able to synthesize, evaluate, analyze. Don't assume that students know how to do this without some time-on-task and opportunity to see how it is done. Sharing with the class both good and poor examples of former students' essays will help students learn how to respond appropriately.

If you tend to favor essay tests, you might want to encourage students with poor writing skills to get assistance early in the academic term. Possible sources of help are the university's writing center, private tutors, or retaking basic English courses. Writing skills aside, to do well on an essay test, students generally must be able to demonstrate a clear and concise understanding of the material. Encourage students to create an outline prior to writing their responses. This will help them think about what they need to say as well as help them stick to the question being asked. Students often do a beautiful job of answering the wrong question, without realizing they have done so, perhaps due to nervousness, sleep deprivation, caffeine overdose, or a mere desire to prove they do know something, even if it's not the answer to the question at hand.

If you become aware of a student who suffers from test anxiety, an actual tendency often experienced by well-prepared students, encourage this student to get assistance for this difficulty through available written materials, workshops, or counselors at the university. The keys to overcoming test anxiety are for students to be as well prepared as possible and to engage in systematic desensitization, a method of removing the link between tests and anxiety that employs cognitive coping and relaxation exercises (Davis, Eshelman, & McKay, 1995).

Other helpful hints to tell students about test-taking include the following:

- Get up early on the exam day and review the content to be memorized, writing it out several times.
- Eat breakfast.
- Come prepared with everything needed (e.g., pens, pencils, calculators, identification, etc.).
- Arrive at the testing site in plenty of time to get settled, sharpen pencils, and so on.
- Avoid trying to cram in the final minutes before the exam; it's better to try to relax and be confident.
- When handed the exam, check it to make sure there are no missing pages.
- Assume that most questions are straightforward, not "trick" questions.
- Read all response choices.
- Attempt to eliminate the distractors and the obviously incorrect responses.

- On difficult questions, underline the key words as an aid to understanding.
- Avoid second-guessing and changing responses.
- Look over the exam when finished to double-check your work.

References and Resources

Anderson, J. A., & Adams, M. (1992). Acknowledging the learning styles of diverse student populations: Implications for instructional design. *New Directions for Teaching and Learning, 49,* 19–33.

Brock, K. L., & Cameron, B. J. (1999). Enlivening political science courses with Kolb's learning preference model. *PS: Political Science & Politics, 32,* 251–256.

Davis, M., Eshelman, E., & McKay, M. (1995). *The relaxation and stress reduction workbook* (4th ed.). Oakland, CA: New Harbinger Publications.

Dorough, D. K., & Rye, J. A. (1997). Mapping for understanding: Using concept maps as windows to students' minds. *The Science Teacher, 64* (1), 37–41.

Ellis, D. (1997). *Becoming a master student* (8th ed.). Chicago: Houghton Mifflin.

Felder, R. M. (1993). Reaching the second tier: Learning and teaching styles in college science education. *Journal of College Teaching, 23* (5), 286–290.

Felder, R. M. (1996). Matters of style. *ASEE Prism, 6* (4), 18–23.

Felder, R. M., & Henriques, E. R. (1995). Learning and teaching styles in foreign and second language education. *Foreign Language Annals, 28* (1), 21–31.

Hadwin, A. F., & Winne, P. H. (1996). Study strategies have meager support: A review with recommendations for implementation. *Journal of Higher Education, 67,* 692–715.

McWhorter, K. (1992). *Study and thinking skills in college* (2nd ed.). New York: HarperCollins.

Miller, L. (1980). *Developing reading efficiency.* Minneapolis, MN: Burgess Publishing.

Novak, J. D., & Gowin, D. B. (1984). *Learning how to learn.* London: Cambridge University Press.

Romance, N. R., & Vitale, M. R. (1999). Concept mapping as a tool for learning. *College Teaching, 47,* 74–79.

U.S. Department of Education. (1993). *National excellence: A case for developing America's talent.* Washington, DC: Office of Educational Research and Improvement.

7

*Experiential
Education*

Overview: In real estate, there is a maxim that the three most important things to know are location, location, and location. Similarly, in education, it may be that the three most important concepts are involvement, involvement, and involvement. Indeed, the trick is often finding ways to involve students to a greater extent in the learning process—especially those with low levels of motivation. Helping students to experience firsthand the concepts and principles being studied is a time-honored approach in many disciplines and is being gradually extended to many others. Experiential learning can include such diverse activities as Study Abroad programs and archaeological sitework.

What Is Experiential Learning?

The renown educator John Dewey believed that students learn best by doing. Years later, Carl Rogers (1969) also argued for experiential learning and wrote in *The Freedom to Learn:* "It has a quality of personal involvement—the whole person in both his feeling and cognitive aspects being in the learning event" (p. 5). Experiential education requires that the student make meaning out of his or her experiences—that "raw" experiences are transformed into usable knowledge (Katula & Threnhauser, 1999).

We know from our own personal experience and from observing students that human memory is a capricious thing. It is possible to memorize formulas, world capitals, all the bones in the human body, and 10 steps of this or that process, and to know these well— only to forget them at a critical moment when it really matters. Does the inability to have complete recall indicate that no learning occurred? Indeed, how much material once committed to memory have we forgotten? At the same time, certain learning, such as how to ride a bike, stays with us most of our lives.

The principle of experiential education is based on the notion that a richer, more comprehensive and accessible knowledge arises from greater involvement with the subject matter. Experiential learning opportunities allow students to integrate knowledge from the classroom and encourage them to think at a more complex level—to analyze and synthesize. It is one matter to memorize the parts of a 20-speed mountain bike and quite another to challenge a rocky hill with two wheels. It is one thing to learn the longitude and latitude of Calcutta, its annual rainfall, the size of its population, and the region's annual per capita income, but an altogether different knowledge comes from walking its streets, smelling human and animal waste in the gutter, watching women wash their saris in the river, and seeing a mother raising her young children in a large drainage pipe.

Many colleges and universities have experiential learning courses or cooperative education programs where students individually can elect to explore possible new fields or careers by shadowing professionals or serving as interns. In co-op programs, students typically alternate courses with work experiences in order to better integrate their learning. Students are attracted to such programs because they help the student:

- Confirm the choice of an academic major
- Gain related work experience
- Earn money for educational expenses
- Test possible career choices
- Explore a particular workplace or industry (Mosser, 1989, cited in Cantor, 1997)

Wallace (1993) has suggested that another value of experiential education is that it creates a personal challenge which, when mastered, increases self-confidence and a deeper level of awareness of one's strengths and weaknesses.

A key component of experiential education is reflection on the student's experience. Hatcher and Bringle (1997) have recommended that students keep personal journals of their experiences. These journals can be daily or weekly records. To link these journals more directly to course objectives, students can be asked to reread their journals and highlight comments that relate directly to course content. Or they can be instructed to keep double-entry journals where they write about their service experiences on the left half of the page and how those experiences relate to course content on the right half of the page. Another variation is to have students factually record their experiences on half of the page and then on the opposite side to relate their feelings about those experiences. Reflection about experiences can also be stimulated by having students ponder and respond to such questions as:

What did you learn that you didn't anticipate learning?
What did you learn about yourself this past week?
What surprised or pleased you?
What made you sad or angry?
What was the hardest thing to learn?
What puzzled or confused you this past week?
What else do you need to learn in order to become more skilled?

Directed writings that invite students to analyze their experiences in light of an assigned reading, theory, or question can also help students make connections and integrate content. Discussions can be focused on those student experiences that illustrate a relevant course concept.

Laboratory science courses also have a fine tradition of involving students with hands-on learning. Ideally, students learn the skills of observing, classifying, measuring, interpreting, predicting, and hypothesizing in these classes. Unfortunately, according to Leonard (1994), because students usually are instructed to follow recipe-like procedures from a detailed laboratory manual, there is little opportunity to make real discovery. Students often have assigned goals in the lab that usually involve a somewhat tedious procedure, instead of thinking about the scientific questions being investigated. Research appears to support the effectiveness of inquiry-based approaches where students are given less direction and more responsibility for determining procedural options (Leonard, 1994).

Leonard (1994) has made the following recommendations for modifying laboratory courses to make them more inquiry-based and less prescriptive:

1. Give students a simple question to answer.
2. Give students only the essential procedures. (Encourage students to figure out some of the steps for themselves.)
3. Have students work in small groups.
4. Coach and coax only when absolutely necessary.
5. Ask meaningful questions at the end of the investigation. (For example, have the students summarize their data; ask if the data support their hypotheses; ask questions about generalizations and implications.)

Service Learning

Certain disciplines (e.g., social work) have relied on an experiential model from their inception. Sometimes known as *service learning,* typically these students intern at social services agencies in much the same way as elementary and secondary teachers acquire valuable skills as student teachers, and as doctors and dentists "practice" on their own patients as a vital part of their educational experiences. In these professions, interaction with real flesh-and-blood clients and pupils provides a level of instruction clearly superior to reading from a textbook or taking notes during a lecture. Service learning allows students to become exposed to real problems, to make decisions, and sometimes to learn from making mistakes. It is a relevant, meaningful way to connect knowledge with critical thinking and application quite distinct from rote learning or recitation.

"Among the more interesting specific outcomes favorably affected by service participation are persistence in college, interest in graduate study, critical thinking skills, leadership skills, and commitment to promoting racial understanding" (Astin, 1996, p. 16).

The difference between *community service* and *service learning* is this: Service learning seeks to integrate academic coursework with the provision of aid. In other words, it is community service that has been thoughtfully organized or prepared so that students achieve certain curricular objectives. Typically, reflection on the experience and seminars in which students can discuss their views accompany service learning but not community service. Further, students must spend enough time in the project for it to be a transformative experience (Chapin, 1998). Carver (1997) has noted that service learning speaks to "the three major goals of 'experiential education' by: allowing students to become more effective change agents, developing students' sense of belonging in the communities of which they are members, and developing student competence" (p. 143).

In order for service learning to be successful, the following standards (adapted from the Alliance for Service Learning in Education Reform) should be addressed:

- Clearly articulated learning and service goals understood by all parties
- Preparatory study of the context, problems, history, and policies likely to be connected with the service project
- Structured reflection involving reading, writing, discussion, and observation
- Concrete opportunities for students to learn new skills and test new roles that contribute in a meaningful way
- An evaluative process

Service learning can be adapted to most courses with a little imagination. Cushman (1999) described a group of Berkeley undergraduates enrolled in a Social Issues of Literacy course who read scholarship on literacy, volunteered at the YMCA, wrote fieldnotes, and then integrated theory and data in case studies. This is an excerpt from her article:

One student's paper noted that Scribner and Cole's famous work on Vai literacy showed their limited access to Vai females' literacy practices. Her paper then illustrated two interactions where she noticed how girls were excluded by the boys during story-telling, playing, and writing. She consid-

Principles of Experiential Education Practice

- The priority or order in which each profession places these principles may vary.
- Experiential learning occurs when carefully chosen experiences are supported by reflection, critical analysis, and synthesis.
- Experiences are structured to require the learner to take initiative, make decisions, and be accountable for the results.
- Throughout the experiential learning process, the learner is actively engaged in posing questions, investigating, experimenting, being curious, solving problems, assuming responsibility, being creative, and constructing meaning.
- Learners are engaged intellectually, emotionally, socially, soulfully, and/or physically. This involvement produces a perception that the learning task is authentic.
- The results of the learning are personal and form the basis for future experience and learning.
- Relationships are developed and nurtured: learner to self, learner to others, and learner to the world at large.
- Because the outcomes of experience cannot be totally predicted, the educator and learner may experience success, failure, adventure, risk taking, and uncertainty.
- Opportunities are nurtured for learners and educators to explore and examine their own values.
- The educator's primary roles include setting suitable experiences, posing problems, setting boundaries, supporting learners, ensuring physical and emotional safety, and facilitating the learning process.
- The educator recognizes and encourages spontaneous opportunities for learning.
- Educators strive to be aware of their biases, judgments, and preconceptions and how they influence the learner.
- The design of the learning experience includes the possibility to learn from natural consequences, mistakes, and successes.

Approved by the Association for Experiential Education Board of Directors, November 1994

Source: C. Luckman, "Defining Experiential Education," *The Journal of Experiential Education, 19* (1) (May/June 1996): p. 7. Used with permission.

ered methods of participant observation that might invite more of the girls to engage in these activities. At the same time, she conducted formal interviews with the YMCA members in order to understand better how their values for oral and literate language shifted along gender lines. She did this with an eye toward filling gaps in knowledge that she saw in the scholarship on literacy that we read in class. (p. 333)

Experiential education approaches have a great deal of face validity, but there is not much research demonstrating its superiority over other classroom methods. Katula and Threnhauser (1999) have noted that "the data on cooperation education are sketchy and often based on anecdotal rather than empirical evidence" (p. 245). They suggested a possible explanation by raising a question, "What good is an internship if the student stands at a copy machine all day and has no program of reflection within the curriculum to process what he or she has learned in some systematic way?" (p. 252). Clearly, internships and co-ops that don't engage students' minds are not providing sound educational experiences. Experiences outside of the classroom must be connected to those inside the classroom. Students must think critically, analytically, and reflectively about their experiences and relate those to larger issues and questions. The "doing" ought to be only one part, not the totality, of experiential education

References and Resources

Alliance for Service-Learning in Education Reform. (1997). Standards of quality for school-based and community-based service learning. *The Social Studies, 88* (5), 215–219.

Astin, A. W. (1996). The role of service in higher education. *About Campus,* (March/April), 14–19.

Cantor, J. A. (1997). *Experiential learning in higher education: Linking classroom and community.* Washington, DC: George Washington University, ASHE-ERIC Higher Education Report No. 7.

Carver, R. L. (1997). Theoretical underpinnings of service learning. *Theory into Practice, 36* (3), 143–149.

Chapin, J. R. (1998). Is service learning a good idea? Data from the national longitudinal study of 1988. *The Social Studies, 89* (5), 205–211.

Cushman, E. (1999). The public intellectual, service learning, and activist research. *College English, 61* (3), 328–336.

Hatcher, J. A., & Bringle, R. G. (1997). Reflection: Bridging the gap between service and learning. *College Teaching, 45,* 153–157.

Katula, R. A., & Threnhauser, E. (1999). Experiential education in the undergraduate curriculum. *Communication Education, 48,* 238–255.

Leonard, W. H. (1994). The laboratory classroom. In K. W. Prichard & R. M. Sawyer (Eds.), *Handbook of college teaching: Theory and applications.* Westport, CT: Greenwood Press.

Rogers, C. (1969). *The freedom to learn.* Columbus, OH: Merrill.

Wallace, J. A. (1993). The educational value of experiential education. In Theodore Gochenour (Ed.), *Beyond experience: The experiential approach to cross-cultural education.* Yarmouth, ME: Intercultural Press.

Note: Organizations for those interested in promoting and discussing good practice with regard to experiential education:

The National Society for Experiential Education
3509 Haworth Drive, Suite 207
Raleigh, NC 27609-7229
<www.nsee.org>

The Association for Experiential Education
2305 Canyon Boulevard, Suite 100
Boulder, CO 80302

8

Use of Instructional Technology

Overview: There's no question that the computer is changing the educational landscape at a breath-taking clip. Not even the invention of the printing press has provided such potential for change in education as that brought on by new technology (Boschmann, 1995). Computers can tutor students independently or collectively, test them, and then score the results in a matter of seconds. Educational games and electronic simulations bring a richness and a realism unimaginable even 10 years ago. Students can navigate through phenomenal databases in a fraction of the time it takes to walk to the library and find a book, then read and store needed information without paper. And no longer must instruction be delivered in person at set times. Students can "attend" virtual classrooms at any hour of the day or night and communicate electronically as questions arise—there is no need to wait for scheduled classes or office hours in order to exchange ideas with an instructor. It also doesn't matter whether the instructor lives across town or is conducting archaeological research in Belize—e-mail provides almost instant access. In short, today's educators have many more instructional tools and resources available to them than ever before.

While more and more computers are being seen inside and outside of the classroom, at the same time instructors in many schools across the country are making greater use of television to reach students who live some distance from their campuses. This chapter provides a look at some of the basic considerations involved with using some of the newer forms of instructional technology.

The Electronic Classroom

Gone are the days when all an instructor needed was a box of chalk, an eraser, and a chalkboard. Computers are continuing to change education. For one thing, students are increasingly computer literate. A recent (1999) survey of University of Wisconsin students found that 77 percent of those responding reported owning a computer. Students know about the amazing things computers can do: the dazzling array of databases and information sources that can be located with a few keystrokes, the vivid graphics, the spell-check and grammar-check features of word-processing programs, and other wonderful applications. Some educators have made maximum use of electronic technology and found that it is possible to correspond with students entirely by e-mail and to use no paper at all in their classes (Navarro, 1998). In such classes, students "hand in" their assignments as file attachments to e-mail. The faculty may even find that there is less need to hold actual office hours; rather, students can contact them in a "virtual office."

"Smart classrooms," where every seat is wired to the school's computer server and the Internet, are gradually becoming a reality rather than a far-fetched vision. In these classrooms, it is possible for instructors to administer a quiz and, minutes later, have the computer grade and record scores. Surveys can be constructed and polls taken; the data can be analyzed almost instantaneously. For most instructors, the fully electronic classroom is still sometime away. But in the meantime, technology has vastly improved on the old-fashion overhead and slide projectors.

Programs such as PowerPoint and Astound make it possible for instructors to incorporate video and audio clips, computer animations, and bulleted slides in multimedia presentations and thus "dress up" lectures that in the past may have been not so visually stimulating. However, concerns have been noted about the use of such powerful presentation software. First of all, these visual software programs take time to learn—especially if one wants to make full use of special effects. Preparing the presentations can also be time consuming. Second, a computer-based presentation is a passive-teaching technique. If presentations are done in a fashion that is too detailed, there will be less need for students to take notes. Less actively involved and placed in a darkened room, some students may find it easier to doze off than in a normal lecture (Parks, 1999; Reinhardt, 1999). Third, complex topics can't always be reduced to cute visual images, and animation on the screen can't be reproduced in the student's notes.

On the other hand, students like to see lectures outlined for them with bulleted points and colorful graphs. There's little doubt but that this type of media is good for the visual learner, and it can reinforce and enhance learning that has already occurred from the student's reading or studies. Using presentation software forces the educator to organize his or her material well in advance, and students could benefit from this as well. The challenge is to create multimedia presentations that convey interesting ideas and stimulate intellectual questions rather than just entertain.

Reinhardt (1999) and Endicott (1999) have made the following suggestions for instructors wishing to present material with such software as Persuasion, ToolBook, Supercard, Astound, and Power-Point:

- Investigate various software before selecting the one to use.
- Start with a handful of target lessons; don't attempt to do the whole course at once.
- Story-board your first several lessons by planning which objects and actions will be highlighted.
- Use sound effects (like the laser sound) sparingly; if used too often, they lose their effect.
- Select one type of text animation and use it every time; choose one primary transition and stick with it.
- Animate graphical images when telling complex stories. Create an animated progression of objects that graphically tell the story so that the presenter's role is filling in the details.

Why Universities Are Interested in Distance Learning

Today the educational landscape is strikingly different. Only 52% of college students are 18 to 21, and fewer than 15% fit the profile of a residential student—young, full-time, and living on campus. (Connick, 1997)

Few would disagree that the portrait of college students today is different from one made of those attending the nation's universities

20 or 30 years ago. There are more working, more nontraditional students who do not live on campus and seek the convenience of taking courses that can fit into their busy schedules. Electronic technology is making it possible for students to receive instruction from hundreds and thousands of miles away without ever venturing onto a college campus. Television instruction is not a recent development, but what is new is the widespread use of the medium as institutions of higher education target students in off-campus locations. Instead of building new classrooms and bringing students onto campuses already suffering from too few parking spaces and other attendant problems, educators today, more than any other time in history, are taking the instruction to the students. Indeed, *distance learning* is the term replacing *extension programs* as the banner for this mission. Technology has provided several avenues through which distance learning programs can be delivered: Besides television, there is the Internet, and even instruction by CD-ROM or hybrid programs relying on combinations of videotapes, computer assignments, and homework sent in electronically or via the U.S. mail.

The development of the Internet has made it possible to teach students in distant locations almost as easily as turning on a computer. Not only are entire courses available from the World Wide Web but also whole degree programs are possible. The number of institutions offering courses by Internet changes so rapidly that it is difficult to keep track. However, a recent Peterson's Distance Learning Guide (1998) counted over 900 "cyberschools." Roughly 1 million students are now plugged into virtual college classrooms— compared to 13 million in brick-and-mortar schools (Gubernick & Ebeling, 1997). The University of Phoenix, a for-profit institution without many of the usual fixtures and amenities associated with universities, has reported having over 10,000 students enrolled in on-line programs (Carlson, 1999). Its rapid growth is due to both distance learning technology and the changing demographics of students.

Needless to say, students are quick to see the obvious advantages in not having to attend 8:00 A.M. classes, but taking Internet courses has some disadvantages, too. If you are thinking about creating a course that would be mostly taught via computer technology, you should be aware of some of the advantages and disadvantages.

Advantages of Internet Instruction

Teaching a course over the Internet or via CD-ROM allows students to participate 24 hours a day. This is an exceptional convenience for students who work or need to be home with small children or elders and for those who find it difficult to travel because of great distances or physical handicaps. Unlike traditional classroom instruction, students accessing courses by computer can set their own pace and interact with the prepared material as long or as often as they choose. With this mode of instruction, there's no lost class time, no class roll to call.

Creed (1996) has enumerated the advantages of electronic communication for instruction: elimination of the "vagaries of handwriting and penmanship," enhanced ability to archive and retrieve students' work, potential for enhanced student interaction outside of class (presuming they make use of e-mail), and this media may "level the playing field" for shy students who would be uncomfortable raising questions in a traditional classroom. Someone phrased it poignantly: "Computers make no personal judgments."

Offering a course via computer also allows for feedback from the instructor to the student to be completely private, unlike graded papers that get passed down rows of students. And, after they overcome their initial fears, students who are apprehensive about using the computer are likely to go on and make other useful discoveries about the vast information resources available from the Internet.

Possibly the chief advantage from an instructor's perspective is that once the course has been loaded into the computer, then there is no further day-to-day preparation. The course can be taught again and again, with no additional brushing up on one's lecture notes, photocopying of handouts, or wrestling with overhead projectors or balky VCRs. (However, there is some maintenance, as the URLs of links and resources that you have placed in your webpages may change.)

Depending on how you view it, another advantage could be that there are also no limitations on the number of students who can participate. A single student could enroll, as well as several hundred— there is no real upper limit. After the instructional material has been prepared, the major time demands consist mostly of grading assignments and corresponding with students.

Still another benefit of web-based instruction is that instructional material can be provided simultaneously to all students at the same time—minimizing the problem of a small group of students monopolizing the resources placed on reserve in the library. Thus, the instructor can scan handouts, old exams, exemplary papers, or supplemental notes into the website without making multiple copies or worrying that a valuable document might be stolen or vandalized. An entire collection of rare writings can be posted electronically. (The University of Virginia makes available William Blake's Songs of Innocence and of Experience at <www.iath.virginia.edu/blake>. The University of Kentucky has the "Electronic Beowulf"—digital images of the manuscript found in the British Library, <www.uky.edu/AS/English/Beowulf/eBeowulf/main.htm>.) The instructor can also provide "hot links" to other networked information located anywhere in the world. Also, when students are all off campus, there's also less need for the educator to keep "office hours" if he or she would prefer to work at home. However, at least one on-line instructor says that he got complaints from students when he checked his e-mail only once a day (Stadtlander, 1998).

Disadvantages and Considerations in Teaching via the Internet

If you are a "people person," you will miss having regular face-to-face contact with your students. Unless you set a special meeting, you may never hear their voices or see their faces. Some faculty feel alienated from their students when the principal form of communication is e-mail. Both faculty and students might miss the informal opportunities to discuss a point further over a cup of coffee, the ability to look the other in the eye to assess sincerity or humor. Even though you may encourage them to call if they have problems or difficulties, students may not contact you as often as you think they should—especially when they obviously need help.

Almost *four weeks* into the first Internet course I was teaching, after I had diligently responded to all assignments and questions by e-mail within 24 hours, one student called and casually wondered why she had not received anything back from me. Delicately, she asked if I was behind in my grading. When we discussed the matter a little further, we determined that she had given me the wrong e-mail address. Why did she wait four weeks to contact me? I still don't know, but this is the kind of glitch in communication that can easily occur.

If you never meet person to person with your students, you'll find yourself reading their communications to you very closely as you try to personalize and understand who these individuals are as people. Instead of noticing a student's ramrod straight posture, the braided hair, or pierced nose, you may be struck by the incomplete sentences, the misspelled words, or the idiosyncratic rules of capitalization. Few students seem to proofread their e-mail communications before sending them. Those who are careless in their writing or who use poor grammar give distinct impressions that may belie their intelligence and give a different impression than you would have received if they had been sitting in front of you raising interesting questions. A dilemma you'll likely face will be trying to decide whether your Internet students really know the rules for good written communication or if you need to teach that, too.

Probably the major disadvantage of teaching over the Internet is that the instructor doesn't experience a great savings in time spent on instructional tasks. In fact, teaching by Internet is often extremely time consuming (Lacina-Gifford & Kher-Durlabhji, 1996). Grading of assignments takes more time. When you meet face to face with a class, it is possible to hand back assignments with only letter grades on them without receiving any objections from students. However, when there's no personal contact with students and when you can't smile at them and explain that they "seem to be on the right track," even a brief comment or two isn't adequate. A frequent criticism of distance education is that it is a packaged product underlaid by a behaviorist model of teaching and learning (Roberts, 1996). In order to keep Internet courses from deteriorating into completely impersonal self-instructional courses, faculty need to give serious thought to the quality and quantity of the feedback given to students.

Teaching Internet courses seems to require writing longer, more detailed explanations to students about why points were taken off for an answer or how they veered slightly off the mark. On one occasion, I realized I was writing the equivalent of a personalized letter to every student after each assignment. And, since weekly assignments were required, I spent much longer than I had originally anticipated responding to students. And this doesn't count the time e-mailing responses to questions when students asked for additional information before beginning assignments.

Until I caught on to what they were doing, one or two students even sent me first drafts of their assignments to see if they were on target with what I wanted. I painstakingly commented on these and then two or three days later the assignments came back to me again as cleaned-up, "official" submissions. The students "forgot" to inform me that their first efforts were drafts that they didn't want graded. When all communication is written and there are no smiles, no body language to read, no tone of voice to assist with interpretation, messages can be unclear. Was it the newness, the unfamiliarity with learning by Internet, the vagueness of my instructions, or were they pulling a fast one? I really couldn't tell.

Although reading first *and* final drafts of students' work may be an educationally sound practice, anyone thinking that launching a course over the Internet will *free up* extra hours each week is mistaken. However, some day, we'll have the technology to electronically circle misspelled words on the screen, write comments, and then forward the whole kit and caboodle right back to the sender. Until then, don't expect any time savings.

The feedback we provide is important because students enrolled in distance education courses feel isolated. They lack the informal support and the casual encounters with other students. Students like to consult with each other and to the extent that they can't, satisfaction with the course will decline. Finding ways to encourage student-to-student interaction can be challenging. Simply circulating students' phone numbers or e-mail addresses to each other will not keep them from feeling isolated, because few of them will make contact with virtual classmates unless they are required to or have an opportunity to meet each other at an initial session and to form friendships.

Although personal computers are no longer a rarity in U.S. homes and workplaces, the instructor must still expect to encounter students who are uncomfortable with computers and their applications. Some students completely unfamiliar with computers may sign up for Internet courses in order to overcome their computer phobia. Even though most elementary, middle, and high schools have computers, 80 percent of all school computers are considered obsolete (Ely, 1996). Also, don't assume that all your pupils have computers configured just like yours or are using the latest version of popular software. You might want to conduct an assessment of students' computer literacy the first time you meet or have contact with them. A brief questionnaire could ask if they have a computer at home or work, how many times a week they send e-mail and look for resources on the World Wide Web, how many hours a week they spend on the computer, what software they know, and so on.

A potentially greater problem is that most students have their own computers at home or in the dorm as well as at work, and their familiarity and facility with e-mail may produce too much volume if the Internet course has a chat room and requires participation. At a recent conference, one Internet instructor revealed that she and her students were receiving on the order of 300 e-mails a week in connection with the course. The volume was so overwhelming that she had to set guidelines on the number of exchanges that students should make.

The first time I taught a course over the Internet, my students were on the campus of another university about 75 miles away. The computers in that lab were set up quite differently than mine and that university used an older e-mail software. Many students' frustrations came from not getting good technological assistance there. For instance, only a handful of computers in that lab had the ability to access the Internet, and these weren't marked well. Students would sit down at other computers and spend 15 minutes or more trying to find the right screen or icon when Internet access wasn't available. Then, students who did get connected and found something they wanted to print occasionally discovered that the printer wasn't hooked up to their computer. Low-tech problems were the undoing of many students who really wanted to have a good experience with this class. Depending on your own expertise and time demands, you may want to make it clear to students that you are not a technician who can be called whenever they lose a file or are unable to get a printer to respond. Of course, the greater your willingness to assist students, the more favorably they will evaluate the Internet class.

Another consideration in planning for distant learning courses is that classes at the off-campus site might not have available to them all of the resources commonly found on the main campus. For instance, if the Internet class is a graduate-level course designed primarily for students 200 miles away in a rural part of the state, the closest library could be a public or community college library and very likely wouldn't be a research library with all the professional journals and resources needed. Thus, the distance learning instructor must anticipate this problem and work out the logistics in order for his or her students to have access to necessary books, journals, and so forth.

Administering tests long distance can be a disadvantage. At the current time, there is no 100 percent foolproof way to verify via computer that the student 150 miles away is who he or she claims to be. As an instructor of an Internet course, you have three basic options for examining students: (1) administer your tests in person at a central location where identity can be verified with a picture ID and the tests supervised by a proctor; (2) require students to take their tests at labs or sites with CU-SeeMe software (tiny cameras that provide a visual image of the person in front of the computer) and scheduled examination appointments; or (3) mail your tests or put them on the Internet and trust your students to abide by the honor system.

Option A, of course, provides the greatest security and is the one I use. However, this option doesn't make it impossible for a "ringer" to pose for the student registered for the class if fake IDs can be obtained. Option B can provide a good measure of protection against cheating if you have had previous contact with your students and recognize each of them. Even if students in your class don't actively cheat on the test you send to them by e-mail, Internet, or the U.S. Postal Service, Option C will require that you continually develop new exams, as it is almost certain that some student will print out and share the current test with friends or students in your future classes. To keep students from cheating, some faculty "legalize" it by giving everyone permission to work collaboratively.

Another consideration is that students with visual impairments may find Internet courses difficult. Most websites contain visual images that are not designed for those who must rely on speech synthesizers to read for them. Instructors creating their own webpages need to present information in a straightforward fashion and to ensure that any important pictures are accompanied by descriptions that can be read by screen-reading software.

Copyright issues can pose a problem—both in the sense of someone stealing material from your webpage and because you may not be able to make public over the Internet copyright protected materials that you have collected or obtained over the years.

Finally, the technology is changing very rapidly in this area and bringing new tools for the educator every day. There are now real-time electronic "seminars" and computer conferencing software where multiple students can log on to a classroom website at a specific hour and raise questions for the instructor, see the questions raised by other students, even read prepared materials posted to an electronic "white board" corresponding to the low-tech chalkboards that we all know so well. Such seminars can feature electronic attendance lists, and even other features such as chat rooms.

Tips for Teaching on the Internet

Given that Internet instruction is not only here to stay but is going to grow and have an even larger role in higher education, it may be wise to begin thinking about what questions you would have if asked to teach an Internet course. It doesn't hurt to be prepared for that inevitable day when the department chair comes knocking on your door with that Cheshire cat grin on his or her face. And when the request does come, here are a few suggestions to help your web-based course to be a success once you have mastered the technology needed to post the course.

1. If possible, hold an initial (orientation) session with students. Ask them to introduce themselves to each other. Use one of the ice-breakers suggested in Chapter 3. This "getting acquainted" meeting allows students the opportunity to build informal support mechanisms and helps them to get some sense of who you are as an instructor. It also combats feelings of isolation. You might want to schedule additional in-person meetings throughout the semester—for instance, to conduct a review of material before the midterm or final exam.

If you can't meet with students in the flesh, you might consider posting one or more photographs of yourself on the Internet. These don't have to be serious portraits; students will enjoy seeing snapshots of you teaching, swinging in a hammock, or walking your pet beagle. You can also invite them to include their photographs on the homepage as well, but don't expect 100 percent compliance. An alternative idea for helping the students get to know one another is to have each one supply a mini-vita (work experience, hobbies, age, long-term goals, etc.) that you could post or make available to all the other students.

2. Carefully examine your syllabus to make sure the directions for assignments are clearly and unambiguously stated. Look for any assumptions that aren't explicit. For example, don't give your Internet students a syllabus structured with weekly readings and assignments and then make the mistake of assuming that the students will proceed methodically week by week through the syllabus. If it is important that students turn in assignments on a weekly basis, then build in incentives to encourage prompt submission. Otherwise, the students may view it as an independent study and deduce that they can turn their assignments in at any time during the semester as long as all are completed by the end of the term.

One estimate is that 30 to 50 percent of all students who start a distance education course drop out before finishing it (Moore & Kearsley, 1996). You may be able to identify some of these students by their failure to turn in assignments on time. Many students need the discipline of going to class every week—falling behind once the novelty wears off. Not having to face a live instructor each week makes it too easy for some of the less conscientious students to put off and forget about their course responsibilities. Distance learning courses require a high degree of self-directedness on the part of the learner (Mood, 1995). State clearly in the syllabus the penalty for turning in late assignments.

3. Expect "down times" when hard drive fails, printers won't work, or the server is not responding. And, following Murphy's Law, you can expect to get a virus or have equipment problems at the most inopportune times, such as on a day you were expecting assignments to arrive by e-mail or had planned to fix some critical problem with your webpage. If students are sending you assignments electronically, it's probably a good idea to keep a log or record of these independent of your computer-based file.

4. Anticipate that students will find creative ways to problem-solve around the obstacles before them. I developed my Internet course over a few weeks of intense, concentrated effort. In worrying more about finding any bugs that might keep it from functioning the way I had wanted, I wasn't overly concerned about finely polishing the text. By the time students were reading the web-based notes associated with the third chapter of their text, I had planned to be going over the notes of the fifth and sixth chapters with a fine-tooth comb and catching all the typos, sentence fragments, and so on. (I had written all the HTML myself and typed the text in my computer's Notepad, which, incidentally, didn't have a spell-check capability. There are other ways of doing it now, but that's how I did it in 1996.)

However, several students who either did not have computers or who were uncomfortable with using them accessed the homepage for the course and printed out, at one time, all the lecture notes, assignments, and so on. By doing this, the students effectively kept me from correcting spelling errors and revising assignments—not that I wanted to change the assignments drastically, but from one student who turned in some assignments early, I could tell that adding another sentence or two would have helped to communicate more clearly what I expected of the students. The problem was further exacerbated because these few students were also not in communication with me or their classmates by e-mail. They chose to send in their assignments through the U.S. mail.

Internet instruction requires students to learn specific course content information as well as to learn more about computers. We can expect that in the coming years this form of instruction will become even more popular and widespread. From a higher education perspective, one benefit may be that it will likely improve the standardization of content, which has always been a problem when courses are taught by diverse faculty. There may also be even other unrecognized pedagogical arguments for Internet courses. A student made this observation:

> *In order to do well in this class, I will actually have to read all of the chapters assigned. This may seem obvious, but . . . in the past, I have merely listened in class, taken notes, and very occasionally skimmed a chapter that has troubled me.*

One last consideration: Because of the relative permanence of a course created for the Internet or captured on CD-ROM, there is an issue of ownership. Many faculty believe that if they create such a course from scratch, then it should be their course—forever. However, universities can have a somewhat different view. Faculty who develop these courses most often do so on "company time." The issue here is that once an Internet course is developed, then it can be given to other faculty or teaching assistants to run with no or slight revisions. If you seek ownership of the curriculum material that you develop, you may want to explore the possibility of obtaining legal assurances in writing before beginning the project.

Television-Based Instruction

Compressed video is a form of interactive television (ITV) that permits a teacher in one location to reach simultaneously students in special studios at distant locations. Fiber optic cable, video cameras, and microphones in these classrooms allow students to see and hear the presenter as well as to be seen and heard by the instructor. It's something like watching television, where the characters in the set are not only watching you but can converse with you, too. This technology can create some interesting combinations: The instructor can teach in front of an actual class at the same time as it is broadcasted to other classrooms (which can pose some minor problems if students from different sites want to ask questions simultaneously). Or the instructor can present in an empty studio to students in a remote site. Some instructors prefer having the live students in front of them because the audience helps the instructor gauge the pacing of his or her material. However, the instructor has to be careful not to be more attentive to those students than to others at some distance. When students from several sites are participating and a question is raised, it is not always easy for the instructor to identify the speaker. In fact, students must be instructed to say something like, "This is Sue Bonner, in Seattle, and I have a question." Some instructors find it easier to attend to the distant students if there are no local students in the television classroom. When multiple sites receive the same instruction, often a facilitator or assistant is assigned to each location to lead discussion after the lecture, to monitor tests, and to take charge of the class when the technology breaks down.

Having multiple sites often creates many more problems than in a single classroom. For instance, because of differences in their composition, or preparation, students in one site (e.g., Cincinnati) may become bored with a student's questions in Columbus and begin talking amongst themselves. If their microphones are open, then the distraction is picked up and broadcast everywhere. Similarly, if a presenter in another location turns his or her back to the camera in order to respond to questions in that audience, there may be little the instructor can do about it from the "home" campus other than to remind the presenter to face the camera. There is a certain loss of control as the instruction goes out to multiple classrooms. And the most serious disaster is when the technology fails altogether such that a remote site loses its visual or auditory signal. Although such problems shouldn't happen all that often, instructors still need to anticipate such emergencies and to have back-up plans and phone numbers (and telephones!) in each of the off-campus classrooms.

Like teaching by Internet, teaching by television, whether by satellite or interactive (ITV), requires a great deal of planning and preparation. The most common mistake with this medium is what is known as a "talking head"—that is, to stand before the class and lecture with a minimum of movement or visual effects. Although it is possible to get away with lecturing behind a podium before a live audience when you are in the same room with them, it is altogether a different matter when students are watching a television monitor. Even though an instructor might be in a studio only 100 feet away from the classroom, television reduces the immediacy and dynamism of a speaker, creating a distancing effect. Attention will lag within a few minutes if the lecturer speaks in a monotone.

Television is a visual medium. Part of the reason why people watch so much of it is because of its ability to dazzle and becharm them with new and novel images. Certainly, instruction by television doesn't have to entertain, but it must provide visual interest. The audience needs to see some kind of a demonstration or illustration of the major points that you are making. It is *not* enough for them merely to hear your words—they must also *see what you say*. Thomas Cyrs has recommended using pictures, key words, animation, graphics, and even audio- and videoclips to reinforce the ideas being presented. He estimates that it takes three to five times longer to prepare for and produce a quality course for television than a regular lecture course. Further, he has suggested that the instructor should have 100 percent release time for a summer or semester to prepare fully for a distance learning course (Cyrs, 1998).

Teacher immediacy behaviors are those that invite students' participation in the course. Sanders and Wiseman (1994) have suggested smiling, using students' names, varying vocal expressiveness, and establishing eye contact. It is also a good idea for faculty to visit the distant locations in person at least once, to incorporate question and answer periods as a part of each televised session, and to provide for telephone access both during the week and during the televised session (when one-way television technology is being employed). It is easy for telecourses to deteriorate into the "talking head" format, where information is relayed in a lecture-type format. Instructors need to use active learning techniques to engage students.

Another mistake would be attempting to develop a new course to teach over the Internet or via television without the necessary resources. What do you need? Laurillard (1993) has identified these:

1. Academic support
2. Administrative support
3. Technical support
4. Equipment provision
5. Facilities provision
6. Materials publishing
7. Materials duplication
8. Materials delivery
9. Maintenance of materials
10. Security of equipment and materials

The necessary support will enable you to plan, to develop resources such as student study guides, and to receive sufficient training in the use of the equipment. Teaching on television does require different skills and you can't go into the studio and teach in the same way as you always have (Cyrs, 1997). Must you learn, for instance, to operate the cameras yourself? Do you know how to zoom in for a close-up or will you have a technician with you? Having the time to practice on videotape and to have a more experienced instructor critique your presentation is strongly encouraged.

On television, it is critical that the presenter keeps eye contact with the camera and that he or she smiles, articulates well, and uses voice modulation. The presentation can't ramble; it must be tightly organized. Transmitting your enthusiasm for the material is crucial. If you need a lot of feedback cues from your pupils, you may not be able to read these as easily over a television monitor (ITV). You will not have them at all if you are teaching by satellite.

ITV can take a little getting used to—there can be a jerkiness at times; words being heard may not always be in sync with those lip movements of the person on the screen. And if you pause for questions and then a student speaks at the same time as you, you'll cancel each other out. One or the other of you will have to pause and wait for the other to repeat the comment.

Pacing of the instruction and parceling it out in just the right amount to fit a given scheduled slot is even more critical, because the instructor usually can't hold the class a few minutes longer in order to squeeze in material before the end of the class.

Because of the electronic distancing effect created by television, students are often reluctant to ask questions. Ostendorf (1997) has recommended that instructors use directed questions—to call on individuals to assure that they are paying attention and understanding the lesson. Do not wait for students to ask you questions. Do not say, "Are there any questions?" but ask a particular person a question that you have prepared ahead of time.

If you are very creative and unflustered by cameras or technological equipment, you may find teaching by television is just your thing. It will require you to go slower probably than you would in person, and it will force tighter organization of content. Some of your favorite stories, examples, or self-disclosures may not seem quite so appropriate when you are no longer in a small classroom with only 15 students. Teaching by television does not require that you are the best lecturer in the state so much as it demands logical organization and visual presentation.

Don't let anyone talk you into doing more than 75 to 90 minutes of television instruction at one time. Two hours would really be pushing it. Freddolino (1996), a distance learning coordinator at Michigan State University, has noted:

> *It has been our experience that for most courses, 3 hours of connected interactive video does not provide the best stimulus for learning. Rather, each session typically incorporates some segment of interactive time—perhaps 90 minutes— together with a segment of "local" time that students spend with their adjunct faculty members, who play an essential role in the delivery of the course content. (p. 207)*

Tips for Teaching on Television

Like a lot of things, *thinking about* being on television and teaching in front of others is a lot scarier than the actual practice. After three or four sessions, you'll be an experienced veteran, ready to give advice to the next group of newcomers. Until then, you can reduce your anxiety and smooth the way for a more successful experience if you take note of the following recommendations:

1. Be well prepared. Because of time limitations, many instructors find it necessary to prepare everything ahead of time. For example, instead of taking class time to write key points on a flipchart, these can be prepared in advance of the class. It is also useful to practice in front of the camera. Stage a timed "dress rehearsal." You might even want to prepare a "script" of your lecture. This script can include instructions to the technical coordinator who may need to activate a VCR, or music, or move the camera in response to certain cues from you. Organize your materials so that they can be easily found. Disorganization on television is amplified and exaggerated, making even a few moments of the instructor seeking the right transparency seem like an eternity.

2. Be familiar with the operation of the equipment you'll be using. Learn how to direct the camera to the audience, to zoom in on an individual and then how to bring it back to focus on you, the speaker. Learn how to turn students' microphones on and off. (Someone who is coughing or loudly rustling paper can be most distracting to the rest of the students.) Learn how far you can move from your podium and still be seen and heard well.

3. Anticipate technology problems. Prepare for the occasion when the system "crashes." Have phone numbers and phones of the coordinators in the distance learning classrooms. Have an assignment ready that students can be given if a class has to be canceled because of mechanical problems. Ideally, have a coordinator or facilitator in the distant location who can lead a discussion, break the class up into small "buzz" groups, or distribute an assignment based on the day's topic.

4. Make ample use of visual graphics, displays, and illustrations. Television is a visual media. Visually interesting materials keeps students interested and focused. Break up and punctuate your lecture with slides and graphics.

5. Prepare detailed syllabi. Write your syllabi with a little more detail than you might ordinarily do. List, by date of the class meeting, the topic, the presenter, and key points to be discussed or questions that students should be able to answer afterwards. Make sure students know how to reach you (by mail, e-mail, and phone) and any other faculty or facilitators who are assisting with the class.

6. Direct questions to students. Because students will be in a passive "receptive" mode, you'll probably not experience as many questions as you might get in a "regular" classroom.

7. Get frequent feedback from students. Ask them what is working and what is not. Have them identify the most annoying problem as well as the things that they wish you would do more or less of.

8. Allow more time for class preparation. Televisions require more effort than traditional lecture classes. More organization and succinctness is required and more time is spent developing or locating visual resources.

References and Resources

Boschmann, E. (1995). *The electronic classroom: A handbook for education in the electronic environment*. Medford, NJ: Learned Information, Inc.

Carlson, S. (1999). U. of Phoenix reports 22% rise in enrollment. *The Chronicle of Higher Education,* October 14.

Connick, G. (1997). Issues and trends to take us into the 21st century. In Thomas Cyrs (Ed.), Teaching and learning at a distance: What it takes to effectively design, deliver, and evaluate programs. *New Directions for Teaching and Learning,* #71. San Francisco: Jossey-Bass.

Creed, T. (1996). Extending the classroom walls electronically. In W. Campbell & K. Smith (Eds.), *New paradigms for college teaching.* Edina, MN: Interaction Book Co.

Cyrs, T. (1997). Competence in teaching at a distance. In T. Cyrs (Ed.), Teaching and learning at a distance: What it takes to effectively design, deliver, and evaluate programs. *New Directions for Teaching and Learning,* #71. San Francisco: Jossey-Bass.

Cyrs, T. (1998). Teaching at a distance: A workshop with Tom Cyrs. PBS Adult Learning Satellite Service, October 29.

Ely, D. P., with Blair, P. E., Lichvar, P., Tyksinski, D., & Martinez, M. (1996). *Trends in educational technology 1995.* Syracuse, NY: ERIC Clearinghouse on Information and Technology.

Endicott, J. (1999). PowerPoint pitfalls. *Religious Conference Manager, 11* (1), pp. 19ff.

Freddolino, P. P. (1996). The importance of relationships for a quality learning environment in interactive TV classrooms. *Journal of Education for Business, 71* (4), 205–208.

Gubernick, L., & Ebeling, A. (1997). I got my degree through e-mail. *Forbes,* June 16.

Lacina-Gifford, L. J., & Kher-Durlabhji, N. (1996). Preparing to teach a class by Internet. *College Teaching, 44,* 94–95.

Laurillard, D. (1993). *Rethinking university teaching.* New York: Routledge.

Mood, T. A. (1995). *Distance education: An annotated bibliography.* Englewood, CO: Libraries Unlimited.

Moore, M. G., & Kearsley, G. (1996). *Distance education: A systems view.* Belmont, CA: Wadsworth.

Navarro, P. (1998). Notes from the electronic classroom. *Journal of Policy Analysis and Management, 17* (1), 106–115.

Ostendorf, V. (1997). Teaching by television. In T. Cyrs (Ed.), Teaching and learning at a distance: What it takes to effectively design, deliver, and evaluate programs. *New Directions for Teaching and Learning* #71. San Francisco: Jossey-Bass.

Parks, R. P. (1999). Macro principles, PowerPoint, and the Internet: Four years of the bad, and the ugly. *The Journal of Economic Education, 30* (3), 200–209.

Peterson's Guide to Distance Learning Programs. (1998). Princeton, NJ: Peterson's Guides.

Reinhardt, L. (1999). Confessions of a "techno-teacher." *College Teaching, 47* (2), 48–50.

Roberts, L. (1996). A transformation of learning: Use of the national information infrastructure for education and lifelong learning. In *Educational Media and Technology Yearbook 1995-96.* Englewood, CO: Libraries Unlimited.

Sanders, J. A., & Wiseman, R. L. (1994). "The effects of verbal and nonverbal teacher immediacy on perceived cognitive, affective, and behavioral learning in the multicultural classroom." In K. A. Feldman & M. B. Paulsen (Eds.), *Teaching and learning in the college classroom.* Boston: Ginn Press.

Schweizer, H. (1999). *Designing and teaching an on-line course: Spinning your web classroom.* Boston: Allyn and Bacon.

Stadtlander, L. M. (1998). Virtual instruction: Teaching an online graduate seminar. *Teaching of Psychology, 25,* 146–148.

White, K. W., & Weight, B. H. (2000). *The online teaching guide: A handbook of attitudes, strategies, and techniques for the virtual classroom.* Boston: Allyn and Bacon.

9

Examinations

Overview: Most college instructors use some form of an examination proce-
dure. Students may think of exams as the "instructor's revenge" but, in fact,
examinations may have many different purposes. Essay exams, for
instance, could enhance critical thinking skills. Other types of exams can
develop a student's ability to recall and recognize correct answers. This
chapter examines the pros and cons regarding the various types of exams
and offers practical advice for test construction and test administration.

What Do You Want Your Exams to Accomplish?

This sounds like a strange question, but really it's not. Some departments and programs seem to view the purpose of testing as separating the "deserving" students from the "undeserving." Particularly in
selective admission programs—such as electrical engineering, medical school, law, and clinical psychology—where there is great competition for a few slots, much emphasis is put on testing to identify
the "best" and to eliminate the poorer students. Those who don't test
well find that they are discouraged from pursuing careers, even
though they may have innate aptitudes or talents generally desired
of professionals in those fields.

It is also possible (and preferable) to view exams as a means of
assessing what students are learning. Exams provide feedback to
the instructor on what techniques and exercises "worked," how
much students are applying themselves, and what areas of defi-

ciency still need to be addressed. Because students are vitally concerned about their scores on your tests, exams also provide another opportunity for teaching to occur—another chance for students to learn what they didn't understand clearly enough.

Objective test items can be designed so that, through reiteration of important concepts, they reinforce knowledge by emphasizing once more what is important from readings and lectures. Tests can also be creative exercises where there are multiple avenues by which a student could demonstrate that he or she has learned critical material. When tests aren't viewed as filters to catch only the best students, then you as an educator have the ability to use them to identify gaps and deficits in individual students' learning. Thus, tests inform the instructor whether another lecture or another assignment might be needed to help students learn difficult material. When the emphasis is on learning and not on failing, faculty might even be of the mind to let students take exams on a second or third occasion—until the student has demonstrated mastery of the material. This is a much more efficient type of learning, since the student is required to focus only on his or her weak areas. Presumably, once those adjustments have been made, better, stronger students exit our classrooms.

Wiggins (1993) has said this about testing:

Tests should teach the student, not only about how school tests parallel the "tests" of professional knowledge and understanding, but about the questions and challenges that define a given field. (p. 42)

Besides their uses in selecting and assessing what students have learned, examinations can be used to provide valuable feedback on an educational program during a time when evaluative data (either formative or summative) is needed regarding the program's curricula.

Before starting to construct an assessment procedure, the instructor must consider the educational objectives previously developed for the course and then think about what dimensions should be assessed. For instance, *declarative learning* is concerned mostly with the facts and principles that have been learned; *procedural learning* involves the skills or learning how to do something; *conditional learning* is knowing when and where to apply the declarative knowledge and procedural skills; and *reflective learning* involves synthesis, analysis, or evaluation (Nilson, 1998). The instructor might also want to think about educational objectives in terms of Bloom's (1956) taxonomy of cognitive objectives or the scheme outlined by Miller, Williams, and Haladyna (1978), which classified objectives in terms of reiteration, summarization, illustration, prediction, evaluation, and application (Erwin, 1991).

Still another consideration draws from such principles for assessment in the liberal arts as identified by Wiggins (1990). His first principle stated, "The heart of the liberal enterprise is not a mastery of orthodoxy but learning to justify one's opinions" (p. 22). His fifth principle would have students become "intellectual performers" rather than "learned spectators" sitting metaphorically "in the bleachers while others, mostly professors and writers of textbooks, perform" (p. 25). The seventh principle would have the assessors of students' progress look at their ability to "criticize sanctioned ideas, not merely re-tell what was taught" (p. 26). It is closely related to the eighth principle: that the aim of the liberal arts is "to explore limits—the boundaries of ideas, theories, and systems" (p. 27).

The manner and choice of assessment, then, naturally follows from one's view of the educational process and philosophy of teaching, but also, realistically, it may be affected by the educational milieu and expectations within the academic unit.

There are numerous ways to go about assessing students' skills and knowledge with exams. This chapter will review the approaches commonly employed.

The "Pop" Quiz

Pop (unannounced) quizzes of 2 to 10 items are useful tools for the educator. They serve the important function of informing students that you take very seriously your task of teaching them, that they must come to class prepared, and that shirking and attempting to just slide by will not be tolerated. Especially in those classes where a lot of reading is expected, pop quizzes help the educator know who is keeping up and who is not. These brief exams motivate students to stay abreast with their assignments. When students know to expect pop quizzes, their greater level of preparedness has other positive repercussions in the classroom, such as richer discussions and more peer learning.

To minimize the chorus of groans and complaints whenever a pop quiz is announced, be sure to explain to the class during your first meeting with them that this is a teaching technique you will use to ensure that everyone is staying current. Explain that the 5- or 10-item quiz is simply a checkup, and that if they do the reading, then they should do well on the quizzes. You may then want to predict that there could be a quiz as early as next week. Keep your word and make the quiz easy enough that most students will do well *if* they have read the material or done their homework. There will be less resistance to these quizzes if students feel that the quizzes are fair and if they really do separate the prepared from the unprepared students.

As an instructor, you can plan pop quizzes every week or announce to the class how many times during the semester they might expect a quiz. If you decide on weekly or almost weekly quizzes, then you might "forgive" (throw out) the lowest one or two for each student. If you have large classes, you might employ a strategy of either having the students exchange papers with each other and grading them or simply not recording the result of every quiz. Thus, the instructor might administer quizzes on 10 occasions, but decide ahead of time to grade only half of those. You might collect only those quizzes that you plan to grade, allowing the students to keep and grade those that you do not intend to record. Even when the instructor does not record the results of their quizzes, students still benefit from getting feedback from fellow students or grading their own papers, and it is worth taking the extra 5 or 10 minutes of class time so that everyone has the correct answers and can compare those with their own.

The Essay Exam

Besides allowing the instructor the opportunity to see how well the student can write unassisted, essay exams also provide a perspective on students' ability to integrate, analyze, and evaluate. Essay exams let students show original thinking and creativity—or their absence. The essay exam provides an occasion to get to know students as individuals, to "see" into their thinking and reasoning processes. Students reveal more of themselves and what they value or have observed, which permits the instructor to personalize his or her remarks in a way that cannot be done with more objective forms of testing.

Essay exams are the quickest to construct, but the most labor intensive to grade. It's relatively easy to dash off an essay question or two in 10 minutes or less. By contrast, creating a 25-item multiple-choice exam can eat up a whole morning. However, you can grade a large number of objective tests in several hours, but it may take days to grade a similar number of essay exams.

Both essay and objective exams have their advocates. Those favoring objective exams generally make that decision either because (1) they have big classes or (2) the course covers a lot of factual content, and instructors feel they can get a better sampling of what students know by asking multiple questions. Instructors who utilize essay tests feel that these communicate the importance of written communication skills and ultimately help students learn to write better. A drawback is that students who already have good writing skills have a distinct advantage over students who may know the material but who have a difficult time communicating through their writing. Also, there's probably a tendency to give more points to students with legible handwriting than to those with terrible penmanship. If a student's essay *looks* sloppy, the instructor probably makes unfair inferences about the quality of the students' thoughts and associations—at least when compared to the nicely lettered and attractive essay that shows the writer took great pains with his or her handwriting.

Students are often equally divided over their preferences. Sometimes you'll hear them argue for essay exams, sometimes for the objective tests. Those who like essay exams feel that if they can write long enough (an essay as opposed to a short-answer or fill-in-the-blank item), they are bound to get at least partial credit. Sooner or later, they hope they will say something that the instructor was looking for all along. Students arguing for objective tests often feel that they can eliminate the obvious distractor items and improve their chances of getting a correct response from 1 in 4 to 1 in 3 or 1 in 2. Often, these are the students most self-conscious about their writing.

Although most educators agree that essay exams test higher-level cognitive skills, many feel that essay exams are vulnerable to test reliability problems. In other words, subjectivity may enter into the grading process. Every educator has had the experience of seeing a bright student's name on a paper and then reading it with the expectation that the student will do well and get a good grade. This expectation usually works to the student's advantage, even when his or her performance is less than exemplary. The tendency is to give the good students benefit of the doubt, even when it is not clear from their responses that they really know the material. And conversely, given the same situation, it is probably human nature to assume that a student who has done poorly on previous tests does not know the current material when his or her essay is ambiguous. To counter the problem of consistency expectations, attempt to read the essays "blind." Instruct students to use only their student IDs or social security numbers on their tests. Another idea is to grade a single question for the whole class before moving on to the next question—as opposed to grading all of one student's paper and then all of the next student's paper. Shuffle papers after you read them so that those at the top of the pile aren't always evaluated most harshly (while you're the freshest) and those at the bottom graded more leniently (when you are fatigued).

Steel (1997) has recommended that before beginning to grade the essays, the instructor should list or outline the major points expected for a "correct" essay response. If you have the time, another approach is to make several passes through the essays— grading them first for grammar or mechanics, then reading them again for content. Such a procedure allows for greater accuracy and less influence on the grade from extraneous factors.

Ory and Ryan (1993) have suggested that you design essay questions for which there is a particular correct response. In fact, you might want to write out the response you desire before you decide to include it as a test item. The exercise of writing out the answer will help you think about the various ways students might respond and what you would consider completely wrong and partially correct replies. What you want to do is to eliminate those essay questions where students can bluff their way through by answering some other question of their choosing. Writing out answers to the essay questions also helps the instructor estimate how long it will take students to respond.

According to Nilson (1998), do not start off the essay question with *why, how,* or *what;* rather, use a descriptive verb and specify how elaborate the response should be. She has provided this example:

> *Describe three ways that social integration could break down in the modern world, according to Durkheim. Then assess how closely each one applies to the United States in the 1990's. (p. 189)*

By all means, be unequivocal about how the essay is to be graded. Writing down your criteria is recommended, because students will ask and have a right to know how their responses were evaluated. Decide ahead of the test and then inform the class if they will be penalized for spelling errors and problems with syntax. Other questions to consider are: Can students bring their dictionaries? Will you grade for organization of ideas as well as content? Can students simply list their main points? Do they have to use complete sentences?

Ideally, the essay question will allow you to discriminate between those students who have a good understanding of the material, those who have a moderate understanding, and those with virtually no idea. If the question can't do this, throw the item out, for it will have no validity.

It is recommended that instructors not give students too many choices of essay questions. Each essay question should allow the instructor to assess the extent to which students achieved educational objectives and therefore reflect content mastered by the whole class. There a slight danger that optional questions (e.g., for extra credit) could be less difficult or could be graded with a different standard—particularly if only a few students choose to write on these.

Mini-essay questions are sometimes a good compromise, allowing the educator to examine the student's written communication skills yet not being enormously burdensome from a grading standpoint. Several shorter essay questions rather than one or two long ones allow the instructor to cover more of the course material while reducing the risk for students of completely "blowing" one question representing 50 percent or so of an exam. It is recommended that the point values for each question be listed (Nilson, 1998).

For those who love the idea of requiring essays but hate the thought of grading them, help is on the way. Computer software is being developed by the Educational Testing Service and others that can grade essays. One program, known as the Intelligent Essay Assessor, uses a "gold-standard" essay written by the professor or other student essays already graded for comparison. The software is reported to be reliable but works best when there are factual questions. Another program (the e-rater) looks for phrases such as *first, second, and third, by comparison,* and *for example.* The e-rater's agreement with human graders is said to be high, between 87 and 94 percent <www.apa.org/monitor/aug98/grade.html>. Despite such continuing and forthcoming advances, it will be difficult for software to evaluate creativity and reflective thought. Where it may be most useful is in grading essay questions of specific content in large lecture classes.

Writing Multiple-Choice Test Items

Multiple-choice questions reduce the need to agonize over essays that meander and ramble as the instructor tries to assess what the student really does know. Objective forms of testing also reduce the impact of the student's personality (and the instructor's feelings about that student) on the testing situation. If the correct answer to item 16 is (d), then that response is either circled/marked or it is not—there is no room for subjective impressions to color or affect grading based on prior assumptions or encounters with students.

The use of multiple-choice items allows the educator to evaluate the course of instruction as well as the test itself, to see which items the whole class missed, and to look for consistencies and possible flaws in construction. For instance, if students got items 4, 8, and 12 correct, did they also get item 16, which used the same concept or formula? Multiple-choice questions truly are more objective, but they have some problems of their own. For one thing, it is easy for test creators to seize on some small statement with the book open before them, and to then rationalize that a particular fact should be known by students now and forever more. The challenge is not to play "stump as many students as possible" with trivial facts, but to evaluate what students can carry from your class and apply to life outside the classroom.

Wiggins (1993), who, as discussed earlier, sees the value of tests in teaching, cautions us about multiple-choice tests: "Testing that operationally defines mastery in terms of the student's ability to recognize sanctioned answers make clear that the student's contributions as a thinker are unimportant" (p. 115).

The statement or question upon which the multiple-choice test item is based is called the *stem* and the choices are known as the *response set* or *response alternatives*. *Distractors* are incorrect response alternatives. Typically, multiple-choice responses contain three or four distractors in addition to the correct answer. However, there is no valid reason why all the items in a test should have the same number of distractors (Osterlind, 1989). Distractors that are absurd and that do not have a "ring of truth" may serve only to make the test longer to administer. Humorous distractors do not serve the purpose of sound measurement and should be avoided (Osterlind, 1989). Fewer distractors make for more efficient tests and the ability to administer more test items in the same amount of time.

There is much to commend the objective form of testing. If this is the approach that you favor, you might want to follow these helpful guidelines (Ory & Ryan, 1993; Nilson, 1998):

- Avoid excess verbiage.
- Avoid negatively stated items if possible. (If you need to negate something, give it emphasis as in: Which is **NOT** a factor in the ...?)
- Address one problem or concept per question.
- Be sure there is only one correct or best response.
- Avoid questions with multiple correct answers.
- Make all of the alternatives equally attractive and of the same length.
- Present alternatives in a logical order (e.g., chronological).
- Be sure alternatives are mutually exclusive.
- Eliminate alternatives that are ridiculous.
- Avoid sexist or other language that is not inclusive.
- Randomly distribute the correct response positions in order to avoid having a "favorite" position (e.g., making most correct answers "e").
- Minimize the use of *all of the above* or *none of the above*.

Writing True-False Items

From the educator's perspective, one of the advantages of true-false items is that they can be developed relatively easily and quickly and thus are often used for brief exams or "pop" quizzes. Also, students can read and respond to true-false items faster than multiple-choice items, which means that more true-false items can be packed into a test designed for a short (e.g., 50-minute) examination period. Obviously, the more test items that are employed, the greater the sampling of the course content. True-false tests have often been maligned by those who assume that students with no knowledge of the material can, by guessing, still obtain high test scores. However, this is not true. On a 100-item true-false exam, the odds of getting a passing score of 70 by blind guessing alone is less than 1 in 1,000. The chance of getting a perfect score on the same 100-item exam by guessing alone is less than one chance in a million trillion trillion (Ebel & Frisbie, 1991, p. 138).

True-false items need not be limited to just factual recall regarding dates, places, persons, processes, symbols, steps, or stages. Ebel (1972) differentiated a number of ways in which true-false items can be utilized:

1. Evaluative statements about events or phenomena
2. Applications of numerical or other computations
3. Steps in processes and procedures
4. Predictions about chemical reactions and other phenomena
5. Evidential statements
6. Examples of concepts or principles
7. Explanations of why events or phenomena occurred
8. Statements about relationships between two forces, factors, principles, and so on
9. Comparisons among concepts (e.g., size, chronology, etc.)
10. Generalizations about a particular topic or phenomenon

The following guidelines may be helpful in writing true-false items (Ebel & Frisbie, 1991; Miller & Erickson, 1990):

- Items should require understanding of concepts as well as memory. Avoid constructing items that test for specific, but trivial, details.

- Test for knowledge of important propositions and ideas—the tools that can be used in other situations and problems.
- Construct the true items to be completely true and the false items to be completely false so that each correct response can be easily defended.
- Construct the items so that the correct answer is obvious only to those who have a good command of material being tested. To those without the specialized knowledge, the wrong answer should appear more plausible than the correct one. Make wrong answers consistent with popular misconceptions.
- Each item should hinge on a single important idea.
- Each item should be worded concisely. Statements longer than 20 words are too lengthy. Statements with dependent clauses and phrases are more likely to be true.
- Do not turn true propositions into false statements by inserting the word *not* into the original proposition. (Negatively worded statements are more difficult and often perceived as "tricky" by students.) Especially avoid double negatives.
- *Always* and *never* tend to be used mostly in connection with false statements, whereas the qualifiers *some, sometimes, several, as a rule, should, most, may, often*, and *generally* tend to be most often associated with true statements. Review your draft test to see if your items fit this pattern. If they do, try rewording your statements so that *always* and *never* are the correct responses for the true statements.
- If the term *not* must be used, place it in bold or italics to make it easier to see.
- When finished writing your draft, check to make sure you have approximately the same number of true and false items.

Writing Short-Answer Items

Short-answer items are used to test mostly for factual content. Because these items depend on recall and not recognition, it is more difficult for students to guess the correct response than when they can see the response categories arrayed before them. Short-answer items or fill-in the blank items are of this form:

1. What president is credited with coining the phrase and concept of a Military-Industrial Complex?   *(President Eisenhower)*
2. Who founded an organization called the Moral Majority in 1979?   *(Reverend Jerry Falwell)*

Guidelines to improve your writing of short-answer items include:

- Make the stem so specific that there is only one best response. (For example, avoid items such as, "Sacajawea was a(n) _____?" where the range of possible correct answers could include: *a woman, a Native American, a mother, a member of the Shoshone tribe, a guide for Lewis and Clark, an interpreter for explorers, a lake, a river,* and so on).
- Avoid using the exact language or phrasing as in the students' reading, as that wording will aid their recall.
- To facilitate grading, design the test so that the students' answers can be written in a column to the right or left of the text.
- Be careful to omit only significant words
- Avoid supplying clues in the stem. Instead of asking "H_2O is composed of what two gases?" ask, instead, "Water is composed of what two gases?"

Improving Your Tests with Item Analysis

As a conscientious educator, you will want to know how well your tests fare in terms that can be documented and quantified—what might be referred to as their *psychometric qualities*. This issue may be of concern to you because of one or more troublesome questions that you thought were absolutely brilliant but that the students complained about.

The first step in assessing test items is to look item by item at how many of the response alternatives students chose or avoided. If, for item 23, for instance, 12 students chose response (A), 11 chose response (B), 0 students chose response (C), and 2 chose (D), then the distractor of item C really didn't work as intended and should be revised or a new one inserted if that test item is to be retained. If, on this same item, the correct answer was (D), then this item and its distractors need to be reviewed, since too few of the students (8 percent) got the correct answer. A possible explanation might be that both distractors (A) and (B) both were partially correct.

In the following example, the examinees spread their responses more or less evenly among the possible alternatives. In this case, the three distractors appear to have done their job well.

Test Item 14

Response	A*	B	C	D	Total
Number	12	6	6	6	30
Percent	40%	20%	20%	20%	100%

*correct answer

Item difficulty is computed by dividing the number of students who responded correctly to that test item by the total number of students taking the test. Thus, for item 14, 12 divided by 30 is .40, or 40 percent; if 20 of 30 students answered question 1 right, then the item difficulty is .67. If 18 students responded correctly out of a class of 24, the item difficulty would be .75—meaning that 75 percent of the students answered correctly. If item difficulty is above .70 or below .30, then the item is, respectfully, too easy or too difficult.

Item discrimination allows instructors to examine test results in terms of how the best and poorest students fared. One starts this process by arranging the test scores in order from highest to lowest. Then, the best test scores (highest 27 percent) are placed in one group and the lowest test scores (the lowest 27 percent) placed in another group. For each item, the number of those in the lowest scoring group who got the item correct is subtracted from those in the highest scoring group who got the number correct. That resulting number is divided by K (the number of students equal to 27 percent of those taking the test). The value that is produced is the discrimination index. For example:

With item 17, the discrimination index is .545 (10 – 4 divided by 11), indicating that more of the best students got the item correct than the poorest students. In other words, that item has a good abil-

Test Item	# Correct High-Scoring Group	# Correct Low-Scoring Group	K (27% of Class)
17	10	4	11 students
21	2	5	11 students
25	7	7	11 students

ity (power) to discriminate between the highest- and lowest-scoring groups. Item 21, on the other hand has a negative discrimination index of −.27 (2 − 5 divided by 11), which indicates (as the example shows) that proportionately more of the poor students than the good students got this item correct. Item 17 could be retained for use in future tests, but item 21 should be scrapped. Similarly, item 25 does not have the ability to discriminate between the groups of high-scoring and low-scoring students and should be rejected or reworked if the instructor wants to continue to use this item.

As a rule of thumb, items with an index of .40 or higher are considered good; those between .30 and .39 are reasonably good; those between .20 and .29 are marginal and usually need improvement; and those with an index of discrimination below .19 need to be revised (Ebel & Frisbie, 1991).

This information obviously has to do with test construction, particularly with those major exams (e.g., end-of-the-semester, comprehensive exams) that the instructor can revise and improve over repeated administrations. Do students have the right to know what you know about the performance of various items making up their exams? Years of experience in the classroom advises against giving this information to students. Once you do, if only to settle a disagreement about a particular item, students being naturally resourceful and clever will ask for item discrimination data on each of the items they missed on their tests. It doesn't take much imagination to see what could happen in a classroom as every item that any student missed is questioned as students seize upon any information about psychometrically weak items to try and improve their test scores.

The Test Taker's Bill of Rights

Several authors (Rogers, 1995, 1997; Wiggins, 1993) have proposed a test taker's Bill of Rights to ensure that students are treated fair and equitably. Students should be entitled to the following basic rights:

- Worthwhile, authentic intellectual problems that are validated against real-world problems, roles, and situations
- Clearly written and consistently applied criteria for grading
- Minimal secrecy in testing and grading (students deserve to know what will be covered and what constitutes a correct answer)
- Multiple and varied opportunities to display achievement
- The freedom to question grades and test practices without fear of retribution
- Opportunities for students to justify or ask about answers marked wrong but they believe to be correct
- Genuine feedback providing usable information about strengths and weaknesses (Wiggins, 1993, p. 28)

Handling Student Complaints about "Unfair" Tests and Test Questions

It is a given that no matter how many hours you labor over fine-tuning a test, checking to make sure it is fair and adequately represents the material your class has heard in lecture or read, someone (or multiple students) will raise challenges after they've received their graded exams. There's several points to remember here.

First of all, you are in charge. This means that if the question seems too hostile, if the student is too argumentative and the rest of the class is ready to move on, simply announce that the two of you can discuss the matter after class. You don't need to explain why or become defensive. If you find yourself angry or need more time to think about the student's position, set an appointment for the next day.

Second, although it is a good idea to give back tests and go over the correct answers during the very next class, decide beforehand how much time you'll spend, so that going over the test won't consume the whole class period.

Next, be prepared. If you have drawn test items from the reading assignments, write the page numbers on your scoring key. When students say, "That question isn't fair; we didn't discuss that," then you can say calmly, "Please refer to Chapter 12, p. 295. I think you'll find the answer there in bold typeface, middle of the page." Similarly, with essay questions, be prepared to list for the students the points they should have made for full credit.

Fourth, don't argue. Sometimes we make mistakes in scoring or counting missed items. Once in a while, a key word might get dropped when typing the test that changes the whole item so that it is different from what you intended or thought was there. Contentious students are best handled by saying, "Circle that item on your paper and write me a note on the top of the page. I'll consider your answer when I've got more time."

When a good portion of the students have the same complaint (e.g., many misinterpreted the question or read it in a different way than you had intended it), you can be magnanimous and throw out the question so that it doesn't count against anyone.

Last, I collect the exams after I let students see what they've missed. This action is a good way to signal the "end of discussion" on matters of debate about whether a response should be counted right or wrong. It's also a good idea to keep these tests for a while (in my university, it is one year) so that if a student does challenge a grade, you will have the necessary documentation.

Letting Students Keep Their Tests: Pros and Cons

The argument for letting students keep their tests is that they can use these to review for any comprehensive exams at the end of the semester. On the other hand, you can also bring their old tests to any review sessions (e.g., the last class) and let them make notes and look over what they missed earlier in the semester.

If you allow your pupils to keep their tests, you will be spending a lot more time writing new tests. If you pick up the tests and keep them, then you might be able to reuse the same tests the next semester or even several times before having to construct new ones. Early in my career, I always let students keep their tests—perhaps because I thought it was a very empowering, democratic thing to do. As I've matured, I value my time more, and even though I have a large test bank of questions, I like to administer the same items that have good discriminatory ability to sort out those who understand and those who don't comprehend the material. These items/tests have good reliability and I can often predict with a fair amount of confidence the student's final grade from his or her first test score. Because I don't want to surrender these items to the fraternity/sorority/commercial sector test pool, my decision in recent years has been to not allow students to keep their tests.

Missed Tests

When you are preparing the syllabus at the beginning of an academic term, it is a good idea to consider how you want to handle students who miss a key exam. Particularly if you have a large class, you can count on one or more students asking for a make-up exam at sometime during the semester.

There are two issues here. One is the additional work required on your part to construct a new and different test for one or two students (to say nothing of the time necessary to administer or supervise it). A second issue is one of fairness. On one hand, if you get a reputation for being "easy" and have a permissive policy regarding make-up exams, then students who are at risk academically may see an advantage in taking the test after their buddies have passed on such information as they can recall. On the other hand, it is unfair to give a zero to the student who misses the test because of a legitimate excuse. Here are some alternatives available to you:

- If you have taught the class on several occasions and have alternate versions of the test already prepared from prior semesters, then allowing a make-up exam is not problematic. If possible, however, you might want to administer make-ups prior to giving back the exams to the rest of the class. If that isn't practical, you might want to excuse the individual needing the make-up during that part of the class period when you return and discuss the regularly scheduled exam.
- If the missed exam was of the multiple-choice variety, then give an essay-type exam to the students who were absent on the date of the test. Most of these students, even if they learn what was

on the initial test, won't feel that they gained an advantage by their absence—other than they possibly gained an additional day or two to study.

- Instead of an exam, require a project of such proportions that only those students with legitimate excuses would seriously consider a make-up. (This has to be announced or stated well before the actual test in order to act as a deterrence. Later, you can scale back the project to a reasonable level if the students who missed really seemed to have honest excuses.)
- When multiple exams are planned for a course, another option is to hold neutral the effect of missing an exam. Thus, if four exams were planned (say, 400 points possible all total from the tests) and a student missed one exam, then compute that student's final grade based on the number of tests actually taken (e.g., 300 possible points from testing).
- Adopt a policy (be sure to put it in your syllabus) that all make-up exams will carry an automatic 10 percent penalty unless the student can bring a doctor's excuse or other suitable evidence *and* the instructor is called within 24 hours of the test.
- When multiple exams are planned for a course, require that a student has to take any three of four tests. (If you do this, however, students will want to know if they can take all four tests and drop the lowest grade.)

Examination Smorgasbord

Insofar as it is possible, try to vary the types of exams you use. Depending on one type of exam consistently (e.g., the multiple-choice variety) will give something of an advantage to those students who do well with this type of assessment procedure. The steady use of essay-type exams plays to the advantage of students who write well and who are creative thinkers. Students do use different strategies in studying, depending on the format of the exam they are expecting.

As an instructor, you will find students more engaged with the material to the extent that you implement more than just midterms and final examinations. Short weekly quizzes can be very effective in encouraging students to read. While from an instructor's standpoint it might be possible to justify giving only one or two "major" exams, students with test anxiety and those who do not do well on standardized tests sometimes argue against course grades based solely on one or two tests. Even though most students don't like to take tests (who does?), they very likely would rather have three or four minor tests rather than a single one that constitutes 85 percent of their grade.

No matter how many exams you ultimately decide to administer, try to give one early in the academic term so that students have some idea of the way you test. Those who don't do well can decide to redouble their efforts or possibly to drop the course. This early test doesn't have to count a great deal, but whether they say so or not, students will prize this insight into the way you construct tests.

Give exams back promptly. Don't return essay exams with only letter grades, but provide students with comments about what they did well and where they went astray. Be fair, encouraging where possible; never be demeaning in your remarks. They may not love you or the course you teach, but following just these simple guidelines will result in students being much less critical in their evaluations.

Carefully proofread your tests before making multiple copies of them. Check your spelling, and make sure all the necessary instructions are included. If there is time, put it aside for a day or two and read it "cold," as a student might. You want to catch any problems before examination day to minimize student questions and/or complaints (e.g., a misnumbered item that shortens the test from 50 to 49 questions).

Last, anticipate that the copy machine might make mistakes and, when there are multiple-page tests, that some might be short a page or two. Have extra copies on hand for such emergencies. Also, instruct students to count the number of pages they have. For instance, say to them: "There are 50 questions contained on five pages. If you have fewer than five pages or duplicates of the same page, please raise your hand." Such steps should result in a smoother examination process.

References and Resources

Bloom, B. (1956). *Taxonomy of educational objectives. Vol. 1: Cognitive domain.* New York: McKay.

Ebel, R. L. (1972). *Essentials of educational measurement* (2nd ed.). Englewood Cliffs, NJ: Prentice-Hall.

Ebel, R. L., & Frisbie, D. A. (1991). *Essentials of educational measurement.* Englewood Cliffs, NJ: Prentice-Hall.

Erwin, T. D. (1991). *Assessing student learning and development: A guide to the principles, goals, and methods of determining college outcomes.* San Francisco: Jossey-Bass.

Miller, H. G., Williams, R. G., & Haladyna, T. M. (1978). *Beyond facts: Objective ways to measure thinking.* Englewood Cliffs, NJ: Educational Technology Publications.

Miller, P. W., & Erickson, H. E. (1990). *How to write tests for students.* Washington, DC: National Education Association.

Nilson, L. B. (1998). *Teaching at its best: A research-based resource for college instructors.* Bolton, MA: Anker Publishing.

Ory, J. C., & Ryan, K. E. (1993). *Tips for improving testing and grading.* Newbury Park, CA: Sage.

Osterlind, S. J. (1989). *Constructing test items.* Boston: Kluwer.

Rogers, T. B. (1995). *The psychological testing enterprise: An introduction.* Pacific Grove, CA: Brooks/Cole.

Rogers, T. B. (1997). Teaching ethics and test standards in a psychological testing course: A test taker's Bill of Rights. *Teaching of Psychology, 24,* 41–46.

Steel, C. W. (1997). Essays—Well worth the effort. *College Teaching, 45* (4), 150–152.

Wiggins, G. P. (1990). The truth may make you free, but the test may keep you imprisoned: Toward assessment worthy of the liberal arts. *Assessment 1990: Understanding the implications.* Washington, DC: The American Association for Higher Education.

Wiggins, G. P. (1993). *Assessing student performance: Exploring the purpose and limits of testing.* San Francisco: Jossey-Bass.

10

Grading

BRADFORD W. SHEAFOR
BRANDON A. SHEAFOR

The student in front of me was complaining about his grade. He'd gotten a B! When my turn came I fell to my knees in front of the harried graduate student.... The people in line behind me looked away in disgust.

"You got a fifty-eight."

"Yes, ma'am, I know."

"You also flunked the final."

"Yes, ma'am, I know," I pleaded, "but I did the best I could. I was here every Saturday, as regular as an insulin shot." She paused. I held my breath.

"I'll pass you on one condition."

I looked her in the eye and said, "Anything!" I could picture myself doing her laundry all summer or chewing buffalo hides to make her new sandals....

"If you promise never to take calculus or trigonometry again." (Black, 1997, p. 58)

Overview: Probably no part of the teaching experience is enjoyed less and is more problematic to new faculty than deciding grades. Sometimes we want to recognize a student's tremendous effort or persevering attitude; at times we may choose not to give a student a break because of his or her attitude. Despite often elaborate efforts to minimize subjectivity, the grades we award are often affected by some inner set of experiences or beliefs and not based entirely on empirical data.

Many factors impinge on the grading decision. We recognize that our assessment instruments are not as accurate as we would like, that the directions for assignments weren't as clear as they could have been, that it is possible for students to misunderstand what we wanted. We want to be liked, to encourage students—not bludgeon them with grades. We also don't want too many to fail or do poorly. At the same time we must have academic integrity and the backbone to do the right thing, to be fair to all students. But how do we decide what is fair in grading? This chapter presents several perspectives on grading along with some suggestions for grading specific kinds of activities.

Physicians give shots, the clergy deliver sermons, and lawyers offer advice. In every profession, certain actions are the centerpiece of the professional/consumer interaction. For the teacher, this action is to assign a grade. The final grade recorded by an instructor, however, is somewhat unique from the actions of other professionals, because it remains a permanent part of the student's record and is interpreted as a meaningful indicator for many unintended purposes.

An instructor must address grading at two levels. First, the manner in which each assignment will be assessed must be established and the student should receive feedback from the instructor on his or her performance. That feedback is an important part of the teaching/learning endeavor. What was correct or incorrect? Did the student accurately apply the subject matter, procedures, or skills that the assignment was intended to assess? Did the student reflect an innovative idea that should be pursued? What might the student do to improve performance if there was a deficiency in the response? The expectation in American higher education is that this feedback will also include a summary statement that reflects the student's level of performance; that is, a grade must be given for each assignment.

Second, in addition to deciding how to grade individual assignments, the instructor must assign a final grade for the course that summarizes the student's performance on all assignments and reflects the student's relative mastery of the course content. The instructor must address such questions as: How should each assessment be weighted? How will grades on team or group activities be translated to individual grades? Should students be compared to a standard of performance the instructor determines or should they be compared to the performance of other students in the class? Addressing these matters is particularly important because it is the final grade that becomes a part of the student's permanent record. A single letter or numerical score is the most typical form of the summary communication about a student's performance in a course, although a few academic settings utilize narrative descriptions for this purpose.

A grade typically takes the form of a one- or two-digit symbol (e.g., B+, 87, 2.8). This symbol is all that represents the outcome of the considerable expenditure of time, energy, and intellectual effort the student devoted to the various assignments and other activities related to the course. When an instructor is fair and uses a well-defined and appropriate methodology for assigning a grade, the process should be relatively straightforward. Why, then, is grading so controversial?

If grades were only interpreted as an indication of a student's level of learning on an assignment or in a single course, they would probably not be particularly controversial. However, grades are also considered significant symbols of the student's intellectual capacity, level of effort, and commitment to learning. Students and instructors alike recognize that grades often are inadequate indicators of the student's effort, ability, and accomplishment because they fail to account for the many factors that might affect a student's performance. For example, the grade on a test or in a course would unlikely be sensitive to such extenuating circumstances as the student experiencing the death of a loved one, an episode of physical or mental illness, stress resulting from difficulties in personal relationships, roommates who are disruptive, or even time conflicts with employment schedules that divert time and attention from meeting course expectations. Yet, this number or letter is all that represents the student's accomplishment and, when combined with grades from other courses (i.e., one's grade-point average), it becomes a significant factor in decisions that can affect the remainder of that person's life. It is the significance attached to grades beyond their initial purpose as an indicator of learning that makes assigning grades one of the most important and, often most frustrating, parts of teaching.

Who Is Concerned about Grades?

The parties concerned with grades include, but extend well beyond, the teacher and student. It is primarily due to the multiple interpretations of the meaning of grades that they can become a point of contention between teachers and students. Following are some of the ways that various audiences attribute meaning to grades.

Students

Among those concerned about grades, students have the most at stake. They typically interpret grades as important signals about the amount of effort they need to devote to completing course assignments, their success in mastering the course content, and even their potential to succeed in college and eventually earn a degree. More importantly, grades become central to a student's self-image. The hopes and dreams of the student and others may be pinned on succeeding in a college or university. This is particularly true for many first-generation students and members of minority ethnic and cultural groups who feel a special pressure to "prove themselves" to the dominant culture. Campus counseling centers are filled with students who have difficulty living up to the pressures to succeed—often as measured solely by their grades. One apprehensive undergraduate summed up her situation by indicating that this phase of her life was devoted to attending college and if she failed college, she was failing life. Indeed, grades are not taken lightly by students.

Perceptive students, perhaps correctly, recognize that one's grades can affect many of their life goals. For example, securing desired employment upon graduation, a primary reason students attend colleges and universities, is often affected by one's academic record. Another reason students typically seek a college education is to obtain a sufficient knowledge base in various subjects to become well-informed citizens who can contribute to society. If one does not maintain sufficient grades to remain in college, it is more difficult to acquire the background necessary to make such contributions.

Instructors quickly learn that for many students, the grade assigned for a course is the most important outcome of the teaching/

learning endeavor. For some students, unfortunately, it would appear to be the only outcome that is important.

Instructors

For many instructors, the emphasis on grades is viewed as a distraction from the important emphasis on student learning and the related concern for providing accurate feedback regarding the quality of the work produced by the student. Nevertheless, grades carry significant meaning and must be assigned responsibly and accurately. It takes considerable time and effort to construct and apply criteria that will serve as a valid symbol of the student's performance—time that in the minds of many instructors may more productively be devoted to class preparation, research, or service activities.

Instructors must be wary of the ethical, legal, and safety issues related to holding the power associated with grading because it is a commodity that is so highly valued by students. Stories abound on university campuses of students offering favors in exchange for grades or, even more aggressively, threatening professors who fail to give them the grades they desire.

Often, instructors are frustrated about what appears to be wasted time spent with students complaining about their grades. That the instructor recognizes the limits of a grade in reflecting the full story of the student's learning experience is of little solace to the disappointed student. It takes considerable effort for an instructor to clearly explain his or her rationale for the method of grading he or she has adopted and to show how the student's performances in the course were translated into that single symbol reflecting the level of accomplishment—especially when the student does not want to accept the outcome. As a result, the pressure for the instructor to be prepared to defend a grade often forces artificial and inflexible grading criteria.

Finally, grades are sometimes interpreted as a commentary on the instructor by his or her colleagues. Too many high grades can create a reputation that the instructor is not rigorous, playing to students to obtain favorable student evaluations, or perhaps on an ego trip wanting to achieve high student popularity. If an instructor's grades are consistently low, however, that might be interpreted as an indication that he or she is not able to teach the material well. Promotion and tenure decisions are not immune to influence from a faculty member's grading practices. Clearly, the instructor's grading practices are an important aspect of his or her responsibilities.

Parents

Sending a child to college is a major investment for most families. Usually without regard for the student's maturity or readiness for higher education, parents expect their child to make the difficult life transition from home and family to college life as soon as he or she has completed high school. Sacrifices are made for years in order to save enough money to pay tuition and support at least part of a child's living expenses while in college. Will the child make a similar commitment of energy and effort to succeeding in the classroom? Is the child capable of mastering the requirements at this educational level? Is the hoped for career and associated quality of life attainable? Will the family's social status be increased or maintained by this child's performance in college? Clearly, parents have a major stake in the student's success, and their primary indicator of this achievement is a grade report. The angry telephone calls instructors sometimes receive from disappointed parents regarding a grade, therefore, are concerned with much more than what the student did or did not learn in the course.

Colleges and Universities

In many ways, grades have become the "coin of the realm" in higher education. They are the currency through which colleges and universities sort students (Kohn, 1994) in order to label their performance and justify various rewards. Usually, students must achieve prescribed grade levels for receiving or maintaining scholarships or fellowships, entering honors programs, receiving financial aid, or even entering some baccalaureate majors. Further, few students are admitted to graduate-level education with less than a 3.0 GPA (B average) on their undergraduate record and, at many universities, if exceptions to that minimum are made, the student enters the graduate program with a probationary status and is vulnerable to dismissal if he or she does not perform well in the first term.

Grades also serve as indicators of the relative status of academic programs on a campus. In coffee-room conversation at colleges or universities, one can hear both students and faculty discussing which majors require "strong" students (i.e., high GPA students) and which majors are appropriate for "weaker," less academically oriented individuals. Serving a few select students with high GPAs often generates far more political capital in higher education than meeting the learning needs of larger numbers of less successful students. Despite knowing the limitations of any grade in serving as an accurate indicator of a student's knowledge and ability, educators, too, attach significant credence to grades.

The General Public

Throughout U.S. society, there are a number of places where the grades of individual students are used as criteria for making decisions about the student. A student's grade-point average has become the primary gatekeeper for remaining in a college or university and, eventually, being awarded a degree. Each graduate becomes, in the eyes of the public, a product of higher education and an indicator of the success or failure of his or her college or university. Legislators, governing board members, and even donors take actions based on their judgments regarding the quality of those graduates who have survived the gatekeeping function of higher education. The images portrayed by these graduates as educated members of society serve as a continuing referendum on higher education and its prudent use of both public and private funds that have been provided to the nation's colleges and universities.

In a society that embraces credentials as indicators of ability, the college degree itself, which depends on maintaining a minimum grade-point average, is a prerequisite to many jobs. In addition, those job applicants with high GPAs have a strong competitive advantage over those who do not. In this litigious society, employers find it to their advantage in job screening to attach considerable weight to a factor such as an applicant's grade average, because it appears to be an unbiased and defensible selection criterion.

Dealing with Grade Inflation

Due to the significance placed on an individual's grades, grade inflation has become an ongoing area of concern at colleges and universities worldwide. The worry is that professors are handing out high marks to undeserving students and, in turn, may be preventing grades from serving as useful tools of appraisal (Cahn, 1994). In other words, if all students get As or Bs regardless of the quality of their work, it may become difficult for future employers, graduate schools, or scholarship committees to discern the exceptional student from the average student. There is little argument that grades are higher, on average, than they were several generations ago, and studies show that average GPAs have increased 15 to 20 percent from the mid-1960s to today (Milton, Pollio, & Eisen, 1986; Basinger, 1997). However, this increase in grades does not correspond with a similar increase in intellectual performance. Despite receiving higher marks, modern students have shown lower proficiency in reading, writing, calculating, and reasoning than did their counterparts in past generations (Milton, Pollio, & Eisen, 1986; Leo, 1993).

Why are instructors giving out higher grades than they have in the past? It may be that many instructors find it easier and safer to give As and avoid controversy; those who give low grades may be harassed by students, parents, administrators, or other faculty members (Gose, 1997). It has been suggested that, unlike previous generations, modern students may be avoiding low marks by negotiating with professors and administrators for higher grades and dropping classes in which they are doing poorly. Thus, students may be artificially increasing the mean GPA without increasing their knowledge base (Gose, 1997). Another reason instructors might be awarding high marks is to receive higher evaluations from students (Wilson, 1998). Studies have shown that professors who are easy graders receive better student evaluations than do tough graders (Greenwald & Gilmore, 1998). Because student evaluations are used by many colleges and universities in determining the continuation, promotion, salary increases, and tenure of faculty members, the pressure to please students with high marks may push professors to inflate grades. Finally, some argue that professors are giving grades that accurately reflect the students' mastery of the material presented, but that academic standards have slipped and too little is now asked of students in order to receive a high mark.

When assigning final grades, it may be difficult for an instructor to remain unaffected by the concerns surrounding grade inflation. There may be pressure from students and parents to deliver high grades, a product they believe they have paid for through their tuition. At the same time, there may be pressure from administrators and colleagues to award low marks in an attempt to curb grade inflation and demonstrate the institution's high standards. Certainly, an instructor who consistently assigns grades that are higher or lower than the school's norms will come under scrutiny from some group or other. However, it appears that the standards an instructor applies to assigning grades do not affect what students gain from a class. Studies have shown that what students learn in a class is essentially the same regardless of whether the instructor is an easy or tough grader (Vasta & Sarmiento, 1979; Abrami et al., 1980). With this in mind, most schools of thought contend that instructors will do best not to be intimidated by grade inflation issues and assign the grades they consider valid. If an instructor is fair, follows the college or university's procedures, adheres to the school's norms, remains consistent in grading, and maintains sufficiently rigorous courses, the grades awarded should not become an issue.

Selecting a Grading Philosophy and Approach

What should an instructor consider when selecting his or her approach to grading? The story is told of a conversation between Jerry Reinsdorf, Chairman of the Chicago Bulls basketball team, and Phil Jackson, the Bulls' highly successful coach during most of the 1990s. Sportscasters have suggested that a difference in philosophy about what motivates athletes was at the root of Jackson's decision to leave his coaching job with the Bulls after the team had won six world championships in the previous eight years. Reinsdorf expressed the belief that players are motivated by greed and fear, whereas the coach embraced the philosophy that love and pride are the fundamental factors that serve as the incentives for the players to make the sacrifices necessary to perform at their highest levels. It is not clear which is the dominant philosophy that contributed to the Bulls' success and there are, no doubt, elements of truth in both philosophies. It is clear, however, that whatever philosophy a coach adopts will affect how he or she approaches the work that is to be done and the level of engagement of the players.

Similarly, the philosophy an instructor adopts about grading will influence the teaching and learning that occurs in the classroom, laboratory, studio, or internship setting. The following distinct schools of thought characterize the grading philosophies that might be adopted by a faculty member.

The "Hold Them Accountable" School

Perhaps the most common approach used to assign grades is to construct a grading scale based on criteria established by the instructor in advance to reflect different levels of accomplishment. The instructor judges the degree to which the student meets the criteria and assigns the appropriate grade for that level of accomplishment. Each student is evaluated independently and might receive any grade from an A to an F. A whole class could theoretically receive A grades, or even F grades if they do not meet the instructor's standards. Sometimes referred to as *criterion-referenced grading,* the message to students is that they will be rewarded for the amount of content that they demonstrate they have learned.

The basic philosophy underpinning this school of thought is that the responsibility for earning the grade rests entirely with the student. A finite amount of content is selected for the course and the instructor constructs measurements that will sample each student's mastery of that material. The instructor, the expert in the subject matter, is assumed to be the person qualified to judge what portion of the course material is learned. Therefore, the instructor's assessments are presumed to be accurate measures of learning. The "hold them accountable" approach is most commonly used in courses where the primary objective is to acquire information or when the course material allows relatively little room for students to creatively apply the information.

A strength of this approach is that it is relatively easy to defend as being eminently fair. Students do not compete among themselves for grades. Rather, they compete with themselves as their pride drives them to perform in a manner that yields high grades. It is an approach where the student who wishes to excel will know exactly what it will take to succeed and every student in the class will have an opportunity to reach that level. Also, this is an efficient approach for an instructor to implement. The scores on the various assessments are summed, the percent of content learned by each student is identified, and the grade is assigned. Given that students (and, if appeals are made up the administrative chain, perhaps the department chair and dean) accept the instructor's judgment that the most relevant course content has been selected for testing or other assessments and that the mechanisms used for making the assessments are valid, there is relatively little for the dissatisfied student to contest.

The "Make Them Fit a Curve" School

A second grading philosophy is based on the assumption that in each course there will be a range in the levels of student ability. The best, brightest, and most diligent students will score high relative to those who are not so capable and motivated. Rather than depend on a predetermined set of criteria for assigning grades, the instructor adopting this philosophy uses *norm-referenced criteria* (i.e., the students are compared to each other based on the assumption that the ability levels in the class represent a normal curve). As compared to the "hold them accountable school," the focus of grading shifts from how much of the content is mastered to how the student performed relative to his or her peers. As opposed to the grade being primarily influenced by knowledge of the subject matter, it is also influenced by the mix of students who happen to be enrolled in that section of that course during that term.

This grading philosophy does not assume that the instructor is the sole judge of the most relevant content and that he or she is unfailingly able to construct valid assessments of student learning. Rather, if most students in a class don't perform well when an assessment is made, it is recognized that the instructor and students may have had a different understanding regarding the importance of specific content or that the assessment tool was in some way inadequate or confusing to students. Curving the scores reduces or eliminates the penalty to students when the failure to succeed may, in part, have been the fault of the instructor.

Curving grades is thought to have mixed outcomes regarding its influence on student motivation. At times, competent students are viewed as "curve raisers," and may be viewed negatively by other students in the class and subtly pressured to perform at a lower level. This competition may take more overt forms, such as back-biting or even sabotaging a classmate's work, in an effort to lower the curve. Regression to the mean can result. Another view, however, is that to the extent that Jerry Reinsdorf's philosophy is correct, the competition for the few top grades will motivate student effort, and the level of production for the whole class should increase.

To curve the grades for a class, an instructor must assume that the composition of the class could yield a normal distribution—a concept in itself that is disputed (Jacoby & Glauberman, 1995). However, if curving is judged to be an appropriate format, the instructor needs only to provide a common stimulus, such as uniform test questions, writing on a common theme, researching a similar topic, or completing a laboratory experiment unaided.

Once the assessment scores are compiled, the next step would be to determine the midpoint of scores for the class by computing either a median or mean for the class. Depending on the level of the class and the norms of the school or department, the student(s) at the midpoint would be assigned the grade that represents the typical grade for a student in the course. In undergraduate courses, the typical grade might be a C or B; and in a graduate course, it might be a B+ or an A–. With the median grade established, it is relatively simple to move up the scale to assign the higher grades and down the rankings to establish the lower grades. To avoid a too rigid application of the numerical scores when assigning letter grades, an instructor might look for natural breaking points in the distribution of scores that could be used to separate grade levels.

A more strict application of curve-related grading involves a forced distribution. Based on the philosophy that competition is a fundamental driving force in student learning and that there is a limited supply of any unit of grades, this approach parcels out grades based only on a comparison of the performance of the students in the class. It is relatively straightforward to determine at the beginning of the course that a specific grade distribution will be achieved and that the student's ranking in the class will determine that grade. For example, 10 percent will earn an A, 25 percent a B, 30 percent a C, 25 percent a D, and 10 percent will fail. Of course, the percentages might be adjusted in relation to the objectives of the course, level of students, and so on.

The "Everybody Should Make an A" School

At an opposite end of the grading continuum from the forced distribution is a school of thought that minimizes the emphasis on grades by guaranteeing students a specific grade at the beginning of the course. This philosophy assumes that grading is a barrier to learning and should be eliminated; skills in teamwork and cooperation are valued, and Phil Jackson's contention that pride is the prime motivator for learning is embraced.

Of course, an instructor cannot arbitrarily discontinue giving grades, and the difficulty for one who wants to take competition for grades out of the teaching/learning equation revolves around what grade to assign. Should all students receive a C? Or a B? If a student's 4.0 GPA is sullied by the instructor's decision to eliminate grades from the teaching/learning mix, the situation most likely would end up in the department head's or dean's office. The option, then, that virtually eliminates complaints about a grade is to give all As. After all, what student would complain about getting a A? Some students might grouse about doing much more for his or her A than other students, but the case is unlikely to end in a grievance.

In some schools, it is permissible to implement this philosophy by assigning pass/fail or satisfactory/unsatisfactory grades. Using this approach, all students who perform at a satisfactory level receive a passing grade and only the very poor performers fail the class. This format is especially useful in instructional situations such as internships or highly individualized assignments where students do not all have the same stimulus as a basis for comparing their responses or where the learning environment is only partly under the control of the instructor. Using a very broad measure such as Pass or Fail minimizes the potential influence on a student's grade from the element of chance affecting the assessment of the student.

This approach, obviously, is highly efficient regarding the time the instructor invests in determining and defending grades. A risk associated with this approach, especially for new instructors, is that it is often viewed as lacking rigor, neglecting the responsibility to accurately assess students, and contributing to grade inflation.

The "Negotiated Grade" School

A final approach to grading involves developing a contract with students at the beginning of the term for the grade they want to receive. Although each student's set of activities can be individually negotiated, typically an instructor sets out a menu of papers, presentations, lab assignments, and so on, that must be successfully completed at each of the grade levels in order to earn a specific grade in the course. This philosophy links the student's production to his or her goal for a particular grade, making the grade the central pawn in the student's motivation to engage in course-related activities.

At the heart of this philosophy is the student's pride and drive. In this case, the student is very much in charge of his or her fate. The process of student selection of tasks takes time for both the student and instructor, but can be accomplished by the student and faculty member developing a contract through a checksheet, an interactive e-mail process, or individual interviews. The more difficult aspect of implementing this approach is establishing qualitative standards. For example, an instructor may determine that to earn an A grade, the student must complete a specified number of written assignments which are evaluated as meeting established levels of quality and receive A grades on three of the five tests given in the course.

Applying a Grading Philosophy

Determining the best approach to grading in a particular class is an important part of the teaching/learning endeavor and should be considered an essential part of course design. It is far too late to begin considering these factors when a test is constructed, an assignment prepared, or a stack of papers is awaiting the instructor.

Three factors should be considered when an instructor adopts a philosophy or combination of philosophies for grading in a course. First, it is imperative that the requirements of the college or university be understood. One's flexibility in method of assigning grades may be constrained by established policies or procedures. Although an instructor may choose to stretch or even violate those requirements, such an action should be done knowingly and the personal risks recognized.

Second, the objectives of the course should be considered. For example, if the primary purpose of the course is for the student to individually master a certain amount of content or develop particular skills, a philosophy such as the "hold them accountable" approach would appear most appropriate. If the objectives include teamwork and peer learning, one might more appropriately lean toward the "negotiated grade" or the "everyone should make an A" school. Or, if the student's ability to function in a competitive environment is central to the course objectives, grading on the curve or the "forced distribution" philosophy might be the best approach.

Finally, the instructor needs to adopt an approach that is compatible with his or her own conscience and philosophy about student learning. One side of this issue is the view that the effective instructor needs to draw on a variety of teaching strategies ranging from entertaining presentations to the (implied) threat of low grades to capture students' interest and motivate them to devote the necessary time and attention to the subject matter. Grades, this side of the argument contends, can be a powerful tool in the teaching/learning process, and the instructor should use that power to maximize student learning. At the other side of the issue is the perspective that students make sacrifices to be in college and their desire to learn should be sufficient motivation to perform at their highest level. Therefore, grading is an unnecessary impediment to learning and should be minimized. Most grading plans reflect a mix of these perspectives. Whichever approach is adopted, it is important for the faculty member to model consistency and remain with that method throughout the academic term.

Issues in Assigning Grades

At the end of a course, an instructor is usually required to designate a final grade for each student that represents a summary of the assessments made through examinations, quizzes, and projects that have been assigned. The following are some issues surrounding the incorporation of the evaluative components into a final grade.

Incorporating Student Self-Evaluations

An increasing number of college and university instructors require students to undertake self-evaluation assignments in which the students contemplate their academic work and evaluate it in writing. Self-evaluation is a valuable teaching tool that reinforces analytical, communication, and assessment skills. It also encourages students to articulate what they have learned, understand it in their own context, and through this process, discover new insights (Waluconis, 1993). Proponents of self-evaluation feel that the skills it teaches are some of the most critical that students will acquire.

Whether self-evaluations should be judged and incorporated into a final grade is a subject of debate. There are instructors who feel that students will not take the evaluations seriously if they are not graded. Some instructors grade self-assessments as they would any assignment and they have constructed a variety of rubrics with which to grade them. Others do not grade individual self-assessments, but use them when assigning final grades as another indicator of what students have learned (Waluconis, 1993). Finally, many instructors feel that self-evaluations should never be graded. They believe that grading defeats the purpose of this type of exercise by encouraging students to try to guess what the instructor wants them to write, rather than to reflect honestly on their own work and progress. Instead, detailed, constructive feedback is recommended without any incorporation of the evaluation in final grades (Malehorn, 1994; Hobson, 1996).

Grading Group Projects

Instructors regularly assign projects that require students to work together in groups, believing that there are many benefits associated with this practice. First, having students work in groups may force cooperation and reduce competition for grades. Second, a combined effort rather than individuals independently working toward a goal may increase the potential for productivity. Also, working in groups allows students to share learning resources, which may be required if the availability of these resources is limited. Finally, group projects are thought to teach real-world social skills. After leaving college, students will almost certainly be required to serve on committees, be part of task forces, or work in conjunction with colleagues, all of which involve refined teamwork skills (Eble, 1988; Culp & Malone, 1992). As an added bonus, instructors may have fewer projects to grade if group assignments are utilized. If handled properly, cooperative projects have been shown to produce better student performance than do individual projects (Slavin, 1983).

However, there are also drawbacks to group projects. Grades awarded can be unfair if some group members work harder and con-tribute more than others. Students who have a strong understand-ing of the presented material and have put forth effort may have their grade pulled down because they are paired with unmotivated group members. Conversely, students who do not have a solid grasp of the course content and do not work hard may act as parasites on the group and gain undeserved high marks. If a student's grade from a group project ends up reflecting someone else's work, it may make the grades an unreliable appraisal tool that cannot accurately be interpreted by parents, scholarship committees, admission offic-ers, or potential employers (Kagan, 1995). This approach may have legal ramifications in that an instructor would have a difficult time defending a grade that is not solely based on a student's individual work. Group projects have been implicated in undermining student motivation, weakening the relationship between effort and reward, and communicating to students that individuals are not necessarily accountable for their actions (Kagan, 1995).

The manner in which grades are assigned to group projects can have a profound outcome on the effectiveness of the assignment. For a group assignment to promote learning, group members need to have an incentive and the performance of each individual should be visible and quantifiable to other group members (Slavin, 1983). The most common way to grade a group project is to assign the same grade to each member of the group based on the quality of the final product. This method provides an incentive, the grade, but there is no individual accountability and no way to quantify the input from each member. Also, group members may not have an interest in whether all groupmates are understanding or succeeding, thus compromising the learning value in the assignment (Johnson & Johnson, 1974).

Another method is to assign grades based on the mean of all the group members' performance on an exam asking detailed questions about the project (Miller & Hamblin, 1963; Slavin, 1983). This not only supplies incentive and individual accountability but it also encourages groupmates to make sure all members have a clear understanding of the project. If group grades are not averaged and members are awarded individual grades, this circumvents the problem of the grade reflecting someone else's work, but cooperation is undermined and members have been shown to learn less from the assignment (Slavin, 1983).

A final way to assign grades to group activities is to break the project into separate tasks. Each student can then be assigned a task and the performance on each task graded individually. For this to be effective, the tasks must be interdependent and the group's success should hinge on the results of each task (Miller & Hamblin, 1963). Although this method might be difficult to implement, it maintains cooperative working while assigning grades based on an individual's work. A variation on this method is to quantify the percent of contribution that each group member has made to four tasks of the project: creativity/ideas contributed, research/data collected, writing/typing/artwork, and organizing/collating (Culp & Malone, 1992). In this method, group members independently rate each other's contribution to the various tasks and the average percent of contribution is converted to a numeric grade.

Grading Oral Reports

Most grading is based on some tangible piece of written work, such as a paper, a worksheet, or an exam. This allows an instructor to critique the work carefully and go over it multiple times, if necessary. It also allows the instructor to point out exactly where the student may have gone wrong and how he or she might improve. Oral projects, although valuable tools for improving students' communication skills, are one-time events that are either graded at the time of the presentation or evaluated at a later date based on the instructor's memory of the presentation. The transient nature of oral presentations can make grading disputes difficult to resolve, as the instructor and the student may have different recollections of the project's content.

A way in which the drawbacks of grading oral reports can be minimized is to clearly define how the presentation will be graded at the outset of the project (Butler & Stevens, 1997). This will give the students a clear picture of what is expected and will indicate that the grade weighs both style and content. Often, an instructor's overall impression of an oral report and the subsequent grade assigned are influenced by the effectiveness of the presentation, rather than by its content. It may be difficult to decide if a confident presentation that displays little understanding of the material merits the same grade as a stumbling report that has strong content. A prearranged grading scheme will allow an instructor to decide what percentage of the grade should be devoted to presentation components (delivery, syntax, clarity, persuasiveness, use of visual aids, etc.), and what should be awarded for content components (understanding of material, linkage of concepts, etc.). The percentages assigned will vary according to the focus of the course (e.g., a speech course would likely have a high presentation percentage, whereas a biochemistry course would stress content).

One aid in grading oral reports is simply to videotape all presentations. Although this may not make for edge-of-your-seat viewing, having a visible record of the presentation allows the instructor the opportunity to reevaluate both the performance and content and can be used to give feedback to students concerning the strong and weak areas of the report. A written outline or report that is submitted by the students prior to the presentation can also serve as a record of the presentation's content and may aid in evaluating the project.

Grading Laboratory Work

In many disciplines, particularly in the natural sciences, laboratories are a major component of the curriculum. Labs are essential for demonstrating the techniques used within a discipline and how the information gained by these techniques have added to the student's understanding of the subject. They also can supply hands-on acquisition of knowledge that cannot be learned through lecture. However, labs differ from lecture courses in that (1) they frequently require students to spend large amounts of time in the lab, perfecting techniques; (2) they typically require students to work cooperatively; and (3) they involve the coupling of concepts and theories to the implementation of techniques and procedures. For these reasons, assigning grades for labs can be difficult.

It may be tempting to grade students on the amount of time spent in the lab, but this practice has the drawbacks associated with giving any grade based on effort. At the same time, it may be hard for an instructor to determine whether students who finish labs quickly are shirking responsibility or are simply more efficient than their peers. Instructors can spend the majority of their time policing labs and calculating participation, which detracts from time spent teaching. At many institutions, labs are open in the evenings after instructors have gone home, and this makes it impossible for the instructor to get a reliable measure of the time each student has spent in the lab.

Labs frequently require extensive resources, which often forces an instructor to have students work in groups. Labs performed in groups need to be graded with the considerations applied to the grading of any group project. Using criterion-referenced grading rather than grading on a curve (norm-referenced or forced) is advisable in labs utilizing group projects, since curves can encourage competition and discourage cooperation (Wright, 1996).

It can be difficult to ensure that the final grade in a lab course reflects both a student's understanding of concepts as well as his or her ability to perform techniques. However, one approach is to test these two different aspects separately. Comprehension of theory and concepts can be evaluated with written exams and/or quizzes, while the ability to execute procedures can be appraised using laboratory practicals that involve the independent reproduction of lab results. Practicals can also be useful in determining a student's understanding of the appropriate application of techniques. The weight given to each type of evaluation should depend on the goals of the course and the emphasis placed on theory versus procedures. Another option is to base grades on either research papers or oral exams that require understanding both theoretical and practical aspects of the course (Heidcamp & Beard, 1979). Although this approach can be extremely time consuming, it can yield a clear picture of whether the student is synthesizing the various aspects of a lab course.

Grading Individualized Learning Experiences

Grading internships, practica, independent studies, original research projects, and other forms of individualized learning poses a particular problem for the instructor. In most teaching/learning situations, the instructor has, at a minimum, the ability to compare students' performances within the class. A test can be constructed for all students, the parameters of a term paper written out in detail, the student's ability to follow the established protocol for conducting a chemical analysis or dissecting a frog can be assessed, and guidelines for preparing an oral report can be explicated, making it possible to compare responses to similar stimuli provided under comparable conditions. But what if the learning assignment is to practice teach in an elementary school, create a painting using an innovative technique, demonstrate counseling skills, or observe and analyze the social interaction patterns of a herd of deer? Here, the stimuli are inconsistent, the student's creativity and style are essential factors, and one's past experience may lead to a satisfactory product with little new learning. What should be the standards for grading these individualized learning experiences?

Inherent in an individualized learning activity is the fact that the experience is adapted to the unique learning needs of the student, and only very general comparisons of performance among students can be made. In an internship, for example, student learning assignments are dependent on the opportunities that arise during the internship, and, because these are real-world experiences, sometimes they will provide excellent learning opportunities and at other times they will simply not yield the anticipated learning through no fault of the student or instructor. Similarly, an idea for an independent research project may or may not pan out when the student delves into the topic or, to take another example, when the performance choreographed by a dance student may be mediocre due to the quality of available dancers. How, then, can these students be fairly graded?

It is important that the expectations for learning are clearly stated (i.e., the knowledge and skills that should be mastered) and it should be understood that there are many ways to demonstrate the expected outcomes. To establish expectations for learning, it is most typical for the student and instructor to engage in some form of negotiated learning contract at the onset of the experience. Nevertheless, there is a much higher degree of subjectivity in grading individualized learning experiences than when evaluating the work of multiple students. In this form of learning, fine distinctions such as letter grades or numerical scores are difficult to assign in a way that is equitable. In many colleges and universities, pass/fail or satisfactory/unsatisfactory grades are used in this type of situation. Where traditional grading is required, a three-tiered grading plan might be used, with B representing the expected quality, A denoting exceptional or honors level work, and F reflecting work that falls below the agreed upon standard for the performance or product.

Addressing Effort and Improvement

According to Mick Jagger, "you can't always get what you want, but if you try, sometimes . . . you get what you need." When it comes to grades, most students will concede Mick's first statement, but many doubt the second. Rather, they feel that if they try they should always get what they think they need. It is not uncommon for students to expect a high grade based on the effort they have put into a class, rather than on how clearly they have demonstrated their understanding of the subject. Yet, grades are supposed to reflect a student's level of learning in a course—and learning and effort are not necessarily connected.

An instructor may be tempted to adjust a grade based on the student's effort and attitude. Although many students do not achieve because they fail to put forth the required effort, it is natural to want to reward those that do. When polled, many college and university professors confess that they have bumped up grades for students who did not perform well in a course but who tried extremely hard (Becker, Greer, & Hughes, 1968). However, this practice undermines the appraisal function of grades, making it impossible for those examining a student's marks to determine whether the student genuinely understands a particular subject or, rather, works hard but has limited proficiency.

Similarly, when students appear to be apathetic toward their studies, an instructor might be inclined to assign a low grade for effort that will be factored into the final evaluation. This practice, some have argued, may generate resentful obedience, but can also damage a student's self-esteem and impede the desire to learn. For example, students who receive low marks for effort may feel that they are failing in the most basic elements of the course and consequently lose motivation. Conversely, students who receive high effort marks, yet fail to excel in a course, may be discouraged because they feel that even with a strong effort, they did not have the intellectual ability necessary to succeed. Either way, this practice has the potential to undermine learning by reducing student motivation (Kohn, 1994).

Adjusting a student's grade based on amount of improvement made during the course may also be tempting. However, this practice can devalue grades and may encourage students to play the game of withholding effort at the beginning of a course in order to receive improvement points at the end.

Constructing a Grading System

When developing a grading system, it is important for an instructor to begin by deciding the type(s) of learning that students will be expected to master within a course. This involves linking established course objectives with the instructor's expectations for student learning. At its simplest, learning types can be broken down into (1) knowledge-based learning, (2) understanding-based learning, and (3) doing- or implementation-based learning (Gordon & Gordon, 1982). In this context, *knowledge-based learning* refers to the acquisition of facts, concepts, and explanations that are the building blocks for a particular field of study. Most introductory-level courses are primarily knowledge based. *Understanding-based learning* deals with the direct or vicarious utilization of knowledge to yield explanations and predictions. This objective leads a student to reexamine knowledge-based learning and stimulates a deeper comprehension of fundamental knowledge. *Doing-* or *implementation-based* learning is the practical use of conceptual material (i.e., knowing and understanding) in a real-world setting. As with understanding-based learning, this approach is intended to stimulate students to reexamine both knowledge- and understanding-based learning and further strengthen their grasp of the subject.

Once the learning objectives of a course are defined, the course-grading philosophy(ies) can be adopted or adapted to reflect student learning. For a course that emphasizes knowledge-based learning, almost any philosophy can be incorporated, although criterion-referenced grading is most commonly used and most easily applied. This approach permits the content of the course and the criteria for grades to be uniformly applied to all students and allows for the subtle differentiation necessary to assign letter grades. A course in which understanding-based learning is stressed might likewise use criterion-referenced grading, but might also effectively utilize norm-referenced or curved grading, which would emphasize the relative understanding each student has gained when compared to his or her peers. The full application of content (i.e., doing or implementation learning) often does not lend itself to the use of grading schemes that directly compare students to each other. Therefore, contract grading schemes may be most appropriate when the primary objective is an individualized student experience.

In addition to adopting appropriate grading philosophies, there are several key elements that will strengthen any grading system. Hammons and Barnsley (1992) have outlined the following eight principles to keep in mind when developing a grading plan:

- Communicate the grading system in writing—let students know what will be measured, the weight attached to assignments, tentative due dates, and so on.
- Measure a variety of behaviors—to accurately assess learning, base grades on the assessment of student performance in several types of activities.
- Match evaluation measurements to course activities and objectives—ensure that course objectives are clearly defined and test only on those objectives.
- Provide prompt feedback—inform students on how they have performed on a previous task before assigning the next.
- Evaluate on different levels—if the objectives of a course are to present both knowledge- and understanding-based learning, make sure each are evaluated.
- Weigh types of performance according to importance—decide what aspects of the course are the most important and weigh them accordingly in the final grade.

- Be creative in evaluating student performance—avoid using the same grading scheme for each assignment. Tailor the grading scheme to the specific assignment.
- Decide on retest possibilities—from the outset, decide if retests will be offered, how they will be graded, how many retests will be allowed, and determine if they will be given in the same or a different format.

Following these guidelines can improve an instructor's satisfaction with his or her grading and reduce student complaints. Careful planning up front can save considerable time and frustration later in the process, although it is virtually impossible to construct a scheme that will satisfy everyone. Clearly, there is no right or wrong approach to grading, and ultimately it is the responsibility of each instructor to thoughtfully arrive at a grading scheme with which he or she has the most comfort.

Changing Grades

At some point in his or her career, every instructor will be asked by an unhappy student to change a grade. This frequently occurs when a student is on the borderline between two grades (e.g., between a C+ and a B–) and it may be difficult for the instructor to justify why the student has received the lower of the two grades. When confronted with this scenario, an instructor should first make sure that there is not an error in the grade computation. Sometimes errors may have been made in scoring questions, points may have been added incorrectly, or grades entered on a wrong line in the gradebook. Instructors should promptly fix these mistakes. However, more often than not, students want grades changed because they feel that they have been unfairly treated and that the instructor does not understand and/or appreciate their individual circumstances. Like Baxter Black in the opening quote of this chapter, they ask for pity as they plead for a higher grade.

Perhaps even more disturbing than the student who challenges a grade is the occasional parent who feels obligated to advocate for his or her son or daughter. A parent's disappointment may be genuine and understandable, but do they really have all of the information? This is complicated by the fact that parents do not have a legal right to know the grades of their college-age children. Instructors can't provide the information parents seek without the permission of the student. However, the new instructor, in particular, must wonder if the department chair will be supportive if a complaint gets moved up the line—even when there is a clear grading process in place. The instructor is, too often, in a no-win situation.

Ultimately, the decision to change a grade requires a judgment call by the instructor. Some questions to consider are: Were there truly extenuating circumstances that affected the student's performance? Would a change of grade be fair to other students in the class? How considered and thoughtful is the student's appeal? Given that grade appeals may lead to a grievance or possibly litigation, it is important that the instructor is sure of his or her rationale for grade assignment—whatever grading approach is selected. Students should be provided a description of how grades will be assigned at the beginning of the course (preferably in writing), the plan should be even-handedly applied, and the instructor should keep accurate records of all factors that are the basis for assigning grades.

Be aware that changing even one grade sets a precedent. You can't swear students to secrecy and they *will* talk to their friends. Once you do change a grade, be prepared to get other requests. One suggestion that might help you avoid agonizing over grade changes: Adopt the policy that if a student is within one point of a higher grade, go ahead and give the better grade. This reduces the amount of time you might otherwise spend splitting hairs and fretting over rounding up or rounding down decisions.

Although there is relatively little case law to guide instructors, it is evident that at a minimum, the instructor should avoid any grading approach that could be interpreted as arbitrary and capricious (Phillips, 1993). In a study of 59 cases concerned with academic decisions in higher education over 17 years, Ford and Strope (1996) concluded that the "philosophy of judicial nonintervention was rousingly affirmed." The reluctance of the courts to intervene in academic judgments is perhaps best summarized in the following decision related to the case, *Susan M* vs. *New York Law School* (566 N.E.2n at 1107):

As a general rule, judicial review of grading disputes would inappropriately involve the courts in the very core of aca-

demic and educational decision making. Moreover, to so involve the courts in assessing the propriety of particular grades would promote litigation by countless unsuccessful students and undermine the credibility of the academic determination of educational institutions. We conclude, therefore, that, in the absence of demonstrated bad faith, arbitrariness, capriciousness, irrationality of a constitutional or statutory violation, a student's challenge to a particular grade or other academic determination relation to a genuine substantive evaluation of the student's academic capacities, is beyond the scope of judicial review. (Kaplin & Lee, 1995, p. 474)

The courts have consistently held in favor of a student's right to a fair hearing if he or she elects to appeal a grade that an instructor has assigned. Each college or university should have a published grade appeal process that informs students and instructors regarding how such concerns should be addressed. It is important for each instructor to become familiar with the school's policies and processes regarding grade appeals as background for preparing a grading system.

Grading is a fact of life in higher education. Because of the importance U.S. society attributes to a person's grades, their assignment has become a significant part of the teaching/learning endeavor.

References and Resources

Abrami, P. C., Dickson, W. J., Perry, R. P., & Leventhal, L. (1980). Do teacher standards for assigning grades affect student evaluations of instruction? *Journal of Educational Psychology, 72,* 107–118.

Allison, L., Bryand, L., & Hourigan, M. (1997). *Grading in the post-process classroom: From theory to practice.* Portsmouth, NH: Boynton/Cook.

Basinger, D. (1997). Fighting grade inflation: A misguided effort? *College Teaching, 45,* 88–91.

Becker, H. S., Greer, B., & Hughes, E. C. (1968). *Making the grade: The academic side of college life.* New York: John Wiley and Sons,.

Black, B. (1997). *Cactus tracks and cowboy philosophy.* New York: Crown.

Blynt, R. A. (1992). The sticking place: Another look at grades and grading. *English Journal, 82,* 66–71.

Brown, G., with Bull, J., & Pendelbury, M. (1997). *Assessing student learning in higher education.* London: Routledge.

Butler, F. A., & Stevens, R. (1997). Oral language assessment in the classroom. *Theory into Practice, 36,* 214–219.

Cahn, S. M. (1994). Rethinking examinations and grades. In P. J. Markie (Ed.), *A professor's duties: Ethical issues in college teaching.* London: Rowman & Littlefield.

Culp, L., & Malone, V. (1992). Peer scores for group work. *Science Scope, 15,* 35–36.

Curren, R. R. (1995). Coercion and the ethics of grading and testing. *Educational Theory, 4,* 425–441.

Eble, K. E. (1988). *The craft of teaching.* San Francisco: Jossey-Bass.

Ford, D. L., & Strope, J. L., Jr. (1996). Judicial responses to adverse academic decisions affecting public postsecondary institution students since "Horowitz" and "Ewig." *Education Law Reporter, 110,* 465–474.

Gordon, W. E., & Gordon, M. S. (1982). The role of frames of reference in field instruction. In B. W. Sheafor & L. E. Jenkins (Eds.), *Quality field instruction in social work* (pp. 21–36). New York: Longman.

Gose, B. (1997). Efforts to curb grade inflation get an "F" from many critics. *Chronicle on Higher Education, 43,* A41–A42.

Greenwald, A. G., & Gilmore, G. (1998). How useful are student ratings? *American Psychologist, 53,* 1228.

Gribbin, A. (1992). Making exceptions when grading and the perils it poses. *Journalism Educator, 46,* 73–76.

Hammons, J. O., & Barnsley, J. R. (1992). Everything you need to know about developing a grading plan for your course (well, almost). *Journal of Excellence in College Teaching, 3,* 51–68.

Heidcamp, W. H., & Beard, W. R. (1979). Biotechniques for freshmen. *The American Biology Teacher, 41,* 52–53.

Hobson, E. H. (1996). Encouraging self-assessment: Writing as active learning. In T. E. Sutherland & C. C. Bonwell (Eds.), *Using active learning in college classes: A range of options for faculty.* San Francisco: Jossey-Bass.

Jacoby, R., & Glauberman, N. (Eds.). (1995). *The bell curve debate: History, documents, openness.* New York: Times Books.

Johnson, D. W., & Johnson, R. T. (1974). Instructional goal structure: Cooperative, competitive, or individualistic. *Review of Educational Research, 44,* 213–240.

Kagan, S. (1995). Group grades miss the mark. *Educational Leadership, 52,* 68–71.

Kaplin, W. A., & Lee, B. A. (1995). *The law of higher education: A comprehensive guide to legal implications of administrative decision making.* San Francisco: Jossey-Bass.

Kohn, A. (1994). Grading: The issue is not how but why. *Educational Leadership, 52,* 38–41.

Krumboltz, J. D., & Yeh, C. J. (1996). Competitive grading sabotages good teaching. *Phi Delta, 78,* 324–326.

Leo, J. (1993). A for effort. Or for showing up. *U.S. News and World Report,* (October 18), p. 22.

Malehorn, H. (1994). Ten measures better than grading. *The Clearing House, 67,* 323–324.

Miller, L. K., & Hamblin, R. L. (1963). Interdependence, differential rewarding, and productivity. *American Sociological Review, 28,* 768–778.

Milton, O., Pollio, H. R., & Eison, J. A. (1986). *Making sense of college grades.* San Francisco: Jossey-Bass.

O'Connor, K. (1995). Guidelines for grading that support learning and student success. *NASSP Bulletin, 79,* 91–101.

Ory, J. C., & Ryan, K. E. (1993). *Tips for improving testing and grading.* Newbury Park, CA: Sage.

Perrin, N. (1998). How students at Dartmouth came to deserve better grades. *The Chronicle on Higher Education* (October 9), p. A68.

Phillips, S. E. (1993). Legal issues in performance assessment. *West's Education Law Reporter, 79,* 708–738.

Popham, W. J. (1998). *Classroom assessment: What teachers need to know.* Boston: Allyn and Bacon.

Seeley, M. M. (1994). The mismatch between assessment and grading. *Educational Leadership, 52,* 4–6.

Slavin, R. E. (1983). When does cooperative learning increase student achievement? *Psychological Bulletin, 94,* 429–445.

Vasta, R., & Sarmiento, R. F. (1979). Liberal grading improves evaluations but not performance. *Journal of Educational Psychology, 71,* 207–211.

Waluconis, C. J. (1993). Self-evaluation: Settings and uses. In J. MacGregor (Ed.), *Student self-evaluation: Fostering reflective learning.* San Francisco: Jossey-Bass.

Walvoord, B. E., & Anderson, V. J. (1998). *Effective grading: A tool for learning and assessment.* San Francisco: Jossey-Bass.

Wilson, R. (1998). New research casts doubt on value of student evaluations of professors. *Chronicle on Higher Education, 44,* A12–A14.

Wright, J. C. (1996). Authentic learning environment in analytical chemistry using cooperative methods and open-ended laboratories in large lecture courses. *Journal of Chemical Education, 73,* 827–832.

11

Managing Problem Situations

Overview: We all probably have some version of a prototypical classroom image in the recesses of our mind. Without too much effort, we can see students sitting in neat rows at rapt attention, hanging on every word of the instructor, the only sound being that of the lecturer's voice and pens moving swiftly across notebooks. That image, however, may exist more in our imaginations than in reality. Writing recently (1998) in the Chronicle of Higher Education, *Paul Trout, an associate professor of English at Montana State University, observed, "A sizable segment of students now entering college does not love to learn, and does not have anything resembling an intellectual life."*

Possibly as a result, faculty across the country are encountering uncivil student behavior, which may range from disruptive conversations on cell phones and in small groups in the back of the classroom, to reading newspapers and napping, to showing up drunk. The problem of insolence has been so bad on some campuses (e.g., Virginia Tech, Montana State, Indiana University) that special committees have been formed (Schneider, 1998).

Although most students aren't ill mannered, only a few in a class can be demoralizing—especially when they have no respect for anyone in authority. The problem has been blamed on everything from consumerism and media violence to poor parenting examples and the "dumbing down" of elementary and secondary education. However, there is historical evidence that students have been quite rude and abusive of faculty, even in the most prestigious of universities. That issue aside, some faculty feel that the problem is currently worse that it was for our mentors (Schneider, 1998).

212

Today's instructors must be prepared to encounter disruptive students, classes that are hard to call to order, unmotivated pupils, students who are frequently absent, and even hostile and angry students. Sawyer, Prichard, and Hostetler (1992) have stated, "If you think you're going to have a peaceful and quiet existence as a new professor, you've made a big mistake in choosing university teaching in the 1990s. Those halcyon days when professors, no matter their ability, were captains of their classrooms are largely gone" (p. 205). A little later they added, "Students are rarely intimidated either by subject content (especially in the humanities and social sciences) or by you. They are likely to bypass your office and head for that of the chairperson, dean, or president in an effort to seek justice or an explanation for having received a low evaluation from you" (p. 210). And as if these problems weren't enough, there may arise other problems of a slightly different nature, as when we are attracted to a student or a student in one of our classes makes a pass at us. This chapter provides advice on how to handle some typical classroom problems as well as how to protect oneself should there be more serious and threatening behavior.

The Noisy Classroom

Walking into a noisy class and getting its attention can be a daunting task at times. However, having a set, "signaling" procedure—such as closing the door, calling roll, writing something on the board, turning on the overhead projector, or distributing handouts—can be helpful. Often, it is necessary simply to project one's voice and to speak authoritatively (e.g., "Open your books, please, to Chapter 9") or to make a request (e.g., "On a scrap piece of paper, jot down two questions you have from today's reading").

Sorcinelli (1994) has recommended preventive measures to avert troublesome situations and disruptive behaviors. The first strategy is to spell out your expectations ("lay down the law") at the first class meeting. Define what is acceptable and what is unacceptable. If you are a stickler for starting the class on time, communicate this to the students. If there are others things that really bother you, address them preventively by listing "class rules" in the syllabus. Call attention to the rules and go over them with the class. You can avoid sounding like a rigid authoritarian by explaining the logic behind your rules, such as: "I find it hard to concentrate when students talk as I'm trying to lecture—it distracts others in the classroom." You can go on to say, "I value your opinions and thoughts, but please, let's just have one speaker at a time. If you raise your hand, I will always share the floor."

The Talkative and Rude Student

If, after you have gone over the class rules, a small pocket of two or three students persist in talking, make and maintain eye contact with them. If that doesn't work, move in their direction and stand beside them. Occasionally, it may be necessary to hush them by making the "shhhh" sound and placing your index finger to your lips. If they persist, you might need to call on them to answer some question or you might need to be more direct and say something like: "Tim, class has started now."

When these approaches fail because Tim and his buddies are persistent talkers, you have two alternatives. The first of these is to assign seats so that this clique is broken up and dispersed around the classroom. Another strategy is to talk with the offending student after class and ask for his or her cooperation. Tell the student that you have a problem and aren't quite sure how to handle it. Be honest. If the talking persists, give the student a task, such as taking lecture notes for someone who is absent. Alternatively, you could give the talkative student a larger role by asking him or her to highlight the important points in the readings for that day. Talkative students seldom view their behavior as rude or inconsiderate; you should not take their behavior as a personal affront. Many times, they are not even aware that they are being disrespectful. Use a light touch of humor if possible (e.g., "I know it's exciting that the team is playing in the Final Four this evening, but since we're not coaching...").

Lies, Damn Lies, and Diabetic Cats

The instructor who requires attendance is guaranteed to hear the standard drab and mundane excuses ("My car broke down", "My roommate forgot to set the alarm clock", "My computer crashed and I had to get it fixed in order to print out a paper due tomorrow") as well as some wonderfully creative excuses ("My cat is diabetic and we had to have a blood sample drawn", and my all-time favorite: "My grandfather is having a kidney transplant—and my mother is donating a kidney"). Actually, there are diabetic cats (check out the extensive webpages devoted to this topic) and the last "excuse" was legitimate, too. Sometimes it is hard to know when a student is lying and when he or she is telling a bizarre but true tale.

Some faculty capitulate all together and don't even try to take attendance or decide what are valid excuses. Other faculty are extremely rigid in granting "excused absences." One instructor I heard about recently informed a student that she would have to bring in a copy of the obituary showing the day and time of her relative's funeral before the student's absence could be excused. However, the middle ground is often the best place to be. Personally, I believe it is important to note who's absent and who's present in each and every class. Taking roll helps me identify the serious students from those who have a more cavalier attitude about the course. Attendance data contribute in a small way (10 to 15 percent) of each student's grade. But students also need a reason to come to class. If class discussions and lectures aren't stimulating, it may be difficult to consistently get good attendance. To improve attendance, many professors draw test questions from lectures so that students won't be able to do well on tests by just reading their texts. If the class is too easy or too boring, students won't attend, even if they lose points for attendance. More students than you would guess never pay attention to the syllabus and don't have any idea of whether attendance counts for 5 percent or 50 percent of their grade. If attendance is important to you, make sure you orally discuss it during the first class meeting and remind the students at other times as appropriate.

Graduate students usually are better about attending class than undergraduates. I did, however, once get a phone call from one who was complaining about a faculty member who was going to give her a failing grade for missing class. The student railed on about the unfairness of it all until I asked how many absences she had. She couldn't, or wouldn't, tell me. Later, the instructor said that particular individual had missed all but one class.

Responsibilities at work, small children, unreliable transportation, and poor health are frequent explanations for classroom absences. Rather than put yourself into the role of judge and jury—

to hear each excuse and then try to decide whether it is legitimate— I find that it is best to follow a scheme like this: (1) Students are informed that the attendance portion of their grade directly corresponds to the number of classes they miss. (2) Roll is taken in each class. (3) The following information is displayed prominently in the course syllabus:

For Semester Classes That Meet Twice a Week (30 Meetings)

1–2 absences = A for attendance (e.g., 95 points/100)
3–4 absences = B for attendance (e.g., 85 points/100)
5–6 absences = C for attendance (e.g., 75 points/100)
7–8 absences = D for attendance (e.g., 65 points/100)
9 + absences = F for attendance (e.g., 55 points/100)

Obviously, you would want to make adjustments if your class meets weekly or only 10 times in one quarter. A variation of this scheme might give everyone something like two "free" absences without any penalties (provided the absences weren't on a day when an examination was scheduled or other major assignment was due). Even the best students have days when the car doesn't start or illness strikes.

The benefits of adopting such an attendance policy is that students have an incentive for attending and know the penalty if they decide to cut class in order to start their spring break a week early. They can make these decisions because they can weigh how the attendance portion of their grades will be affected without wasting your time dealing with specious explanations and arguments.

This policy will work well for the vast majority of students and classes. However, there will always be exceptions: the student who is involved in a car wreck and is hospitalized, the mother-to-be confined to bed rest during the last month of her pregnancy, the star center of the university's basketball team who misses classes because the team is playing out of state. And there will be students who try to take full advantage of your understanding and gentle nature. Trust your instincts; if you feel that a student is fabricating excuses, then demand to see notes from the physician when there are claims of illness.

It is entirely conceivable that a pupil could be unable to attend class for legitimate reasons and yet still be able to keep up with readings and assignments. In such a situation, when there is a medical or otherwise legitimate excuse, it seems only fair to grant the student a waiver from the attendance policy. Must we always be afraid of making exceptions? I think not. Sometimes compassion should temper our rules.

However, it is not unusual to hear of faculty who take the position that students who miss a lot of classes cannot expect to get an A for the course—even if the absences were legitimate. Their explanation is that students who are not present cannot contribute nor learn from class discussion. These faculty have often combined attendance and "participation" and want to give one grade for both. In one situation brought to my attention, a student was able to earn all A grades on her exams and assignments yet received a C for the course because she was in a body cast and unable to attend class. If you weigh class participation that heavily, then make sure the syllabus reflects it as a substantial portion of the grade.

An argument can be made, however, for separating attendance from participation. That way, you can award points differentially to the student with perfect attendance who never utters a sound in class and the one who misses class occasionally but contributes heavily when there.

You may not always agree with the student's need to be excused from class. For instance, athletes at my university, when they are officially traveling with the team, cannot be penalized for missing class and they must be given every opportunity to make up any work. So, although I may not like the fact that Mr. Three-point Shooter catches a flight on Tuesday for Puerto Rico even though the game isn't being played until Saturday, there's not a thing I can do about it. Experience has shown me, though, that those who are frequently absent from class even with legitimate excuses will, more times than not, often still miss class enough times that their overall attendance grade ends up being lowered. Students who are not interested in learning usually find it hard to attend class.

Students Who Need Special Assistance

Most of us are able to recognize students with obvious disabilities, such as the paraplegic, the young woman with a seeing-eye dog, and the young man with dual hearing aids. Many students, however, have invisible disabilities and will not be aware of the disability or will not tell us that they have a learning disability. A faculty member once told me of administering a test to a group of distance learning students only to discover that a mistake had been made and the last page had not been photocopied. He happened to have a rough, handwritten copy of the last page and proposed to read those questions to the students sitting in another classroom receiving him by television. A student strongly objected, saying that she had a neurological impairment and had to visually see the questions—orally received information was often jumbled to her. Other students will be dyslexic (inability to read well) and have problems translating printed matter. Usually, these students struggle with reading comprehension and may have to read even relatively simple material many times before they begin to understand it. These students may be poor spellers (*eqiupment* for *equipment*), confusing the proper sequence of letters (e.g., *no* for *on*).

Another form of invisible disabilities is: *dysgraphia*—the inability to write. These students may be unable to copy correctly from a chalkboard and unable to write complete sentences. *Dyscalculia* is the inability to do math, and these students may be unable to acquire the basics for math computation (because numbers are reversed, *123* looks the same as *321*). Students with learning disabilities can have difficulty comprehending word problems and can experience time management difficulties as well as reasoning deficits. Learning disabilities are permanent disorders. They can be quite specific (e.g., manifested only in math computation). They are not to be confused with emotional disorders or mental retardation.

Here is a list of reasonable accommodations for assisting students with learning disabilities:

- Allow them extra time on tests.
- Provide someone to read the test questions to them if they request this.
- Consider essay tests over objective tests.
- Allow the student to take the exam in a separate room.
- Allow tape-recording of lectures.
- Allow test answers to be dictated to a proctor or oral responses to essay questions.
- Allow proctors to rephrase questions that are not clear.

- Avoid negative questions.
- Underline key words in tests.

Because other students may wish to be given the same advantages (e.g., extra time on tests), it's usually a good policy to grant these only when students have documentation of their disability. Further, testing students with special needs at a separate time or in a separate room also helps to minimize requests from unimpaired students wanting these privileges.

Federal law requires that students with disabilities have a legal right to "reasonable accommodation." Most universities have an office that provides services to students with disabilities and can be contacted if one of your students needs special assistance (e.g., books on tape) or if you need to consult with someone about what constitutes a reasonable accommodation.

Motivating Students

The unmotivated student is usually quite apparent to the college instructor. Such students may not complete assignments or will turn in required work late. They do not participate in class, do not contact the instructor to explain absences, and probably are performing at a lower level than the average student. At times they look like Boredom Incarnate sitting or lounging there in your class.

There are numerous reasons why students may not be motivated. To start with, the *required course* scenario is a likely explanation. Although you may have decided to make politics in colonial America your life's work, it is safe to assume that not everyone will share your enthusiasm. In fact, more than half of the class might be enrolled not because of interest in the topic but because it meets some requirement in a liberal arts curriculum. Students have also been known to enroll in classes because their girlfriends, boyfriends, roommates, or teammates have signed up or even because it is held at a convenient hour—either late in the morning or back-to-back with another course that was required. Students may also show lack of interest after they have decided, midway into the semester, to change majors, to join the military, to drop out and start an Internet business, or to do something else other than continue at your college or university.

In addition, there are understandable situations, such as the death of a loved one, divorce, the loss of a breadwinner's job, recieving news about a serious or chronic illness, and any number of other situations where a student will be thrown for an emotional loss. Reeling from such blows, these students may be unable to concentrate on their work. Worse yet, they can be depressed, unable to sleep at normal times, or simply lethargic. Their depression can stem from being in an abusive relationship or from drug and alcohol addiction. These students should be referred to the counseling office on your campus. They may benefit from psychotherapy, a support group, or medication for their depression.

There are even other possible nonintellectual factors that might explain why some students don't perform well in your course. They may, for instance, have a deep-seated fear of failure or severe examination anxiety. Particularly with students who have small children, or who are caregivers for elderly family members, or who are working in addition to going to college, the pull of responsibilities outside the classroom can give the appearance of an unmotivated student when, in fact, the major problem is that they are overextended. If these students share with you some of their day-to-day activities, you'll be amazed and perhaps appalled at all that they are attempting to do. Your best approach might be to talk with them about time management and to help them prioritize their tasks. If they are hopelessly behind, they may need to reduce the number of academic hours they are carrying or even withdraw from school altogether for a while.

Whenever you detect a pattern that you assume to be due to lack of motivation (e.g., missing classes, not handing in assignments on time), arrange to have the student meet with you outside of class. Candidly express your concerns and then listen. The student will often have very legitimate reasons why he or she hasn't been meeting your expectations. Once it becomes clear that the student is not unmotivated but suffering from too many competing demands on his or her time, then you can decide whether to give him or her a little extra time to make up uncompleted assignments or to assist by working out a plan to keep the student from falling further behind. If the student has no excuse but is simply uninterested in the course, you can decide whether you want to redouble your efforts to reach the student or to let him or her suffer the consequences of lack of interest. Even if you are a wonderfully skilled educator, you will still experience students who are flatly not inter- ested in your topic. Don't take it personally. If students choose not to apply themselves, that is their choice.

However, the effective teacher is always reading the classroom, evaluating his or her own instruction methodology, and trying to reach even the most hard-core, uninterested student. Motivating students is part of the faculty member's responsibility. Writers on the topic of motivating students tend to mention the same remedies time after time: the importance of the instructor showing enthusi- asm for the topic, the use of various media to present material, humor, and employing activities that involve the students in active learning. Remember the adage, "Nothing succeeds like success"? Students who experience some measure of achievement are usually much more motivated than those who've had no taste of success. Instructors who are concerned about students with an apparent lack of motivation ought to consider whether it is possible to create some opportunity for these students to succeed or do well—even if the assignment is relatively small or insignificant.

Additionally, Davis (1993) has recommended:

- Giving frequent and positive feedback that conveys to students that they are doing well or have the potential to do well
- Creating assignments that are neither too difficult nor too easy
- Valuing students' contributions and helping them relate person- ally to the material
- Holding high but realistic expectations for the students
- Specifying what students need to do to succeed in the course
- Allowing students some choice of topics in their reading and in their assignments
- Varying teaching methods (e.g., debates, small group activities, guest speakers)

When one sincerely looks for reasons explaining why students may be unmotivated, it often becomes very apparent: Weaker stu- dents can be discouraged when there is too much competition for grades and not enough emphasis on what's important or useful to learn. Our instructions regarding assignments are sometimes too convoluted or vague, or perhaps we give the students more than they can read, or fail to challenge their intellect altogether. It is not unusual in any class of 30 or so to have 1 or 2 students who constantly wear that "I-don't-want-to-be-here" expression, but if you find more than that or if you are troubled by even those few, by all means begin asking some questions of yourself and of the students. There may be a problem with the way you are teaching. Students' interest and motivation can rapidly decline, for instance, once it becomes apparent to them that a course is too easy and that only a little exertion will produce a good grade. If this is not the general perception, the opposite could also be true: Students may feel that because you are demanding too much, they will get a lousy grade no matter how much time they invest. Having students give you a mid-term evaluation (leave it open ended and ask them to comment on what is and is not working within the class) is one way to ferret out problems that you might be able to correct.

Sometimes you may just get a whole class that is a dud, an assemblage by chance or circumstance where most of the students are not highly motivated. There's not a great deal you can do in such a situation except to innovate and try to bring some excitement to the classroom. You might employ games, simulations, role-plays, videotapes, compelling speakers, or even use candy for rewards for students who raise questions. If nothing else is working, don't be afraid to try new techniques to reach out to the unmotivated. With such classes, keep them actively involved—they are not going to do well at passive forms of learning.

With a little luck, you won't acquire too many classes where you have to fight the urge to give *every* student a Zig Ziglar motivational talk. Your problems will usually be small—two or three under-achieving pupils. One of the major challenges and yet greatest joys of teaching is in finally connecting with the reluctant student, helping that individual to make new discoveries and to develop new insights.

Rip Van Winkle and Sleeping Beauty

Even a young college instructor in his or her twenties soon realizes that there's more than 10 years difference between being age 18 and away from home for the first time and being an "old" 28-year-old who tries to get seven or eight hours of sleep each night. Sometimes students fall asleep in class because of problems not of their own making. Freshman dorms are notorious for the practical jokers who pull fire alarms at 2:00 A.M.; fraternities and sororities subject their pledges to all sorts of creative harassments and minor tortures. Relationships break up and former or present lovers "have to talk" about this issue or that—conversations that extend into the wee hours of the morning. And then there are the larks: driving all night to try and get into the last game of the World Series, the "road trips" to Florida or Texas for spring break, the parties that last all night, the "bull sessions" in the dorm, the poker games, and so on. Some campuses have a tradition of Tuesday night being a drinking night because—follow this logic—Wednesday is the middle of the week, and one can rest on that day in order to make the assault on Thursday and Friday. If campus restaurants and bars are open practically all night, is it any wonder that your students look bleary-eyed? Just for fun, go into one of the all-night or after-hour bars sometime and visit. Odds are, you'll find some students you know.

What should you do about sleeping students in class? One approach is to walk over beside them and ask the class questions while standing in the vicinity. If that doesn't work, or if more than one student is having trouble staying awake, ask the whole class to stand and stretch, to touch their toes or wave their arms, or to do any type of minor exercise that might get the blood flowing again.

If there is poor air movement, a carbon dioxide build-up in the room can contribute to sleepiness. Also, most people get a little sleepy during the notorious early afternoon slot right after lunch. You may want to open the windows, even for a brief time. Even if it's too cold to leave them open for long, the exchange of air will be stimulating and you won't be bothered as much as your audience because you'll be moving around and have more adrenalin pumping. When it's a little too warm, particularly after lunch or in the late afternoon, you may have more problems than in the early morning, when students often drink coffee to help them stay awake.

The student who is always falling asleep may be working all night in order to make money to attend school. When a student regularly has problems staying awake, it is worth at least a conversation with him or her to see if the two of you can come up with any strategy to deal with the situation. It may be that the problem can't be resolved—the student may have to work at night and is so sleep deprived that he or she can't help falling asleep in your class. In such a case, the kindest thing to do might be to allow the student to catch a few winks and not to continually call attention to the problem. However, I would draw the line at snoring and would gently shake or wake any student whose babbles and wheezes distract the class or the lecturer.

"Danger, Danger, Will Robinson": When There's Sexual Interest

Will Robinson, from *Lost in Space* fame, had the advantage over the rest of us mortals in having a protective robot who would loudly announce, "Danger, Danger, Will Robinson" whenever Will was in or about to be in a perilous situation. Without such a robot, you've got to learn to read the signs and signals, both internally and externally, in the environment that indicate hazards and pitfalls for your professional career. Becoming sexually involved with students is one such hazard.

Administrators at most colleges and universities would, if polled, probably prefer that faculty, especially the nontenured ones, not date students. Although these relationships are often overlooked, ignored, and seemingly even accepted in some institutions, that's only when the relationships themselves are harmonious. When relationships break up and bitter recriminations and accusations come to the attention of deans, department chairs, or senior faculty, prior tolerance of the faculty/student liaison will rapidly evaporate. The instructor will find himself or herself on the hot seat, reputation frayed, future uncertain.

How do you know when you are in danger of seeking a student's affection? You are attracted to a student if:

- You have recurrent pleasant thoughts about this individual, even if you think of your relationship as just a friendship.
- You find yourself frequently calling or wanting to call and talk with this person, even when you really don't have a good reason to call.
- You want to invite the student to your apartment or an equally private place where you can escape the possible notice of other faculty or students.
- You give the student special little gifts of something you've made or written (e.g., poetry, some flowers you grew yourself).

- You want to know everything you can about the student—birth-day, favorite music and authors, preferred foods, and so on.
- You fantasize about kissing or touching the student.

Similarly, a student might be attracted to you when there is flirtation, frequent visits to your office, small gifts, requests for "special" tutoring or help, or some excuse is given to provide you with his or her phone number. When these events begin to occur, then program yourself to say, "Danger, Danger."

What's the problem with dating students? The most obvious difficulty is that it is a formidable, if not an impossible, task to be objective when you are grading the work of someone with whom you are romantically involved. So, it is not fair to the particular student nor to the rest of the class. Even if you hold your sexual partner to a higher academic standard than the rest of the class to ensure objectivity, that's not fair either. It may also not be fair if you provide your partner with more help or resources than other students receive— these are ethical and moral issues.

Further, as a new educator, you've got to think about your reputation and whether you want to be known as "the new assistant professor—you know, the one who sleeps with the president of the Student Government Association." That kind of tarnish can remain years later, even if your fling was brief.

Romantic involvements with students might not blow up, of course, but when they do, your formerly precious love object may go to the dean or the academic ombud because you gave this individual a B instead of an A. He or she might file charges of sexual harassment and you may have to retain an attorney or at least have the university's counsel represent you. (This topic will be discussed in Chapter 15.)

A friend of mine, a mental health therapist, says that danger signals ought to go off whenever you find yourself wanting to lower the boundaries that ought to be in place between you and a student; for instance, you loan your car to a student, you let him or her use your office when you are not there, you write long, detailed letters or e-mail to this student but not to any others in your class (assuming you're not working on a research project together). If you are guilty of these offenses, you are in danger of being in too close a relationship with a student. You should not date any student over which you have power to affect by grading, influencing the course of a dissertation, program of study, and so on. Dating after the semester is over may or may not be a problem, depending on your position within the university, what you will be teaching in subsequent semesters, and any other responsibilities, such as being part of a committee that would prepare a qualifying exam or read the student's thesis. The safest counsel is simply not to date students until after they graduate or leave the university.

The Instructor as Therapist and Money Lender

Whether or not you want to hear their stories of woe and hardship, chances are good that you will hear them if you are perceived as a warm, open, or approachable faculty member. Often, we faculty expect our pupils to reveal why they've missed so many classes or didn't show up for a test. And, if you ask, they will tell you. Some of their hardships or difficulties are relatively minor problems: a car that wouldn't start, a sore throat, the death of a grandmother. Other problems are much more serious: the student who is, for all practical purposes, homeless, sleeping in his car; the student with an alcohol or drug problem; the depressed and suicidal student.

Faculty members may learn of students' problems even before the students have acknowledged having a difficulty or have decided to go to a counseling center for help. Faculty may discover the presence of a serious personal problem when, for instance, a student misses numerous classes and then offhandedly drops a bombshell or when a student reveals some private distress in a writing assignment. When faculty are viewed as sympathetic and approachable, students are likely to share personal problems. They find this easier than scheduling an appointment with someone they don't know at the university's counseling center. Indeed, almost three-quarters of faculty have provided short-term personal counseling to students (Roberts et al., 1982).

When students disclose an gut-wrenching problem, there may be no choice but to listen and try to offer some helpful advice. I remember a student, Brian, who dropped in one day to show me fresh cuts on his wrists. He hadn't been trying to kill himself, he said, but to "let some of the pain out." We spent some time talking and, much to my relief, I learned he had a psychiatrist whom he was seeing regularly. This young man was also gay and lived in fear of being beaten by an abusive roommate. After the roommate sold Brian's stereo and television to a pawnshop, Brian finally got the courage to move out, but going to school and working part time was a tremendous financial challenge. On another visit, Brian revealed he was in danger of being evicted from his apartment. He didn't ask for a loan, but I gave him $300, with the understanding that he would repay it. A few weeks later, he came by to tell me that he had been to the doctor about the bad cough he'd had all semester. He had just been diagnosed with cancer of the lung that had spread from a previously undetected malignant melanoma. Brian wanted to tell me he had decided to drive to California, since he had always wanted to see that part of the country before he died. He would pay me back, of course, he promised.

I never heard another word from Brian.

Even though I had a good relationship with Brian and think of myself as a good judge of character, I learned an important lesson about loaning money to students. Were this situation to present itself again someday, I would handle it entirely differently. First of all, I made a mistake in taking ownership of Brian's problem. It would have been a better course of action for me to brainstorm with Brian all of the resources and possible avenues of help available to him. Would his employer give a cash advance? Did he have any relatives who could loan him the money? Had he contacted the housing office or the dean of students to see if there was a vacant room in a dorm where he could live? If no solution seemed apparent, I'd ask Brian for his permission to discuss his problem with some of the other faculty to see if any of them knew of someone with a basement or extra bedroom where Brian could stay.

Unless you have the professional education and training for counseling, you probably should refer most serious problems to your university counseling office. The personnel there will be experienced with diagnosing and assessing such problems as the depth of a student's depression or alcohol problem and can often facilitate, if necessary, inpatient hospitalization for severe problems.

Do not attempt to counsel any student whom you know or suspect is contemplating suicide. Convince these students to contact their therapists or, if they have none, the counseling center. Encourage them to call for an appointment from your office. If necessary, make the call yourself to see if there will be someone available if you walk the student there (to ensure that he or she actually arrives).

Be very cautious about engaging in an ongoing counseling relationship with any student who is also enrolled in one of your classes. Mental health professionals discourage "dual relationships" because of the confusion that can result. A dual relationship exists anytime an educator takes on additional roles (e.g., sexual partner, friend, employer, therapist). For instance, after a young Mexican American woman has disclosed an absolutely horrific experience of growing up with a schizophrenic father, an emotionally distant mother, and rape by a stepbrother, are you going to be able to grade her literature essay as objectively as you will the essays of your other students, about whom you know nothing?

An even more serious problem is that if you give the young Mexican American woman a low grade, will she feel rejected? Could she conclude that it might not be safe to confide anything else in you? Will she fail to keep her next counseling session? How would you respond if you believe she desperately needs your counseling but she refuses to participate and possibly quits coming to class? What if she wants to continue in counseling and makes you promise not to reveal her big secret—that she's been thinking about suicide? Alternatively, what if her secret is that she's planning on taking harmful revenge on her stepbrother or former boyfriend?

Counseling students can get very sticky. Your intentions may be honorable, but emotionally disturbed students may confuse your interest in helping with sexual interest and feel spurned when you clarify matters. Counseling also goes on behind closed doors, and you might possibly be accused of inappropriate touching or sexual harassment, having no witnesses to come to your defense. Even if that doesn't happen, counseling a student might lead to your learning some things that you'd just as soon not know (e.g., that the sexual partner who treated your student so callously is a colleague in the same department).

Because of the difficulty in being objective once you have insight into students' problems and personal lives, many faculty have a policy of never attempting to counsel students. Not only is counseling a somewhat risky business if one isn't professionally trained but it can also be very time consuming when an exceptionally "needy" student sees you as his or her lifeline and stops by or calls three or four times a week for that pep talk or boost that you provide.

Even if the relationship is not characterized as counseling with poignant and moving disclosures but is more of a friendship based on common interests (e.g., rock climbing or mountain biking) outside the class, the instructor's ability to evaluate and grade impartially may still be hindered (Congress, 1996). Be especially cautious of engaging in close friendships with students as long as they are in your classroom or as long as you have the ability to boost or thwart their academic progress.

The Angry and Hostile Student

Occasionally, you may encounter a belligerent student who feels that you "robbed" or "cheated" him or her out of a desired grade. Usually, the best thing you can do is to listen to these students and allow them to ventilate. Don't become argumentative or threaten them. Don't raise your voice, although you may feel quite angry yourself about the unfair or inaccurate accusations being made. Keep a pleasant and cooperative demeanor.

Sometimes faculty make mistakes in computing grades (e.g., transposing 58 for 85) or forget about some statement that might have been made in half-jest ("I'll drop your lowest quiz grade if you have perfect attendance at the end of the semester and if your last quiz grade is twice as high as your first"). Honest mistakes occur and when they do you should quickly rectify them. However, when it's not likely that you made a mistake, but a student is claiming something else, such as favoritism (that you graded students that you "liked" with a different set of criteria from those you didn't like or that you were unfair in some other way), then a wise course of action is to make no decision on the spot when the student is in your face and glaring, but to take notes and announce that you need some time to consider the information that the student has presented. Take a day or two to think it over—you may even want to consult with a colleague to get another opinion. Communicate your decision to the student after you've had time to consider all perspectives and possible evidence.

If that decision does not favor the student and you expect that person to be angry all over again, state the reasons behind your decision in an objective fashion. Be somewhat dispassionate and don't allow yourself to be brought into an argument. After you have rendered your decision and listened to the student's rebuttal, then conclude the meeting by informing the student of his or her alternatives, such as taking the course over again with a different instructor, filing a complaint with the department chair or dean, and so on.

There is no reason to let this meeting or conversation go on as long as the first meeting. Bring it to a conclusion by announcing, "I must go now" or "I have something else I need to attend to right now" and stand up. Don't touch the angry student or push him or her from your office. If the student is blocking the door in what you take to be a threatening manner, say as pleasantly as possible, "Excuse me, John, but I really must make a phone call" and then call someone on your floor to come to your office. Often, the presence of another person will help terminate the conversation.

When a student has a complaint that doesn't have much merit, such as "your tests are too hard," and this isn't one of your best students, sometimes it is helpful to ask the student such questions as: How many hours did you spend studying for the test? How did you study for the test? You could also ask the student to bring in his or her study notes or materials so that you can see the extent of the student's preparation. It could be that the student does not know how to prepare or has lousy notes. Your demeanor should be that of a concerned and interested problem-solver—the mystery, of course, is why the student didn't do better. The clues will likely be numerous, but don't browbeat the student; rather, let the evidence speak for itself.

To minimize episodes with angry students, be fair in your grading practices. The syllabus should clearly state the cut-offs for grades, penalties for assignments turned in late, and that kind of thing. Return phone calls and e-mails from students who want to challenge or complain about a grade. No one likes to be ignored. However, you don't have to drop everything and schedule a meeting the same day. Setting a meeting date later gives the student time to cool off.

Students Who Stalk

Very rarely do you need to be concerned about students who want to vandalize your property or hurt your person. Even so, if you teach long enough, you will likely encounter an occasional mentally ill individual. The highest rate of psychiatric disorders, almost 17 percent, is found in young adults between the ages of 18 and 44 (Reiger et al., 1988). Surveys of counseling centers at colleges and universities across the country reveal that psychopathology among college students is ubiquitous and extensive (O'Malley et al., 1990). In one situation at my university, a disturbed student threatened to kill a faculty member and an administrator when he received a failing grade and his appeal wasn't granted. It turns out that the student's family deliberately sent him to the United States in hopes that the young man would receive psychiatric assistance that was not available in his home country.

While the chances of someone threatening you with harm are very, very remote, it's best to follow the maxim of "an ounce of prevention is better than a pound of cure." There are several things you can do to protect yourself—particularly if you have already had a run-in with a student or someone has threatened you:

1. Do not list your address in the city or university phone directory.
2. Do not invite students into your home unless you know them well. (Some student might disclose your address to someone else who you would not want to know where you live. This is primarily a concern if you are presently being stalked.)
3. Do not stay late at night when there is no one or few people in your building.
4. Keep the phone number of the campus police displayed where you can see it on the telephone.
5. If someone does storm into your office and is obviously agitated, do not argue with that person. Do not try to meet force with force. Don't raise your voice, but talk calmly and softly. Sometimes allowing these persons to voice their concerns or unhappiness is enough to defuse the situation. Try to understand their position and offer empathy, if possible. Encourage the individual to sit. Don't blame the other person, ridicule, or find fault. Also, don't be excessively familiar, but show respect and maintain a professional role. If you sense that you are in danger, make an excuse to leave the room: Say that you have to get something, that you have a tickle in your throat and need a drink of water—any excuse will do as long as it is somewhat believable.
6. If you are concerned that someone may wish to harm you, plan out possible scenarios in your mind. For example, consider when you are most vulnerable and what steps you can take to protect yourself. Plan a set of emergency procedures—how you might escape or signal others if you get trapped in your office.
7. Let your colleagues and the administration know any time a student makes a threat.

8. Arrange your office furniture so that guest chairs are farthest from the door and your own chair is closest to the door. Try to position yourself so that nothing is between you and the door.
9. Buy a can of pepper spray and keep it where it can be grabbed quickly.

Most of these same steps are also applicable when there are students who don't want to harm you, but who may be romantically fixated. Perhaps in most of the cases of faculty being stalked by students (or even other faculty), the stalkers are would-be or erstwhile lovers who want nothing more than to catch sight of you, to deliver some letter or poem they've written, or to ask your opinion on some "weighty" matter. Students who are infatuated may simply want to know what your house or apartment looks like. They may have images of you reading in your study or working in the garden or jogging in a nearby park. These individuals are curious, wanting to test their notions about you and your private life. They become stalkers when their behavior is too obsessive or whenever you become uncomfortable with it. In many cases, they have erotomanic delusions that they are loved, despite receiving rather clear signals to the contrary.

Stalking is defined as willful, repeated, and malicious following or harassment (Coleman, 1997). About half of stalkers might be mentally ill. Because they tend to have been reared in physically or emotionally abusive homes, these individuals may be "needier" than others. You may have spent more time with them because you felt sorry for them. Particularly if you have been informally counseling these individuals for personal problems or difficulties, they will feel a close emotional bond. Erotomanic stalkers, however, have a rather strong delusion that you love them. Any small acts of consideration or kindness are magnified out of all proportion.

If you discover too many troubling "coincidences" of running into someone who you think is attracted to you (e.g., gifts being sent that you don't want), be clear and direct. Tell the stalker that you do not want to be followed, that you are not interested in dating or socializing with them, and clearly end it. Do not attempt to reason with them or discuss this in a detailed manner. Do not say, "But we can still be friends."

Change your patterns and daily activities so that your comings and goings are less predictable. Inform key people that you are being stalked and ask them not to give out information about you. It may be possible to obtain a restraining order against the person if his or her behavior persists. About 20 states have antistalking laws (Coleman, 1997). Talk with the campus police as well as those in your locality if you feel threatened. Do not be embarrassed to ask for help.

References and Resources

Coleman, F. L. (1997). Stalking behavior and the cycle of domestic violence. *Journal of Interpersonal Violence, 12,* 420–432.

Congress, E. P. (1996). Dual relationships in academia: Dilemmas for social work educators. *Journal of Social Work Education, 32,* 329–338.

Davis, B. G. (1993). *Tools for teaching.* San Francisco: Jossey-Bass.

Meier, M., & Long, D. D. (1998). Student disclosures in social work education. Does your program need a policy? *Journal of Baccalaureate Social Work, 4,* 27–36.

O'Malley, K., Wheeler, I., Murphey, J., O'Connell, J., & Waldo, M. (1990). Changes in levels of psychopathology being treated at college and university counseling centers. *Journal of College Student Personnel, 31,* 464–465.

Orion, D. R. (1997). *I know you really love me: A psychiatrist's journal of erotomania, stalking, and obsessive love.* New York: Dell.

Reiger, D. A., Boyd, J. H., Burke, J. D., Rae, D. S., Myers, J. K., Kramer, M., Robins, L. N., George, L. K., Karno, M., & Locke, B. Z. (1988). One-month prevalence of mental disorders in the United States. *Archives of General Psychiatry, 45,* 977–986.

Roberts, G. T., Murrell, P. H., Thomas, R. E., & Claxton, C. S. (1982). Ethical concerns for counselor educators. *Counselor Education and Supervision, 22,* 8–14.

Sawyer, R. M., Prichard, K. W., & Hostetler, K. D. (1992). *The art and politics of college teaching.* New York: Peter Lang.

Schneider, A. (1998, March 27). Insubordination and intimidation signal the end of decorum in many classrooms. *The Chronicle of Higher Education.*

Sorcinelli, M. D. (1994). Dealing with troublesome behaviors in the classroom. In K. W. Prichard & R. M. Sawyer (Eds.), *Handbook of college teaching: Theory and applications.* Westport, CT: Greenwood.

Stone, G. L., & Archer, J. (1990). College and university counseling centers in the 1990s: Challenges and limits. *The Counseling Psychologist, 18,* (4), 539–607.

Trout, P. A. (1998, July 24). Incivility in the classroom breeds "Education Lite." *The Chronicle of Higher Education.*

12

Cheating—What You Need to Know

Overview: There is quite a bit of evidence that many students cheat on a regular basis and that only a few students have never cheated (Kerkvliet & Sigmund, 1999). Cheating is a major problem in higher education, and every educator needs to (1) recognize its pervasiveness, (2) understand the conditions that might support or encourage cheating, and (3) be prepared to implement procedures and actions that can minimize the problem. This chapter discusses cheating on tests and plagiarism as well as offers advice on how to reduce these problems within the classroom.

Prevalence of Cheating

Cheating is widespread and has been increasing since the mid-1960s. McCabe and Trevino (1996) have noted that "large numbers of students have cheated since time immemorial, and they continue to do so." In a study conducted at nine medium to large state universities in 1993, 70 percent of students admitted to one or more instances of test cheating; 52 percent copied from other students, 27 percent used crib notes, 54 percent copied material without footnoting, 29 percent falsified a bibliography, and 49 percent collaborated on assignments requiring individual work. Two out of three students reported engaging in at least 1 of 14 questionable academic behaviors (McCabe & Trevino, 1996). In surveys conducted in 1990, 1992, and 1995, involving 7,000 undergraduates on 26 different campuses, almost 80 percent reported one or more incidents of cheating (Center for Academic Integrity, <www.nwu.edu/uacc/cai/research/highlights.html>).

Whitley (1998) has published a literature review of factors associated with cheating among college students. Within the 107 studies he located, 46 provided some prevalence estimates. He calculated averages of the reported rates and found that 70 percent of students reported some form of cheating, 43 percent was the mean for students who had cheated on examinations, and 47 percent admitted to plagiarism. Whitley noted that most of the studies used in his research were based on student self-reports of cheating, which may, in fact, underestimate the actual cheating rates.

The Josephson Institute of Ethics released a national survey of 20,000 middle and high schoolers in October 1998 revealing that 70 percent of high schoolers said that they had cheated "at least once" in the past 12 months; 44 percent had cheated on two or more occasions. Half (51 percent) of the seniors in high school had cheated on two or more occasions and only 27 percent said that they had never cheated <www.josephsoninstitute.org>. The problem, in other words, is serious and one that should concern every educator.

Factors Underlying Student Cheating

From his literature review, Whitley (1998) has noted these demographic characteristics: Younger and unmarried students are more likely to cheat than older and married students, and cheating is more common among students who are male, living on campus, and receiving more financial support from parents.

In terms of motivation, Whitley (1998) observed that cheating seems to be motivated by students' fear of doing poorly in a particular course, rather than by a general lack of academic ability. Further, the more pressure students reported feeling that they had to achieve high grades, the more likely they were to cheat. The greater the amount of the reward for expected success, the greater the likelihood of cheating. Also, students who perceived their workloads as being heavy and to be in greater competition for grades were more likely to cheat.

The review also found that students with favorable attitudes toward cheating were more likely to cheat than students with unfavorable attitudes. Similarly, procrastination and too much partying behavior were found to be positively related to cheating. Colleges and universities with honor codes seem to experience less cheating than institutions without honor codes. Students are more likely to cheat when they think there is relatively little risk of being caught. Whitley's review (1999) also suggested that "students who are likely to cheat are deficient in study skills and are lower in industriousness and higher in procrastination and test anxiety than students who are less likely to cheat" (pp. 261–262).

Rather than being a simple spontaneous act, the bulk of cheating appears to be planned behavior in an environment where there is no perception of strong norms or moral values opposed to cheating and when the perceived risk of cheating is low. Certainly, as Diekhoff and colleagues (1996) have pointed out, academic dishonesty may be "symptomatic of a general social and cultural malaise evident in the lack of ethical behavior in educational, political, and business arenas" (p. 501). And if that is the case, external controls must be applied because internalized controls against cheating appear to be missing.

The Ways Students Cheat

Students are a creative lot and the following examples are by no means exhaustive. Besides copying someone else's answers, probably the most common means of cheating is when students manage to smuggle in "crib notes." Important dates, notes, and formulas may be written under shirt sleeves or socks, inside the bill of baseball caps, on the backside of a tie or scarf, on watch bands, inside the tongue of an athletic shoe. Using masking tape, memos and reminders can be secreted in any item of apparel or just about any part of the body. Torn jeans offer several possibilities for hiding notes. Valuable information can be installed on pencils or even inside clear plastic pens. Then there is always the industrious student who arrives in plenty of time before the test and positions himself or herself in such a way to place notes carefully on a bulletin board, on the floor (where they can be covered by the student's shoe), or on the side of the teacher's desk itself. This practice is known as *doctoring* the classroom. Students who ask to use tape players to listen to cassettes of their favorite music to "help them concentrate" may be listening to study notes that they have prerecorded—even if the cassette is carrying the label of a commercial recording company. Programmable pocket calculators and electronic organizers can contain illegal text. Some of these devices have infrared capabilities and can share information across a classroom. Other high-tech innovations include tiny video (surveillance type) cameras hidden in a tie or other article of clothing which allows a viewer some distance away to see the exam. That confederate can call back the answers on a silent pager (Kleiner & Lord, 1999).

Low-tech methods include sign language as well as answering multiple-choice questions where one has to guess with a *c* because that letter can later be easily altered with a claim that it was incorrectly marked wrong (Kleiner & Lord, 1999). One student stole a physician's notepad and used it to write medical excuses whenever she needed to postpone an exam or qualify for make-up exams. An equally creative approach is for the student to feign a head cold and to write valuable information on tissues. Puffs Extra Thick tissues have been identified as substantial enough for this scam (Chidley, 1997).

Michael Moore (1991) has even written a guide for students *(Cheating 101: The Benefits and Fundamentals of Earning the Easy "A")* that he sells over the Internet for those who want to find ways to cheat. He calls copying from friends the "collegiate bread and butter cheating method" but then goes on to identify a number of sophisticated ruses that range from stealing or buying tests from someone who works in the professor's departmental office, to darting out with a test when the instructor is distracted and then calling and asking to take a make-up exam. Another version that might be attempted in large classes where tests are passed down long rows is for the student at the end of the line to take a copy of the test or answer sheet but not to fill it out. The student can then complete the test outside of class or fill in the computer-scan sheet in class when the instructor goes over the test—even marking a few wrong—and then claim that his or her test was never scored. Or, if the instructor has not counted the number of copies of the test, the student can hide one copy and claim that he or she never got one. This scheme can be used to get the extra copy to a friend in another section of the class, or the student could use it by signing a phony name to one test and then calling the instructor claiming to be ill and in need of a make-up exam.

Still another approach is to have a confederate or substitute take the test. Even when picture identification is required, a scheme that might be called "the sacrifice" is when one individual with a relatively good standing and one in danger of failing put each other's names on their tests. If students are allowed to bring in their own blue books, the blue books may contain contraband notes in light pencil, or full pages of notes may be slipped in between the pages. (A better practice is to have each student bring in blue books, but to deposit them on the instructor's desk, where they can be shuffled and redistributed.)

Signaling is when two or more students work out a code. For instance, tapping the top of the desk might indicate the correct answer is *d*, placing the eraser against the cheek could mean the right answer is *c*. Signals can be visual as well as auditory (e.g., foot taps or taps with the pencil).

In addition to these illegal means, students may have access to old exams from fraternity or sorority files, businesses that buy old exams, friends, family members, and so on. An article in my university's student newspaper recently revealed that two computer science undergraduates had constructed a website that allows students to access a library of examinations. It is reasonable to expect that students in most other colleges and universities are likely to have created similar websites or chat rooms to swap test information.

It doesn't pay to get lazy and reuse the same exams time after time. I once used an exam two semesters in a row, but the third semester I changed not the questions but the items in the multiple-choice response set. After handing back the graded exams, a student held up her hand because she was puzzled why question 25 was marked incorrect. I explained why *a* was the correct response, and she replied, "But *c* was right the last time." And she was the daughter of another faculty member!

Suggestions for Minimizing Cheating on Tests

According to Donald McCabe, the founding president of the Center for Academic Integrity, "Students notice when faculty trivialize cheating" (*Insight on the News,* 1998). Those who engage or want to engage in academic dishonesty gauge the instructor's vigilance, or lack of concern, in weighing the benefits of cheating against the risks. To minimize cheating in your classroom, let the students know that this behavior will not be tolerated. Because students may be of the mind that cheating is a victimless crime, give them examples of how cheating can have repercussions outside the classroom. For instance, the nursing student who "gets by with a little help from her friends" might not know how to compute the correct dose of medicine and in a real-life situation could actually harm a patient (Gaberson, 1997).

Guilt is ineffective in deterring cheaters, because they believe that cheating is a justifiable means to an end, but fear of punishment may be an effective deterrent to cheating (Diekhoff et al., 1999). However, the Diekhoff study noted that only 1.8 percent of Japanese respondents and only 2.8 percent of American respondents had ever been caught cheating in school. This is what Diekhoff and colleagues concluded in a 1996 report:

> *Our data indicate that the traditional mechanisms of social control are largely ineffective in deterring academic dishonesty. Internal controls—conscience and guilt—are weak. Informal controls, such as friends' disapproval of cheating, clearly do not exist. Cheaters know that most other students will not condemn them or report them, especially if those others are cheaters, as the majority are. As for external controls, students might respect official sanctions, but they also feel, with justification, that they will escape notice. Large and crowded classrooms, multiple-choice tests, and lack of close monitoring foster cheating and make it more difficult for cheating to be detected. (p. 500)*

To reduce cheating in your classrooms, take a proactive stance and employ these measures:

- Communicate. Make your expectations clear. Talk about the policies on cheating, the importance of doing one's own work, and the consequences and penalties for cheating. Do this the first day of class, place it in the syllabus, and mention it again immediately before distributing the test.
- Incorporate readings about ethics into class activities. (The Markkula Center for Applied Ethics at Santa Clara University

has an electronic journal, *Issues in Ethics,* that students will find very readable. Back issues can be viewed on <www.scu.edu/SCU/Centers/Ethics>.)

- Minimize copying by using alternative versions of the test (e.g., version B contains the same questions as version A, but the items have been scattered randomly). Or scramble the response set so that if *d* is the correct answer in version A, then *c* might be the correct response for the same question in version B.
- Space the students yourself, assign them to every other seat or new seats for the test, and break up any friendship clusters or groupings.
- Use a checkerboard arrangement so that students on all sides have an alternate form of the exam.
- Move students who are acting suspiciously, even in the middle of the test.
- Don't allow baseball caps, tape recorders, personal organizers, pocket calculators, or computers in class. Require students to store backpacks under desks and don't allow access to these until after the test.
- Require picture identification in large lecture classes.
- Don't give the same exam if there are multiple sections of the course or if you intend to allow make-up exams.
- Make frequent eye contact with those who are watching you. Move around. Don't sit in one place and read a book.
- Don't allow students to pass anything (e.g., erasers, pencils, calculators) back and forth.
- Attend to any suspicious behavior immediately (such as pseudo-coughing or a student pushing a sleeve or pants leg up on more than one occasion).
- Don't allow students to write in or on notebooks that they bring with them into the testing situation.
- Be wary of diversions (e.g., students who want to talk with you at length during an exam may be providing cover for someone else to cheat).
- Use essay questions along with objective test items.
- Once students leave the testing room, do not allow them to reenter.
- To check for cheating, have students leave completed tests face down on their desks. Number them and pick them up in order so that papers of suspected cheaters can be compared.

- Offer study and review sessions prior to your tests to help those students who are deficient in study skills. Make yourself available to students who desire help.
- Keep all tests in locked files; do not leave your computer or office unattended; do not store old tests longer than a year, shred or destroy old copies; do not be careless around photocopy or duplication machines.
- Don't put too much "make or break" weight on a single test.
- Use criterion-referenced grading based on students attaining identified levels of performance instead of grading "on the curve."
- Consider allowing students who do poorly on tests the opportunity to "redo" portions of it for a few extra points.
- Examine desktops during the exam for extraneous material.
- Announce that talking during an exam will be construed as cheating.
- Document all irregularities during the course of an examination.

Kerkvliet and Sigmund (1999) have empirically examined the effects of selected independent variables on the probability of cheating and have concluded the following:

- Students taught by graduate teaching assistants are 32 percent more likely to cheat than students taught by faculty.
- Writing additional test versions decreases the probability of cheating by an estimated 25 percent.
- Issuing a verbal warning at test time decreases cheating by 13 percent.
- Use of an additional proctor reduces cheating by 11 percent.

These researchers also observed that because students use a myriad of cheating devices, mere physical separation is not an effective deterrent measure. However, the authors noted that some of the faculty may not have used as much of the space as was available to them to separate students.

To reframe this problem altogether, instead of making the classroom more of a police state and heightening students' anxieties about tests, another approach is to go to collaborative testing, where students are either paired with another student or placed in small groups. Muir and Tracy (1999) claimed to have observed greater quantity and quality of student responses to items that called for solutions, performance, and open-response explanations, that achievement increased slightly, that text anxiety decreased greatly, and that students engaged in reflective thinking. The authors pointed out the advantages of this approach: It simulates real-world problem solving similar to what students will experience in the workplace, the classroom atmosphere becomes more pleasant around testing periods, and one student's deficits and strengths can complement another student with a different learning style, thus enriching the learning for both.

Of course, this approach is not without problems. Matching a talented student with a student who is not his or her equal can result in complaints about being graded on someone else's product or activities. Allowing students to select their own partners may reinforce cliques and further isolate the loners. Also, because of the time needed for discussion, fewer items (70 to 80 percent of the number usually used) can be administered with this testing procedure.

Plagiarism

Plagiarism is a form of cheating that usually occurs outside of the classroom, where it is harder to monitor; it is the use of the ideas or published work of another person without giving proper credit (Gaberson, 1997). Anytime a student is required to do library work and to write papers drawing on those resources, there is always a possibility that a student may plagiarize. Usually, the sloppy or careless students who accidently forgets to insert a citation can be distinguished from those who deliberately seek to misrepresent what they did not originate. What these students don't realize in wanting to impress us with borrowed phrases or concepts is that the sudden burst of poetic language, eloquent expression, or rapier wit (a friend of mine once coined the phrase *domesticated sexuality*) arising from an affluence of drab and dreary paragraphs is often as obtrusive as the student who enters class dressed as a Norse Viking.

Students with the money have probably always been able to hire other students to write their term papers. Even those without ready cash receive the "helpful" advice from fellow students eager to coach another on how to wow an instructor. (I remember one late-night discussion in the 1960s when my roommate was advised to use high-sounding words such as *nouveau riche* to distract from the fact that he had little content in his essay.) Today, however, the student who plagiarizes is much more likely to buy (or perhaps even take for free) a paper that he or she has downloaded from the Internet. Businesses exist to provide papers on just about any topic imaginable (see <www.schoolsucks.com>). The problem of plagiarism has, in all likelihood, become a lot worse because of the Internet. Documents, even government reports, can often be downloaded or "cut and pasted" into students' papers. The ease with which plagiarism can be executed certainly has made giant strides.

Suggestions for Minimizing Plagiarism

How can you combat the availability of papers written by others? McBurney (1996) has recommended that instead of making the assignment of a term paper and then waiting for it to be turned in, a step-by-step process should be developed for the longer writing assignments. Such a procedure might include the following steps:

1. The students discuss their topics or thesis interests with the instructor.
2. The students list the references that they will be using. (A variation of this is to have students photocopy the first page of each article or book that they will be citing.)
3. The students turn in a tentative outline or a rough draft prior to submitting the final product.
4. Where plagiarism has been a real problem, the instructor could also ask students to submit all of their drafts and notes along with their final paper.

Although there are websites that will provide first drafts with deliberate mistakes, instructors should help students understand that "given the amount of time it takes to cheat, students could devote the same amount of time to just doing the work" (Floyd, 1999).

Gibelman, Gelman, and Fast (1999) have recommended that instructors need to rethink the open-ended nature of most writing assignments. Instead of allowing students complete freedom in choosing their topics, the instructor may want to narrow the array of possibilities and to require students to integrate classroom discussion and lectures as well as assigned readings. Tom Rocklin, at the University of Iowa, has recommended that instructors not assign "generic" topics for papers, but specific concepts that arise from class discussions. He adds this final thought:

> *The plagiarist and the instructor are in an adversarial relationship. Somehow, the student has come to conclude that the goal is to "beat" the instructor, to fool the teacher. If we can convince our students that the assignments we have developed are truly for the students' benefit, they will understand that beating the assignment harms them, not the instructor.* <www.uiowa.edu/~centeach>

Assignments should also be changed from semester to semester, especially when there are multiple sections and a common syllabus. Another idea is to utilize examinations and essay-type questions as a means of checking on what students learned about their writing project.

Of course, these steps don't *prevent* plagiarism; they simply remove the impulsive temptation to cheat because of poor planning or budgeting of one's time. Several authorities have provided anecdotal evidence that this form of cheating appears to occur most often when students are working against tight deadlines. By structuring a process that requires students to work on the project over the course of the semester, there will be less pressure to produce a paper over night or over the course of a weekend.

Proactive steps to minimize plagiarism should include giving the class written examples to show specifically what constitutes plagiarism and what does not. Despite the best efforts of English 101 instructors, many students think that as long as they are not directly quoting but paraphrasing, they are protected from having to cite the original source. If you are particularly concerned about plagiarism, then leave nothing to chance and give students all the information they need about this practice. Also invite them to discuss with you before or after class any problems or questions about attribution and giving proper credit. Encourage students to bring their drafts and original sources when they bring their questions— use it as a teaching moment that will be well worth the time spent.

Last, there is a little glimmer of hope on the horizon that all the new technology that has made plagiarism so easy might also be used to combat it. Entrepreneurs (e.g., <plagiarism.com> and <plagiarism.org>) have developed software that detects sentences that match those from papers in their database. Services from such vendors as IntegriGuard are based on subscription fees that give faculty access to the service. Students send their papers to the site electronically, where the software checks and e-mails a response to the professor about sentences which "fail" the plagiarism test. Another group has developed the Intelligent Essay Assessor, which operates on a similar principle. Still another group sells software that creates a copy of a student's paper with every fifth word missing. With this approach, professors could call students into their offices who they suspect of plagiarism and ask these individuals to fill in the missing words (Guernsey, 1998). Another antiplagiarism service said to uncover even subtle dishonesty is known as the Essay Verification Engine, or EVE2 <canexus.com>.

Alschuler and Blimling (1995), in discussing why students cheat, say that the research has been summarized into two main groups: norms that sanction cheating and benefits that outweigh the costs. If students are of the opinion that "everyone else is doing it" or that "there is little or no punishment if I do get caught," cheating will be more of a problem than if there are strong disincentives and honor codes. The more you do to combat cheating and plagiarism, the less of it there will be.

References and Resources

Alschuler, A. S., & Blimling, G. S. (1995). Curbing epidemic cheating through systemic change. *College Teaching, 43,* 123–125.

Chidley, J. (1997, November 24). Tales out of school: Cheating has long been a great temptation, and the Internet makes it easier than ever. *Maclean's,* pp. 76–79.

Cizek, G. (1999). *Cheating on tests: How to do it, detect it, and prevent it.* Mahwah, NJ: Erlbaum.

Crown, D. F., & Spiller, M. S. (1998). Learning from the literature on collegiate cheating: A review of empirical research. *Journal of Business Ethics, 17,* 683–700.

Diekhoff, G. M., LaBeff, E. E., Clark, R. E., Williams, L. E., Francis, B., & Haines, V. J. (1996). College cheating: Ten years later. *Research in Higher Education, 37* (4), 487–502.

Diekhoff, G. M., LaBeff, E. E., Shinohara, K., & Yasukawa, H. (1999). College cheating in Japan and the United States. *Research in Higher Education, 40* (3), 343–353.

Floyd, B. P. (1999, August 13). Ethics center's site offers essays, case studies, and expert advise. *Chronicle of Higher Education.*

Gaberson, K. B. (1997). Academic dishonesty among nursing students. *Nursing Forum, 32* (3), 14–21.

Gibelman, M., Gelman, S. R., & Fast, J. (1999). The downside of cyberspace: Cheating made easy. *Journal of Social Work Education, 35* (3), 367–376.

Guernsey, L. (1998, December 11). Web site will check students' papers against data base to detect plagiarism. *Chronicle of Higher Education.*

Innerst, C. (1998). Students are pulling off the big cheat. *Insight on the News, 14* (9), 41.

Kerkvliet, J., & Sigmund, C. L. (1999). Can we control cheating in the classroom? *Journal of Economic Education, 30* (4), 331–343.

Kleiner, C., & Lord, M. (1999, November 22). The cheating game. *U.S. News & World Report, 127* (20), 55–56, 57, 61–64, 66.

McBurney, D. (1996). Cheating: Preventing and dealing with academic dishonesty. *APS Observer,* 32–35.

McCabe, D. L., & Trevino, L. K. (1996). What we know about cheating in college. *Change, 28,* 28–33.

McKeachie, W. J. (1999). *McKeachie's teaching tips: Strategies, research, and theory for college and university teachers.* Boston: Houghton Mifflin.

Moore, M. (1991). *Cheating 101: The benefits and fundamentals of earning the easy "A."* Hopewell, NJ: Moore Publishing.

Muir, S. P., & Tracy, D. M. (1999). Collaborative essay testing: Just try it! *College Teaching, 47* (1), 33–35.

Whitley, B. E. (1998). Factors associated with cheating among college students: A review. *Research in Higher Education, 39* (3), 235–274.

Humor in the Classroom

Overview: Humor is said to have a number of benefits. It improves morale by suggesting things could always be worse, relieves stress and reduces anxiety, provokes creative thought, and can unite individuals in a common bond (Wallinger, 1997). Humor works, in part, because of the interaction between the joke teller and the audience.

In attempting humor, the presenter takes some risk, exposes a playful dimension, and usually comes across as being more amiable. Jokes "lighten" topics and may even prolong the attention span of students (Sev'er & Ungar, 1997). The ability to make others laugh is a wonderful gift—that is, of course, as long as the jokes don't offend anyone. What is fair game? Lawyer jokes? And what topics are off limits? When is humor inappropriate? This chapter provides a quick reference of dos and don'ts.

The Classroom Devoid of Humor

Everone likes to laugh. Laughing breaks tension and reduces stress as well as helps people feel more connected with those around them. Victor Borge once said, "Laughter is the shortest distance between two people." Most successful public speakers know that starting with a funny story or joke is often a very effective mechanism for warming up an audience and converting them from being slightly interested to whetting their appetites for the presenter's material. Spaced throughout a lecture, humor can maintain attention and interest. The trick, of course, is to find the "right" story or cartoon to put on the overhead transparency.

If you find yourself asking, "But is humor really appropriate in the classroom?" you need only to think back to the worst lectures, the worst speakers you can recall. The odds are that not many of them attempted to keep your interest by occasionally injecting a joke or relating an amusing story. This is not to say that you have to be a stand-up comic or wear a clown suit to class. However, if you have even a slight sense of humor, you may find that your students will appreciate you sharing it with them. They want to understand you as a person, to discover your slant on life—to figure out if you are a real human being or someone whose obsession is reshelving out-of-order books in the library. What strikes you as funny? Are you amused or saddened when 18 out of 25 students fail their mid-term exams? Your sense of humor (or lack of it) can be *very* important to certain audiences.

Some evidence (cited in Powell & Andresen, 1985) shows that material containing humorous elements resulted in the greatest retention of information—possibly by reducing boredom. Humor is an important consideration for faculty, but probably no more important than promptness in returning papers and tests, fairness, knowing students by their names, creating an intellectually alive classroom, and so forth. Instructors are cautioned to avoid trying too hard to be humorous. Instead, strive to be natural and real. Be alert to humorous material that might be of interest to the class without feeling compelled to toss out 10 zany one-liners at each meeting. If too much effort is made to be funny (particularly if the jokes fall flat), the whole endeavor can backfire and the instructor's credibility can be jeopardized.

A Taxonomy of Humor

Neuliep (1991) has noted that secondary teachers use humor to make learning fun and as a way to keep the class from becoming too formal—not as a pedagogical strategy for increasing student comprehension or learning. When humor is viewed this way, then it is possible to conceive of different types of humor. The following listing derives from Neuliep (1991). I am not, by any means, suggesting that all of these forms of humor are appropriate in the classroom.

What can be seen, however, is that instructors need not think narrowly—that humor is only found in joke telling, for instance. There are many other activities that students might find amusing.

Types of Humor

- Nonverbal
    affect display (making a funny face)
    kinesic humor (physical, bodily humor)
- External source
    historical incident
    third-party humor (cartoon, funny object)
    natural phenomena (e.g., releasing the air out of a balloon and letting it fly around the room to demonstrate a physics principle)
- Untargeted humor
    joke telling
    punning
    awkward comparisons/incongruities ("what's wrong with this picture?")
    tongue-in-cheek, facetious humor (e.g., clumsy analogies)
- Student-targeted humor
    friendly insult
    teasing
    student role-play
- Teacher-targeted humor
    self-deprecation
    self-disclosure (e.g., embarrassing situation)
    teacher role-play

Self-Deprecating Humor

Ron Berk (1998), author of *Professors Are from Mars, Students Are from Snickers* and a self-proclaimed student of humor, notes that self-effacing humor is probably the safest and least offensive type to use in the classroom. It communicates to students that, despite your title or graduate degrees, you recognize your fallibility, your humanness. Students receive this type of humor well because the effort shows your interest in trying to reduce the status/power differential and to reach them on their level. On the other hand, if you are into self-aggrandizement, then self-effacing humor may not be your cup of tea.

Ethnicity, Gender, and Politically Incorrect Jokes

One of the surest ways to get into trouble by using humor is to tell a joke that draws on offensive stereotypes or denigrates persons because of their gender, sexual orientation, national origin, religion, age, or race. Although it may strike you as the funniest joke you ever heard in your life, don't share any jokes or humorous stories that have the slightest possibility of offending someone. The only exception to this rule is if you are a clearly identified member in good standing of that particular subgroup. For instance, if you are a Catholic priest with the last name of O'Sullivan, then it is probably permissible to poke fun at the Irish or other Catholic priests. If you are a blonde, it's okay to tell "blonde jokes."

Oftentimes, humor is about power differentials. Faculty need to be sensitive to the fact that gender-based humor can easily offend because it plays on status differences. This is what Sev'er and Ungar (1997) have noted: "Increasingly, gender-based humor is seen as a manifestation of power imbalances between men and women, which in turn helps to solidify and perpetuate that power disparity. Feminists argue that men define reality for both men and women in work and in leisure" (p. 88).

Don't attempt to become too familiar with your students by using self-effacing humor dealing with your sexual successes or failures. The class will *not* want to know if you "scored" last weekend or how many weeks you've been celibate because your lover moved out. Although they might discuss amongst themselves whether you are married or dating (particularly if they run into you at an off-campus bar), they will regard any mention of your sexual life as creepy.

Similarly, you may find it hilarious that you went into the restroom this morning and discovered, after a few nervous moments, that your boxer shorts were on backwards, but underwear and restroom material runs a high risk of being offensive. Most things that we do in private have no place being mentioned in the college classroom as material for a joke. The exception here would be if that private behavior were investigated or studied as a subject. For instance, if you are running a graduate seminar on sexual addiction, then you might be able to get away with relating humor at the expense of nationally prominent characters who get caught lying about their activities and then want to squabble over the definition of *sexual intercourse*. Similarly, "sick" jokes (e.g., "dead baby jokes") and attempts to make fun of racial tensions may not be viewed in a humorous light by all college students.

Screen your efforts at humor by thinking about how the joke or humorous line could be interpreted by someone who is not a member of your ethnic group, gender, or other "insider" group. Some remarks are truly "barbs" that arise from anger, frustration, or hostility and should not be aired publicly. Never *embarrass* or *ridicule* a student to entertain the class. Such attempts at humor are inappropriate in the classroom and work against "a feeling of camaraderie that permits them to endure difficult times and appreciate the talents and diversity of others" (Wallinger, 1997, p. 29).

Sarcasm

Sarcasm is defined by the dictionary as "a sharply mocking or contemptuous remark, typically utilizing statements or implications pointedly opposite." An example of this might be handing a test with a score of 30 on it back to a student and remarking, "Well, Mr. Jones, once more you gave it your best" or "Thank you, Mr. Jones, for deciding to spend next semester with me again. The third time is the charm, they say."

Any time you try to make the class laugh at someone else's expense, students may perceive this as an attack on that individual. And since none of us want to be attacked, you'll lose any student support—even if Mr. Jones is loud and obnoxious and the whole class was hoping he would fail in retaliation for his snoring during your lectures.

Sarcasm is also a form of emotional abuse, because it can be quite hurtful. Imagine waiting in line behind an overweight student dropping coins in a vending machine. She's already purchased package after package of chips and cookies, and now she's delaying you to the point of making you late for an appointment, and yet she fishes around in her backpack for still another quarter. If you are slender and have never had a problem with your weight, the remark, "Dieting again, Sue?" may seem wickedly funny—but it is more wicked than funny and is an example of a barbed remark. That's the problem with sarcasm and ridicule—it's secret aim is to wound, not to bring joy.

Similarly, it is best to be very cautious with teasing and "friendly insults." Most of us don't like to be teased, insulted, or made to bear the brunt of a repeated joke. The best advice would be to avoid this type of humor and to focus on the "safer" varieties (e.g., cartoons, natural phenomena, historical incidents, etc.).

What to Do When Someone Takes Offense

Because we all wear cultural lenses that keep us from fully knowing the other cultures around us, it is not always possible to anticipate ahead of time which statements or remarks that we intend to be humorous may be experienced by someone else as a "slam." What might pass for humor between close friends doesn't always come across in the same way in the classroom.

About the only thing you can do when a student takes offense with one of your attempts at humor is to apologize. Don't try to prove that you are really a sensitive person or that you have friends who are_____(fill in the blank). Say that you are sorry. Be matter-of-fact; don't draw it out—it's not necessary to grovel.

If this incident was viewed as a particularly serious offense by several students, then you might want to consider eliminating jokes or off-the-cuff remarks from your presentation, because there are, apparently, some holes in your knowledge about what students regard as being disrespectful or tasteless. Most classes have a good sense of humor and appreciate even attempts that fall flat. They may groan or bring in copies of their favorite jokes for you, but they won't complain when they understand that you're not trying to "put anyone down" but to sweeten the lecture by making it more interesting. Other classes, however, won't find anything you say funny, and so there's not much point in trying with such a group.

Humor Resources

The Internet offers a rich source of humorous material on every possible problem, characteristic, or situation. Large bookstores often have sections for humor books. Additionally, there are magazines and journals to which you may want to subscribe. A partial listing of these is as follows:

Humor Digest

Annals of Improbable Research (formerly the *Journal of Irreproducible Results*)

Journal of Polymorphous Perversity

Stitches: The Journal of Medical Humor

Another thing you can do is to start a clipping file for every time you find a one-liner, cartoon, or useable joke. *Reader's Digest* is also a good source of low-risk anecdotes that you might be able to adapt. The best humor is that which doesn't seem forced, but helps to make or demonstrate an educational point. In other words, the humor needs to be relevant to concerns, issues, or topics being discussed or of interest to those in your classroom.

References and Resources

Berk, R. (1998). *Professors are from Mars, students are from Snickers.* Madison, WI: Mendota Press.

Neuliep, J. W. (1991). An examination of the content of high school teachers' humor in the classroom and development of an inductively derived taxonomy of classroom humor. *Communication Education, 40* (4), 343–355.

Powell, J. P., & Andresen, L. W. (1985). Humour and teaching in higher education. *Studies in Higher Education, 10,* 79–90.

Sev'er, A., & Ungar, S. (1997). No laughing matter: Boundaries of gender-based humor in the classroom. *Journal of Higher Education, 68* (1), 87–105.

Wallinger, L. M. (1997). Don't smile before Christmas: The role of humor in education. *NASSP Bulletin, 81,* 27–34.

14

Improving Teaching Performance

JULIE VARGAS

Overview: The teaching skills of faculty in most institutions of higher learning in this country are commonly assessed with student ratings. Unfortunately, this form of evaluation may not be all that helpful (for reasons that are fully explained) for instructors who sincerely want to become better teachers. This is not to say that student opinions are a waste of time—simply that there are many other ways to obtain information about what is actually occurring in the classroom. This chapter discusses a variety of other approaches that inform about one's teaching technique. A heavy emphasis is placed not on the teacher's behavior, but on assessment approaches that focus on student performance—the most accurate way to gauge instructional impact.

My first semester teaching at the university level, I gave a lecture on writing behavioral objectives, complete with transparency slides, lots of examples, and even some practice for students to pick out the best from a list of objectives. The students listened attentively and nodded as I made major points. Their assignment, logically enough, was to write behavioral objectives for a class they might some day teach. I went home happy that I had taught well. Imagine my surprise, then, when looking at the objectives they handed in, to find that most of the students' objectives were not behavioral at all!

Teaching is not presenting—although that is what most people think, even those who should know better. At the beginning of an undergraduate class of over 200 education majors at West Virginia University, students were asked to teach a five-minute lesson on a topic of their choice. All but one student talked the entire five minutes. The sole student who asked for student responses, it turned out, was an older student who had teaching experience.

Not only novices think of teaching as equivalent to presenting. The educational establishment assumes that teachers will be lecturing. For example, in summarizing "over 10,000" studies on teaching effectiveness, Seldin (1991) wrote, "Briefly, these findings indicate that effective teachers are masters of their subject, can organize and emphasize, can clarify ideas and point out relationships, can motivate students, and are reasonable, open, concerned and imaginative human beings" (p. 1). Except for "motivating students," *none* of the characteristics even mentions students! The format in which an individual "can organize and emphasize" or "clarify ideas and point out relationships" is assumed to be the lecture. Seldin does not mean to ignore student learning, as the rest of his book shows, but his summary of effective teachers reveals the pervasiveness of the conception of teaching as lecturing.

No one-to-one correspondence between quality of lecturing and quality of student learning exists. If it did, all students who attended the same lecture would perform equivalently on tests on the material. Teaching is much more than explaining and demonstrating, even clearly. "The essence of teaching is the creation of situations in which appropriate learning occurs; shaping those situations is what successful teachers have learned to do effectively" (Menges, 1990, p. 107). Menges has pointed out that evaluation of teaching is done for a variety of purposes, including accreditation of institutions, decisions about hiring, promotion and tenure, as well as improving teaching. The evaluation methods commonly used for promotion and tenure or for awards and bonuses are summative, norm-referenced, and indirect measures of teaching. They give the *opinions* of students or colleagues about teaching quality. They cannot tell you how the discussion groups you introduced or the exercises you redesigned affected your students' learning. To assess teaching for the purpose of improving your teaching, Menges has recommended that *you* take charge of the information. Or, as Cross (1990) put it, "The role of feedback in the assessment-for-improvement model is to provide a continuous flow of information that is useful in shaping the quality of teaching of learning while it is in process. This is generally referred to as formative evaluation, and feedback is most effective if it is not made public and if it emphasizes competencies instead of comparisons" (p. 124). Cross has recommended that classroom research directly measures the impact on student performance of instructional procedures. Other sources of information, however, are quite useful in informing about your classroom efforts and providing ideas for improving your instructional style.

**Sources of Information to Improve
Teaching Discussed in This Chapter**

Indirect Sources (often documented in portfolios along with direct sources)

- Student ratings of instruction
- Videotapes of your teaching
- Critiques by colleagues or supervisors
- Seminars and workshops on improving teaching
- Books or articles on improving teaching

Direct Sources (information on student performance)

- Lecture fill-in sheets
- Response cards or electronic devices
- Quizzes at the end of lectures
- "No-name" quizzes
- Temporary pairs or groups
- Short, timed quizzes
- Pretest-posttest differences
- Quizzes over the World Wide Web
- E-mail and list serves
- Bulletin boards and chat rooms
- Follow-ups of graduates

Student Ratings of Instruction

Student ratings consist of a series of questions asking students how they feel about the instruction they received using such items as the following:[1]

	NA	Poor	Fair	Satisfactory	Good	Excellent
In general, this instructor's teaching was	—	—	—	—	—	—
The respect the instructor showed toward individual students was	—	—	—	—	—	—

Student ratings of instruction have received a boost from the increased competition for students brought about by the demographics of the 1990s. Colleges and universities increasingly rely on tuition as a source of income. Nationally, only about 63 percent of entering students complete college in five years (USDE, 1996), and each student lost is dollars lost, so retaining students is often an administrative priority.

Students are thus increasingly seen as consumers, and their satisfaction is important to university officials. At my state university, we are continually told, "Students are our customers." In fact, students are only an intermediary. Our actual "customers" are the societies for which we are preparing our students. States do not fund their universities to give students enjoyable, recreational experiences, but rather to produce adults who contribute to society both professionally and personally. Similarly, parents do not pay tuition for their offspring to be entertained for four or five years, but rather so that they can become productive adults. (Of course, you do want students to enjoy their courses, if for no other reason than it may help them complete their degrees, but the main purpose of college is education.)

When university officials judge success by enrollment figures and graduation rates, long-term societal goals get short shrift compared with keeping students happy. Student ratings feed into short-term goals of "satisfying students" and have become a standard way to evaluate faculty—serving the purposes of administrators who must judge faculty for promotion and tenure decisions or for bonuses or awards. When faculty are evaluated on what students say about their courses, they, too, become interested in keeping students happy. Unfortunately, although these evaluations can provide instructors with some interesting information (mainly in the open-ended comments sections), research does not support their helpfulness for improving teaching practices.

Drawbacks of Student Ratings for Improving Teaching

Extensive research has been conducted on student evaluations. What the scores represent, however, is still being debated. An early study looked at how lecturers are rated (Naftulin, Ware, & Donnelly, 1972). In particular, this study wanted to see whether a suitably distinguished-looking actor could get a good rating giving a lecture whose content was "irrelevant, conflicting, and meaningless" but whose delivery was enthusiastic, full of gestures, and sprinkled with humor. The study took place at a teacher training conference. The actor, after being introduced as Dr. Myron L. Fox, addressed an audience of psychiatrists, psychologists, and social worker educators on "Mathematical Game Theory as Applied to Physical Education." The lecture was videotaped and shown later to two other groups, the last of which consisted of educators and administrators. All groups rated Dr. Fox highly on a seven-question anonymous questionnaire. They overwhelmingly felt that Dr. Fox "seemed interested in his subject," "presented his material in a well organized form," and "used enough examples to clarify his material." But they had learned nothing. The material was total nonsense. Yet responses to Dr. Fox's lecture were so positive that one respondent even answered "yes" to the question, "Have you read any of this speaker's publications?" In another, more recent study, a professor teaching developmental psychology substantially improved his ratings (as advised by a media consultant) by adding more hand gestures, varying the tone of his voice, and trying generally to be more exuberant (Wilson, 1998).

In addition to impressive lecturing, what else affects ratings? A series of studies in the 1970s manipulated student grades and observed the effect on student ratings of instructors. In a recent summary of this research, Greenwald (1997) concluded that "the hypothesis that grading leniency-strictness affects ratings...has been supported with some clarity in virtually all published experimental tests. Although the conclusions of these experiments have been questioned by critics, those conclusions have not been empirically refuted" (p. 1183). Other aspects that have been shown to have an impact on ratings include size of class, interest of students in the topics, and a number of other aspects only tangentially related to quality of instruction.

The conclusions from this research suggest that to get good ratings, it helps to (1) grade easily, (2) talk and gesture enthusiastically, and (3) teach small elective courses. Thus, while students may report how much they *feel* they learned in a course, totally irrelevant factors enter into rankings. Even bringing donuts, wearing a clown suit, or meeting students after class for pizza have been offered as ways to improve ratings. Telling a few jokes or bringing food does not subvert the goals of education, but "dumbing down" of courses does. In fact, the average number of hours that college freshmen reported spending per week on homework their last year in high school has declined (Astin et al., 1997). Grade "inflation" has also occurred (Farley, 1995). More students get a grade of A and fewer earn lower grades now than 10 years ago. If the As reflect improved mastery, students are better equipped to contribute to society. If, however, they reflect decreasing standards for an A, the effect on the future is not so bright. Certainly, student evaluations discourage requiring *more* work and setting *higher* standards than your colleagues, particularly for untenured faculty who need good rankings for tenure.

In an article supporting the validity of student evaluations as a measure of quality of teaching, Marsh and Roche (1997) quoted a study that followed 195 teachers over a 13-year period and found "no systematic changes in any of the student rating of Educational Quality factors over that period" (p. 1188). They present this as evidence for the validity of student evaluations, showing that age and years of teaching experience do not significantly affect ratings. However, this same information can also be interpreted very differently: The student evaluations didn't help the teachers improve their teaching; ratings did not improve. There are three possible explanations: Either the ratings did not reflect quality of teaching, or the ratings did not help the teachers to improve, or both. I vote for both. Regardless, you will no doubt experience student evaluations during your career, so you might as well make the best use of them as you can. The next section will tell you how to do this.

Note: Five articles on student evaluations of faculty appeared in a 1997 issue of *American Psychologist.* Those interested in this topic might want to consult:

d'Apollonia, S., & Abrami, P. C. (1997). Navigating student ratings of instruction. *American Psychologist, 52* (11), 1198–1208.

Greenwald, A. G. (1997). Validity concerns and usefulness of student ratings of instruction. *American Psychologist, 52* (11), 1182–1186.

Greenwald, A. G., & Gillmore, G. M. (1997). Grading leniency is a removable contaminant of student ratings. *American Psychologist, 52* (11), 1209–1217.

Marsh, H. W., & Roche, L. A. (1997). Making students' evaluations of teaching effectiveness effective: The critical issues of validity, bias, and utility. *American Psychologist, 52* (11), 1187–1197.

McKeachie, W. J. (1997). Student ratings: The validity of use. *American Psychologist, 52* (11), 1218–1225.

Using Student Ratings Constructively

Reading your student ratings can be traumatic. My first year of teaching, I was so anxious about my evaluations that I took them home unopened and locked myself in the bathroom before I looked inside the package. I did not find the ratings that compared me with my peers useful, though it was nice to see that they were generally positive. The open-ended comments, however, were informative. The class was a required course with about 30 students in it. At the very back, two students, both older that I, had whispered back and forth to each other more or less throughout the whole semester. It had displeased me, but, for the most part, I had just ignored those two students. From the comments on my student evaluations, however, the chit-chat clearly had bothered my students a great deal. "I wouldn't stand for the chatting at the back of the class," one student wrote, and several others made similar comments. Without these student evaluations, I would never have found out how aversive it was for students to hear talking during a lecture. It changed my behavior completely. From then on, I would pause until the students hushed, or would politely say, "It's hard for others to hear when you're talking," or some such comment to quiet the class. In one persistent case, I asked the students to remain after class and explained to them that their talking was bothering others. That was all that was needed. (By the way, I strongly recommend talking to students about inappropriate behavior *after* class, never in front of other students. Not embarrassing fellow students is a large part of what students identify as "treating students with respect.") In general, I have found the students' open comments more useful than the multiple-choice ratings. One needs to pay attention when comments are consistent.

Often, you will find that there is little consistency in students' remarks. Some aspect of your course that one student loves, another will hate. For instance, as part of a research course one semester, I gave my students flash cards on basic terms. In about equal proportions, students singled out the flash cards as particularly helpful and as something to drop.

In cases where comments are diametrically opposed, you must evaluate activities on other criteria, or try to improve the way the activities are conducted, or, if feasible, offer alternative ways to meet the objectives. Sometimes it is necessary to get the "kinks" out of a new technique before deciding to keep or abandon it. Even then, instructors should not be excessively concerned with students' preferences. It wouldn't make sense, for example, to discard Chemistry Lab just because several students "hated lab." In general, the standard university student evaluations can be expected to tell you what students like and do not like, but they will not be of much use to you for improving the quality of your teaching.

You can, of course, make your own feedback questionnaires to solicit student opinions. This allows you to control both the questions and the use of the results. Secure in the knowledge that only you will see what students write, you can ask questions designed to solicit critical comments that you might not want in your teaching portfolio. You can address specifics of your instructional procedures that do not appear on standard questionnaires. Furthermore, you do not need to wait until the end of a semester before giving a questionnaire or asking students which of two alternatives (both acceptable to you) they prefer. These questionnaires can be given as formative evaluation—that is, to help shape the teaching process as it occurs—rather than only as summative evaluation at the end of the term.

There are data that suggest that students appreciate courses in which they feel they learn a lot. One research study found that students evaluated "tough" courses more highly than "easy" ones (Marsh & Roche, 1997, p. 1191). That seems contradictory to the research reporting that raising grades raised evaluations and lowering grades lowered evaluations. In reality, the two are not contradictory. The research that, for experimental purposes, raised and lowered grades given to students in order to see the effect on their ratings, did so at the very end of the semester. All teaching had been completed. The differences found, therefore, did not reflect differences in how much students felt they had learned; rather, they reflected only the grades they were assigned. You can understand this by considering, if you will, two As you received in your educational career. Which one do you feel best about—the one that you got easily or the one you had to work hard for? In general, students find it more personally rewarding to get an A in a course with difficult material or standards that challenged them than the "guaranteed" A in a "gut" course. High standards are not detrimental to good evaluations as long as students are able to reach your expectations.

Student ratings will tell you what students like and dislike, but they are only indirect measures of teaching. They cannot tell you what to do to improve students' performance on the concepts, principles, problem-solving strategies, and creative skills needed for competence in a field. In addition to these ratings, there are other indirect sources you can use.

Other Indirect Sources of Information for Improving Teaching

In addition to student opinions, you can solicit feedback from colleagues or administrators, or you can serve as your own reviewer by watching yourself on videotape.

Videotaping Your Teaching

Videotapes provide a unique kind of feedback—seeing yourself as others do. They thus alert you to both positive and negative aspects of your classroom style, which is a first step in making improvements in that aspect of your classroom performance. Most colleges and universities will arrange to videotape one or more of your classes if requested or you can ask a colleague or student. If you decide to go this route, choose a typical class and make sure the camera operator includes shots of your students as well as of you.

In addition to increasing your self-awareness, videotapes make it possible to quantify data about your performance. For example, if you are interested in increasing student participation during discussions, you might check the number of positive versus critical remarks you make when students respond. Or count the number of open-ended questions you ask compared to questions that are answered with a simple "yes" or "no." You might also be interested in "pause" time, since research shows that teachers who wait after asking a question get better performance from students than teachers who fill in the silence with hints or by turning to a specific student to respond.

Videotapes can document improvement over time—both your improvement and the response of your students—and are useful to include in a teaching portfolio (discussed later) when coming up for promotion or tenure. Also, videotapes provide a vehicle for soliciting suggestions from colleagues or administrators. Asking others to critique a videotaped performance has the advantage of being able to replay specific sections for analysis. But even without videotaping, you can draw on the expertise of others to help improve your teaching.

Critiques by Colleagues or Supervisors

A critique by a colleague or administrator may or may not be helpful. Those critiquing usually suggest what they themselves do, which may or may not be effective or fit your teaching style. Still, colleagues often have good suggestions based on their own experiences. They may be able to spot problem areas and may offer simple suggestions for improvement. For example, if a colleague visiting your class notes that you are not getting many students responding to questions, he or she might suggest asking each student to jot down an answer on paper first, or having students pair up and answer to each other before answering in front of everybody. As a new instructor, you may not have realized that these are simple ways to get all students involved.

When trying some new strategy, you might ask around to see if anyone else has tried something similar. Years ago, I was part of a teaching team of newly hired instructors who decided to include some self-pacing in a required undergraduate course. To complete the course, students had to pass 10 multiple-choice quizzes (in addition to other assignments that were not self-paced). Each week, 10 forms of the test were made up by drawing from a large pool of items, and students could take them at any time, from 9:00 A.M. until 5:00 P.M. six days a week in the learning center. Naively, our team did not set any deadlines. Unfortunately, most of the 500 students put off taking the quizzes until the last two weeks of class, resulting in a colossal jam in the learning center. Roughly 200 students failed the course. Needless to say, we would have benefited from advice about giving bonus points for early completion, a procedure that eliminated the problem in subsequent semesters. Colleagues or administrators who have experience with a procedure are a valuable source of information on how to make it work. If you plan, say, to incorporate e-mail interactions with students into your courses, ask someone who has done it first. That way, you can set up procedures to avoid the onslaught of extra work that such a simple idea may produce, while still maintaining the benefits.

A technique developed by Joseph Clark (Redmond & Clark, 1982), called the *Small Group Instructional Diagnosis,* involves a colleague who comes into the classroom (the instructor is absent) to conduct a brief survey. The colleague might ask such questions as: How is the course going? How could it be improved? What's not working so well? Students discuss these questions in small groups and the consensus from each group is then reported to the consultant/colleague. This feedback is shared with the instructor without any reference to individual students. The instructor may then decide to clarify with the class any misunderstandings or to make any needed midpoint adjustments.

Colleagues who have taught for a number of years are usually willing to meet with junior faculty and help in identifying good textbooks or improving a syllabus or exercises. Most will share their own materials or give feedback on materials you have designed if you meet with them. However, do not just hand over materials for a colleague or administrator to "look over." You will get better feedback if you request a meeting and point out the sections or portions where you most desire their comments and impressions. If you do ask a colleague to critique your teaching materials or classroom performance, be sure to document the date and course. Evidence of steps taken to improve one's teaching can strengthen your teaching portfolio and shows a serious commitment to that part of academia. In addition to consulting personnel within your university, seminars or workshops can be of help.

Seminars and Workshops on Improving Teaching

For faculty involved in committee work, teaching, research, writing, and service, there are never enough hours in a day. Thus, it might be tempting to ignore opportunities to attend workshops and seminars on teaching offered on your campus or within an easy commute. Not only will these sessions help you to become more effective, but they may also help you to save time. Take today's rapid pace in computer technology, for instance. No one can keep up with all of the advances on top of a busy professional career. Yet, software programs are appearing daily that can save you time; you may find it useful, for example, to learn how to use spreadsheets to calculate grades.

Professional development workshops can not only alert you to how to use new programs but also to resources you did not know that your institution provided. There may be an office that will create instructional webpages for you, thus saving you time and frustration when students miss class. Similarly, you may learn about new search engines, library resources, test-making programs, and presentation software, as well as receive suggestions on improving your teaching.

Conventions are also an excellent source of new ideas. The 1999 meeting of the honorary society, Sigma Xi, for example, had a full day of talks and posters on using "inquiry learning" to improve undergraduate science education. Whenever you attend a workshop or seminar, be sure to record it in your teaching portfolio or dossier. Also, try to evaluate the effectiveness of any new techniques that you attempt.

Documenting Teaching Quality via a Teaching Portfolio or Dossier

Assembling a teaching portfolio provides documentation for annual assessment by peers, for promotion or tenure, or for merit pay and other awards. Thus, it mainly serves administrative purposes. However, the process of assembling documentation requires you to spend time reflecting on your teaching goals, and lends itself to the recording of effective teaching strategies.

One of the main advocates of teaching portfolios, Peter Seldin, provides a list of 30 items that might be included, summarized under three headings: "material from oneself," "material from others," and the "products of good teaching" (Seldin, 1991, pp. 9–12). The first two sections contain indirect data on teaching, such as teaching assignments, advising, teaching philosophy, goals, documentation of steps taken to improve teaching, summaries of student ratings, peer and chairperson comments, and comments from advisees. Section two could include invitations to speak about teaching and videotapes of your teaching. Here, too, you would include letters from alumni or colleagues that make statements about your teaching, advising, or other contributions.

Seldin's third section contains only the direct measures of teaching effectiveness and those most useful for improving instruction: "Student scores . . . possibly before and after a course as evidence of student learning"; sample student products such as essays, reports, creative products, or papers; and information about conference presentations or publications by students. Data on the numbers of your students pursuing advanced degrees or even choosing your field as a major or career may reflect on aspects of your teaching not revealed in other documents.

One word of caution: Check out your institution's evaluation procedures before counting on the impact of anything you supply for peer review. Occasionally, submitting material not requested can backfire. Peers doing the judging may not like having to look at portfolios or videos, and they may resist the idea of including student products or test score gains along with student ratings of courses, lest they become requirements for everyone. Having a departmental agreement on documentation prior to evaluation time will help head off resentment toward dossiers or data on student performance as measures of teaching performance. Although videos, documentation of peer visits, summaries of syllabus reviews, sessions on teaching attended, student performance and gains, and other evidence of effectiveness are becoming more common, a survey conducted back in 1966 indicated that, for evaluating teaching performance, 62 percent of the responding 110 deans said their colleges considered colleague opinion. In 35 percent of the colleges, informal student opinion was used as evidence. Only 2 percent used classroom visits and even fewer did any long-term follow-up to assess teaching competence (Lewis, 1998, p. 23). Even if your department does not consider student outcome data as described here, you ought to look at student performance to see the impact of your course procedures on student achievement. This shifts the whole process from a focus on instructor activities to a focus on your students' behavior.

Improving Teaching through Feedback on Student Performance

It rarely occurs to faculty to examine the impact of their teaching procedures by trying something and then assessing its effect on student performance. But to improve instruction, you must do just that. To see the impact of a teaching procedure, you must first decide on the skills your students need to learn, then decide how to measure those competencies. Whatever you base grades on is your operational definition of course objectives. If problem solving and creative behaviors are important, they, as well as basic terms and concepts, need to be assessed. Next, to see what students have learned, you must know the skills students already have when they entered your course; otherwise, you cannot distinguish between what they have learned from what they already knew. Finally, try out the teaching activity and assess student improvement. This may seem overwhelming to someone used to large lecture classes where the only feedback on student performance comes from a midterm and final. Designing effective instruction is not simple. Corporations spend millions of dollars to produce a single instructional module. Colleges and universities are increasingly taking a team approach to instructional development because of the complexity of designing effective instruction, particularly now that web-based components are becoming common. Most courses, however, are still designed and run by an individual, perhaps with graduate assistant help for labs or sections. Fortunately, if you teach a course repeatedly, you can improve it over time. The key is to get feedback on the contribution of each component to student mastery of critical skills.

There are many simple ways to increase the amount of feedback you can get on your students' mastery of course objectives, and all of them also help student learning. The rest of this chapter discusses ways to sample student repertoires in order to keep in touch with your students' progress, thus enabling you to adjust what you do to help them, or to make your next class better. The methods are not offered as examples of ideal instructional design, but rather as approximations that are feasible within college and university settings.

First of all, you must get feedback on student progress more often than twice a semester. Lest you visualize late nights grading stacks of papers, note that most of the following methods do not require grading. The major purpose of these assessments is for *you* to get feedback on performance, and for that, no grading is necessary. The strategies are grouped into those for large lecture and those for smaller classes.

Feedback on Student Performance in the Large Lecture Class

The vast majority of all college and university classes are based on lectures. If you are like most instructors, in planning lectures you concentrate on what you will present and on making content as interesting and understandable as possible. Clear visuals and lots of commonplace examples help, particularly if you start with simple cases and then progress to more complex examples. So far, so good. But what will your students be doing? Hopefully, they will be taking notes, but there is no guarantee that they will take good notes, that they will understand what they are writing, or that they will be able to repeat information or solve problems as a result of attending your lectures, even if you present them with the panache of a Dr. Fox. To find out how much students learn from your lectures, you need to get feedback. Various methods are available but they may not all appeal to you. You have to judge what you would be comfortable using. Anything that enables you to see how students are responding to material will give you valuable feedback on your effectiveness.

Lecture Fill-In Sheets with Quiz Items

One of my first classes at the university was a required lecture course in which 500 students had registered. There was no lecture hall that could hold all 500, so I gave each lecture Tuesday night to half of the students and Wednesday morning to the other half. Although I am a reasonable lecturer, I noticed students in the back who were not paying attention. (This conclusion was not difficult, since they were reading the student newspaper.) That had to stop. My solution was one many other professors have used, and that is to hand out a lecture outline with all of the important parts missing. Say, for instance, that you introduce a new term. Your lecture fill-in would begin with an item such as, "We define *(here you insert your new term)* as _____." The sheets were one or two pages long, and students picked them up as they entered the lecture hall. What a difference! Students wanted to have all their spaces filled in. The same students that were reading the paper before were now watching and listening, and if they missed something (being far in the back), they would come up after class and say, "What was 3b? I didn't get 3b."

Not all the students remembered everything they wrote down, of course, but at least the fill-in sheets got them to pay attention to the basic terms and definitions, and that was a first step. Later, I added quiz items to the fill-in sheets. After introducing a new concept or term, a multiple-choice item would appear such as, "Which of the following are examples of *(new term)?*" Although I could not see which choice they selected, I could see how many readily responded and how many craned their necks to see what those sitting next to them had written. I didn't know then how to find out what they had written (short of collecting their notes), but others have solved that problem with response cards or electronic devices.

Response Cards and Electronic Devices

Another method of both checking comprehension and increasing student responding throughout a lecture uses electronic devices or color cards. A professor at Harvard, Dr. Eric Mazur, read an article that said that although first-year physics students could solve computation problems, they didn't understand the basic principles. The article gave an example of a misconception: When a lightweight car and a heavy car collide, many students think that the heavy car exerts more force. (This is not true, however.) To test student "understanding," an item might show a picture of a heavy truck and light car colliding—asking which vehicle exerts the greater force, the truck, the car, or neither (they exert equal forces). Many physics students, the article said, miss seemingly simple items such as these. As Mazur put it, he thought, "Not *my* students!" (Mazur, 1997, p. 4).

Being a good experimenter, Mazur gave some "simple" questions to his class. To his amazement, he found that as many as 40 percent could not answer these "simple" items. He was appalled. So he redesigned his lecture to include short items he called ConcepTests. He scattered three or four of these questions throughout each lecture. Each student got a little electronic device (remember, this is Harvard) and had one minute to answer the ConcepTest. The answers were displayed on a monitor at the front so that Mazur could see how students responded. To further increase students' reasoning about the practical implications of principles after seeing their first answers, Mazur gave them another minute to discuss their responses with a "neighbor" and then to record their revised answers. During discussions, he walked among his students and listened to student reasoning, picking up better ways to explain as well as misconceptions that needed to be corrected. Inevitably, the revised answers were better than the first. By finding out how well his students could apply textbook principles to everyday situations, he improved what his students learned in class.

Mazur's technique doesn't require high-tech equipment, as he himself points out (Mazur, 1997, p. 18). Others have used cards with large letters written on them for feedback, or colored index cards with each color representing a particular choice. Let's say you ask a question and the correct answer is "red" for choice B. If you see a sea of red, you know the students got the question correct. But if you see many green, yellow, or blue cards, you know those students answered incorrectly. When a misconception is common, you can immediately correct it or, like Mazur, have students discuss among themselves to help each other's reasoning. In small classes, you can follow up with questions to individual students.

Quizzes at the End of Lectures

In addition to sampling understanding with items scattered throughout a lecture, you can give short quizzes at the end of a lecture. One of the problems with a lecture is that the consequences for not actually learning what is being presented are usually delayed. Students write down notes but rarely study them until exam time. Quizzes given near the end of a class can reinforce important points.

A lecturer in a large architecture class, who, by the way, was an excellent lecturer and used wonderful slides throughout his lectures, decided to add more immediate consequences for concentrating on what he wanted students to learn (Cohen, 1968). He was able to schedule two consecutive hours for his lecture sessions. At the conclusion of the first hour, he gave a multiple-choice quiz. Students received two copies, with carbon paper in between. They handed in the original and kept the copy. Then he gave the answers and students graded their carbon copies. At that point, anyone with 90 percent or better could leave. For the rest of the students, he reviewed. The first week, nearly everyone stayed, but as soon as students saw the advantage of mastering the material during the first hour, they began to concentrate harder and more began to test out, so that the professor was left with only those who really needed help. Thus, this assessment method served two purposes: It motivated paying attention and it identified areas that gave trouble so that the lectures could be revised.

"No-Name" Quizzes

All of the preceding methods require multiple-choice responding, but short-answer formats and mini-essays can also be used with a lecture. The problem with short answers and essays is the time it takes to grade them. However, if you tell students *not* to put their names on their papers, they do not expect to get them back and their responses can be quickly skimmed instead of individually graded.

The simplest method is to take the last 10 minutes of class and pass out index cards (they are easier to handle than full-sized papers). Explain that you want to see how well the material is getting across and that students are to answer your questions but not put their names on the cards. You can either construct a quiz item or ask a general question such as, "What did you learn today?" In either case, a quick glance over the cards gives feedback on strengths and weaknesses, letting you see where change would improve your teaching. Since there is no penalty for "wrong" answers, students like this form of assessment.

Temporary Pairs or Groups

Any kind of student responding offers an opportunity for feedback. When students discuss topics, you get a good idea of their problem-solving strategies (and whether they have done the reading). However, when you ask a question to the whole group, many students will tune out, expecting someone else to answer. By arranging for everyone to talk, you give each student opportunities for problem solving, thinking of examples, and creative thought.

Even in a lecture hall with fixed seats, you can pause during a lecture and ask students to pair off with a neighbor. (At the ends of lecture rows, you might have a "pair" of three.) In a 1995 study, Hollingsworth looked at the effect of adding, to his lectures, frequent two-minute discussions between pairs of students. Pairs were asked to discuss the last point covered. Compared with his usual lecture, the undergraduates who took the two-minute discussion section scored significantly higher on the posttest, though on a delayed post-test, there was no difference between groups (Hollingsworth, 1995). When it is difficult to join student groups in the middle of rows, you can ask for their contributions on index cards for feedback. Even in a large lecture hall, feedback from small discussion groups will provide you with some idea of what students are learning.

In any lecture, you will increase student understanding if you ask students to describe to each other a point you just went over, to give a definition in their own words, or to think of an example from their own experience. Asking a group or groups to present their ideas adds a consequence for using the time productively. Handing a transparency blank to each group for their conclusions also helps students stay on task.

Short, Timed Exercises

Many other short activities have been proposed for engaging students in material covered in lectures. Short quizzes covering basic terms or concepts can be timed, using a one-minute format taken from Precision Teaching (see Lindsley, 1991, for a summary). Timing has a magic of its own. Students who were slumped in their seats sit up as the timing is about to start, and everyone concentrates intently while working. Best of all, skills improve. An assistant professor at Fairmont State College, Beverly Born, who was also the coordinator of the physical therapy program, discovered that students in her first-year physical therapy course were not fluent in identifying basic joint motions, even though she demonstrated each one and they were described in the text. However, it is crucial that physical therapists rapidly identify motions in order to tell whether patients are correctly performing therapeutic exercises. So, she began using a new technique. At the beginning of each class, three times a week, Born demonstrated 12 motions at a rate of about one every five seconds. She gave the joint name (e.g., "shoulder") as she demonstrated and the students wrote down the motion demonstrated (e.g., "abduction"). The order was different each day. Born then repeated the motions and gave the names as the students corrected their own work. As students marked their papers, she could see where problems lay. There were other benefits, as well. After a few sessions, Born noticed that students were practicing on their own when she arrived for class, and were talking about their progress. Moreover, she discovered that students were much better prepared for the following clinical course where they had to apply their knowledge. The two students who failed to achieve fluency (naming all 12 motions in one minute) also failed the subsequent practice exam where they had to perform exercise techniques on a live person (Born, 1998).

Pretest-Posttest Differences

If you give multiple-choice or fill-in-the-blank tests (either alone or as part of your evaluation of students), you are in an ideal position to calculate pre-posttest difference indices. This old idea has been reincarnated as *value-added testing*. The procedure can also be done with essays, but calculation and interpretation are more difficult. If you use answer sheets or computers that score automatically, the index is simple to calculate. You must, of course, give a pretest. Items on the posttest are matched with the pretest items, and the percent passing an item on the pretest is subtracted from the percent passing on the posttest. This kind of criterion-referenced item analysis differs radically from traditional norm-referenced item analysis where the purpose is to discriminate among test takers and thus to select items that spread out scores. In fact, a study correlating the pre-post item analysis index with a traditional item analysis index (the difference between the percent of students in the top 27 percent of total scores who passed each item minus the percent in the lowest 27 percent) found a statistically negative correlation (Vargas, 1969).[2] A poor pretest-posttest difference index reveals one of two problems: Either students already could pass an item when entering a course or they scored badly at the end. To improve instruction, you need to attend to both. You don't want to waste class time on things students already know, and you need to redesign instruction if students are consistently missing items on a particular topic.

Like any numbers based on test scores, pretest-posttest difference indices are only as good as the items used to calculate them. If the items are badly designed or fail to assess important outcomes, the numbers from such an item analysis will not improve teaching. But when tests are well designed, pretest-posttest differences pinpoint areas of instructional strength and weakness through the amount of gain in student performance—the best immediate measure of learning.

Quizzes over the World Wide Web

With the advent of the World Wide Web, it is possible to put quizzes onto the web for students to access from home. The technology for web-based programs that can take and evaluate student input is advancing rapidly. Programs exist today that let a professor design multiple-choice, fill-in, or essay tests and to restrict the time available for student access (to help prevent one student from telling others what was asked). Web-based tests can ask students to respond to diagrams, pictures, audios, and even short movies. Furthermore, for any test that has one or a small number of correct answers, grading is done for you. Tests can be set to evaluate each response as it is entered, or only at its end. Results are typically portable into spreadsheets.

Until you have tested a system, however, it is probably best to use web-based quizzes for practice tests or for ungraded homework assignments rather than as a major component of grades. I usually print out a paper copy for students who arrive in class claiming that lightning fried their motherboard, that cat hair jammed the letter *C* on their keyboard, or other problems—real or invented. In the next few years, you can expect to type a test into a web-authoring program as easily as you now create it on your word processor.

E-mail and List Serves

Another Internet vehicle for feedback on student performance is the e-mail system. Many professors have integrated e-mail into their courses. This allows you to see what individual students say. If you have a large class, you probably don't have the time to interact with each student. You can, however, ask for questions to be sent to you individually, but answered on a list serve that goes to every student in the class. If time is scarce, you can answer, say, only the first 10 questions you receive. Using e-mail instead of asking for questions during class permits students to think of questions while doing assignments, and it permits shy students to participate. For you, it provides feedback on what students are thinking in a form that is easily saved for future reference.

Bulletin Boards and Chat Rooms

Instead of receiving individual e-mail messages, you can set up a bulletin board that is accessed by a web address. A bulletin board lets students comment on topics organized into themes or threads. When a bulletin board is opened, the list of topics is displayed and a click on any one will reveal the messages posted on that topic. As the instructor, you can read at your leisure what students are saying. You do not need to send comments yourself, but can do so if you wish. Thus, you get feedback on students' statements without having to respond to everything students say. Unlike e-mail, which appears whether you ask for it or not, bulletin boards are accessed only by going to a particular website.

A chat room provides real-time interaction. It is a kind of on-line conference call, except that contributions are typed rather than made orally. Chat rooms are scheduled for specific times. If you participate, you, too, will have to sign on at a specified time.

For e-mail, bulletin boards, and chat room interactions, some students may dominate discussions. Others may not participate at all unless you set up reasons for doing so.

Feedback in the Smaller Class

All of the methods discussed can be used to obtain information on student progress in small classes as well as in large. Small classes where seats can be rearranged permit group activities. By giving problems during class time, instead of only as homework, you can find out how students go about solving problems, thus enabling you to teach problem-solving activities. Of course, you need to walk around and join each group to get feedback on how students are thinking.

Putting problem solving at the center of teaching has a long tradition in methods such as guided design, discovery learning, and inquiry-based instruction. These approaches to teaching encourage students to contact actual events rather than only talking about them. The "discoveries" that students make are, of course, carefully planned. Students who manipulate the length of string and weights will have a much better "feel" for the principles of the pendulum than those who merely read about periodicity. But you must still monitor performance, lest they play around making swings or yo-yos with the materials. Here, too, you need to determine what students are getting out of the experiences you provide.

In presenting problems to solve, you begin shifting the kind of motivation under which students work. Behavior is governed partly by the world and partly by what people say about that world (Vargas, 1998). Talking about a subject is one thing; doing what professionals in an area do with the material is another. Students may start by hearing or reading about a subject, but they eventually need to develop certain competencies. That is the kind of "understanding" that Mazur built into his physics class. Science labs attempt to shift controls from what people say about physics or chemistry or biology to the effects of the way the physical or organic universe behaves. In other subject areas, students will run a project, write a report, or conduct research.

Logistics enter in immediately. When you consider how much time it will take you, the instructor, to evaluate individual products in, say, a class of 30 students, even if you take only 10 minutes for each one each week, you can see that it will require a minimum of five hours to keep on top of what your students are doing. Rather than omitting a valuable activity altogether, have students work collaboratively, thus reducing the number of projects to manageable proportions while still involving students in activities that enable you to see not only their competence but also their interest in your field.

Follow-Up of Graduates

Good teaching produces more than good test scores. The impact of a well-taught course shows up throughout a student's life. More and more colleges and universities are looking at follow-up data on graduates. You may also be able to track student course choices while students are still at your institution or survey students who took your course several semesters earlier. Occasionally, students write letters of appreciation, telling you how your course impacted their choice of a major or graduate school. Although these sources of information rarely pinpoint the specific parts of a course that made it effective, they document the more difficult-to-measure aspects of teaching, such as ability to motivate and inspire students.

Summary

Improving your teaching is a lifelong process. It involves more than watching your ratings on student evaluation questionnaires. Ratings can be improved by turning lectures into multimedia extravaganzas, such as that presented by a Western Ontario professor who lectures "while pacing a steel catwalk and bounding about an amphitheater much like the set of 'Donahue,'" while flashing computerized simulations and video clips onto a 20-foot screen (Murray, 1999). But while the $500,000 his university spent to refurbish the lecture hall for such presentations may swell enrollment figures, research does not support a relationship between the entertainment value of a course and student learning.

There are many ways to evaluate teaching, but only by looking at changes in student performance can you directly see the impact of instructional procedures. The methods recommended by universities, such as student ratings of instructors and peer evaluations (with or without portfolios), serve administrative purposes of ranking faculty for annual review, for promotion and tenure decisions, or for merit pay and rewards. They are norm-referenced assessments where one professor's score depends largely on how well comparison colleagues perform. Research does not show these evaluations as helpful for improving student learning (as opposed to student satisfaction). They can even work against the benefit of society, by discouraging nontenured faculty from setting high standards. These vehicles are of limited help in improving your teaching.

Instead, you must design your own evaluation methods to show the impact of what you do on student achievement. The effects of good instruction are far-reaching. While only time will tell how your teaching will affect students' future coursework, their career choices, and their approach to the world, performance on course objectives can be measured during a course. To assess impact, you must know how students handle the critical aspects of a field before instruction and what they do after. The more feedback you get on student performance, the better equipped you will be to improve instruction. This chapter has suggested methods of assessing student progress within the constraints of traditional college and university course formats.

Teaching is not just presenting. Teaching is not entertaining. Teaching is setting up experiences that help students gain real competency in a field—becoming fluent with basic terms and principles, learning to solve practical problems creatively, and gaining the enthusiasm that comes from successful discovery and performance. Improving teaching is a serious, nontrivial task, one that requires continued research and effort by those in classrooms, and one that, more than any other, will benefit future generations of students.

References and Resources

Austin, A. W., Parrott, S. A., Korn, W. S., & Sax, L. J. (1997). *The American freshman: Thirty year trends.* Los Angeles: Cooperative Institutional Research Program, UCLA.

Born, B. (1998). *Identifying joint motions: An exercise in fluency.* Course project for Dr. Julie Vargas in Applied Behavior Analysis, West Virginia University.

Cohen, H. (1968). *Training professionals in procedures for the establishment of educational environments.* Silver Spring, MD: IBR Press.

Cross, K. P. (1990). Classroom research: Helping professors learn more about teaching and learning. In P. Seldin & Associates (Eds.), *How administrators can improve teaching: Moving from talk to action in higher education* (p. 142). San Francisco: Jossey-Bass.

Farley, B. L. (1995). *"A" is for average: The grading crisis in today's colleges.* Position paper, Princeton University. ERIC No. 384384

Greenwald, A. G. (1997). Validity concerns and usefulness of student ratings of instruction. *American Psychologist, 52* (11), 1182–1186.

Hollingsworth, P. M. (1995). Enhancing listening retention: The two minute discussion. *College Student Journal, 29,* 116–117.

Lewis, L. S. (1998). *Scaling the ivory tower: Merit and its limits in academic careers.* New Brunswick, NJ: Transaction Publishers. (Reprint of 1975 book).

Lindsley, O. R. (1991). Precision Teaching's unique legacy from B. F. Skinner. *Journal of Behavioral Education, 1* (2), 253–266.

Long, C. D. (1998). Survey shows first-year students apathetic. *Academe, 84* (3), 10.

Marsh, H. W., & Roche, L. A. (1997). Making students' evaluations of teaching effectiveness effective: The critical issues of validity, bias, and utility. *American Psychologist, 52* (11), 1187–1197.

Mazur, E. (1997). *Peer instruction: A user's manual.* Upper Saddle River, NJ: Prentice-Hall.

Menges, R. J. (1990). Using evaluation information to improve instruction. In P. Seldin & Associates (Eds.), *How administrators can improve teaching: Moving from talk to action in higher education.* San Francisco: Jossey-Bass.

Murray, B. (1999, April). Technology invigorates teaching, but is the pazzazz worth the price? *APA Monitor Online, 30* (4).

Naftulin, D. H., Ware, J. E., Jr., & Donnelly, F. A. (1972, July). The Doctor Fox lecture: A paradigm of educational seduction. *Journal of Medical Education, 48,* 630–635.

Redmond, M. V., & Clark, D. J. (1982). Small group instructional diagnosis: A practical approach to improving teaching. *AAHE Bulletin,* pp. 8–10.

Seldin, P. (1991). *The teaching portfolio: A practical guide to improved performance and promotion/tenure decisions.* Bolton, MA: Anker Publishing.

USDE (United States Department of Education, 1996). *The condition of education 1996.* Table 11-1: Percentage of college graduates completing a bachelor's degree within various years of starting college, by selected student characteristics: 1993. <http://nces01.ed.gov:80/pubs/ce/c9611d01.html>. Accessed May 1, 1999.

Vargas, E. A. (1996). A university for the twenty-first century. In J. R. Cautela & WarisIshaq (Eds.), *Improving the human condition* (p. 170). New York: Plenum.

Vargas, E. A. (1998). Verbally-governed and event-governed behavior. *The Analysis of Verbal Behavior,* 11–22.

Vargas, J. S. (1969). *Item selection techniques for norm-referenced and criterion-referenced tests.* Unpublished doctoral dissertation, University of Pittsburg.

West Virginia University. *Student evaluation of instruction, 1998.*

West Virginia University. *Undergraduate catalog, 1995–96.*

Wilson, R. (1998, January). New research casts doubt on value of student evaluations of professors. *Chronicle of Higher Education,* 12–14.

Endnotes

1. Taken from a form used at West Virginia University, 1998.
2. Items that discriminated best among posttest takers showed the least gain from pre- to posttest. In contrast, the highest pre-posttest difference indices, which showed the items on which student most improved over the semester, scored badly on traditional norm-referenced item analysis.

15

Teaching and the
Tenure Track

Overview: In his book The New Faculty Member, *Boice (1992) has claimed that there are three obstacles facing most new faculty: teaching, writing, and collegiality. Thus far, this book has already covered many of the potential classroom problems. This chapter will be addressing issues and problems often occurring* outside *the classroom. Using Boice's scheme, these can be roughly categorized as those associated with writing and publishing, and the academic pitfalls found in most institutions of higher learning sometimes thought of as "office politics" and requiring one to be "politically savvy." To achieve tenure—to make a career out of teaching—one must be at least an acceptable instructor, must not alienate colleagues, and must create a portfolio of published papers that cannot be easily dismissed. How are you going to find time to do all of that? That topic is addressed in these pages.*

Juggling Research, Publications, and *Teaching*

Like it or not, this is a competitive world. Most research universities have the expectation that you will not only teach but publish. At many universities new faculty are commonly instructed that they should seek to publish at least "two solid pieces" of research per year, and this is the advice of Weaver (1992), too. However, the number of required publications varies quite a bit. At smaller colleges and even some regional universities, it may be possible to get tenure without publishing in a refereed journal. The publishing demands are often inversely proportional to the number of courses you teach. If your normal teaching load is four or five courses per semester, then it is unlikely that you'll have to do much professional writing. If, on the other hand, your teaching load is one or two courses a semester, then there is probably the expectation that you should be publishing somewhere on the order of two or more articles per year—and this may be in addition to securing external grant funding.

Most new faculty do not have the option of choosing, say, between teaching and researching in order to publish—they have to do both. The good news is that it is possible to be a good teacher *and* a fine researcher. These two activities do not detract from each other; rather, they complement each other. Reading articles for a literature review, for instance, will turn up wonderful examples of research and hypotheses, even flaws in methodologies or logic that can be used in the classroom. Sometimes it is possible to give students assignments where they not only are able to learn how to do conduct research but also to participate in a way that assists you. For example, students could help you interview subjects or collect surveys from a sample of adults. If you share with them the hypotheses and problems you are working on, a student may find an especially relevant study that you didn't know about. And although you shouldn't give assignments designed only to further your own research efforts—such as requiring your students to conduct exhaustive literature reviews on the topic you'll be writing about next—there is a strong tradition in academia of using students as subjects and research participants. (More about this later in this chapter.)

Besides working smart, which we'll talk about next, making the best use of your time is a critical key to successfully managing the demands of teaching and publishing. Start by finding a quiet place where you can work undisturbed. If that place is your office, so much the better. If it is your home, that's okay, too. But neither of these places count if the phone rings three or four times an hour or if there is always someone stopping by to chat.

Insofar as possible, schedule your social contacts. When there are people you need to talk with or who need to see you, do it when you would normally be stopping for lunch, anyway. Try to find blocks of times (three or four hours at a stretch) when you can work without interruption. Take the phone off the hook if you have to; schedule at least two "writing days" a week when you don't have to teach; let it be known that you won't answer the door even if someone knocks loudly. Plan how much time you will need to develop a lecture, grade papers, and so on, and then stay within that time frame. Boice (1992) found that the most effective new faculty members prepared no more than 1.5 hours per each classroom hour. If you, like many assistant professors, are expected to be engaged in research about half of your time and in activities associated with teaching about half of the time, then schedule your research days or hours and don't let committee work or teaching responsibilities steal that time.

New faculty who love teaching often find it much to their secret liking that students call with personal problems or drop in unannounced to make small talk, to show off a new engagement ring, or to ask for advice about a job interview. If you find yourself truly enjoying these contacts, then you must be vigilant in keeping nonproductive activities from taking over your whole work week. We all tend to engage proportionately more in those activities that are fun and less in those that aren't. So, if you aren't spending at least half of your time involved in research or writing and that's the expectation of your department head, then you are going to be in trouble later when your lack of productivity become obvious.

Time Management Tips

In addition to the suggestions just provided, here are a few others suggested by Parks (1998):

- Identify the "time robber" tasks that waste or are an inefficient use of your time.
- Once your "time robbers" are identified, create a plan to eliminate them. (For instance, are there tasks that you can delegate to a research assistant or a work/study student to do?)
- If you have too much to do, learn to say "no" nicely when new requests are made of your time.
- Break large tasks into small, manageable segments. Procrastination is not uncommon when one feels overwhelmed with the enormity of a task. Dawdling is minimized when only a small amount of time (e.g., 15 minutes or so) is need to complete a chore.

Some efficiency experts recommend that instead of trying to make major adjustments in one's schedule to create large blocks of time, it is often easier to make better use of small parcels. Get to work 15 minutes earlier, stay 15 minutes later. Know when you are most productive and protect that time for your most important projects. Other jobs that don't require as much concentration can be done when you normally get more interruptions or are less productive.

Boice (1992) has urged new faculty to establish a *writing regimen*. His research (1987) found that new faculty who find only an hour per weekday to write generally manage to submit about 1.5 manuscripts per year. Sorcinelli (1992) has recommended drawing up a daily "to do" list, using an appointment book, setting realistic goals, prioritizing projects, and initiating relaxation exercises to restore energy.

Last, keep your eye on the prize. You *can* find the time for the things you *really* want to accomplish. Along this line, here's a great story from novelist Sharyn McCrumb (1998):

> *Procrastinators get no sympathy from me. In 1986 when a publishing company accepted my four-page book proposal, the catch was this: In order to meet their spring deadline, the editor would need the completed novel in six weeks. I did not have six weeks to devote to writing a novel. I was working full time at the university. I was teaching a night class in fiction. I was taking two graduate English courses that semester, both requiring research papers. I had an 8-year-old daughter, and a husband balancing a job with his own graduate course work. I was six weeks pregnant, and I felt awful. . . . I wrote the book in six weeks. It won the Edgar Allan Poe Award for Best Paperback Novel in 1987. It's still in print. (p. 19)*

Working Smart

Working smart means that you must ask for help when you need it. An example comes to mind: Before the advent of the Internet, a student complained to me because she had to spend so many hours in the library—the most of one whole weekend, as I recall. What she had been looking for had been an article that had appeared in the

New York Times. Beginning with the month and year she thought the article had appeared, she began working her way backward, using the cumbersome microfilm reader. For 14 or more hours she labored, although had she asked the librarian a few feet away, she could have found the piece she wanted in a few minutes by looking in the reference book, *Index to the New York Times.*

Working smart means that as a junior faculty member or teaching assistant, you should ask lots of questions of those who are in a position to help you. Senior professors will probably be more than willing to recommend texts or supplements, and more than likely will be, if not glad to share, at least willing to share examples of tests and homework assignments they've used in the past. It also means that if you have very limited experience writing for professional journals and yet you are expected to do this, you ask for consultation. Go to one or more faculty members who have proven track records and ask for a consultation if you need it. Better yet, ask them to review your rough draft. Be open to suggestions and don't get defensive.

Working smart means that you try to recruit students to help with your research projects. There are different ways to do this, from independent studies to class assignments, to even including students as coauthors. If you are hard-pressed for time and don't have institutional support in the form of a graduate or research assistant, then hire a student to run to the library and do photocopying for you, or word processing, or whatever. Sure, you could conceivably spend a few hundred dollars, but on the other hand, how much is your time worth? It's probably worth a lot more than you would pay some undergraduate to photocopy articles.

Working smart also means that you consider teaming up with other faculty and work as coauthors on some writing projects. If this partnership works well, you could have twice as many publications as you would have if you worked by yourself. Of course, working with another person does have its frustrations at time: Your colleague may slip the deadline you both set, may not write well, or may be less informed or capable than you had thought. Obviously, it pays to choose well. The rule here is that someone who already has publications (and preferably a lot of them) is a safer bet for a good writing partner than someone with no publications. Look for a mentor or a coauthor capable of pulling his or her own weight and who is excited about the prospect of writing on the topic and working with you. If you do more than one project together, alternate authorship so that you and your coauthor will both be first authors. Negotiate the order of authorship at the beginning of your endeavor so that there will be no hard feelings later on.

Finally, working smart means that you don't forget about your dissertation. Although you may be so sick of it that you want to bury it in a deep hole somewhere, a well-done dissertation ought to get you at least one and maybe two publications. And the best part is that you know the literature, forward and backward, and have already analyzed the data just about every way imaginable. Cut it down to a findings article where you highlight the most important results. Then, take a look to see if you can get a review of the literature article out of it.

Suggestions for Increasing the Odds of Getting Published

Getting published in respected journals is neither difficult nor as easy as some would have you believe. Above all, you must be disciplined and approach the task logically. Make publishing a priority and give it the time it deserves—don't wait for an opportune moment or push it to the side until everything else is done. Once you've protected some part of your busy schedule just for writing and the preparation it requires, then the following suggestions may help you to think about the component tasks in the writing process:

1. Find a topic, problem, or hypothesis that is interesting and timely. What is hot and possibly controversial in your field? Where is an area with little scholarship? Plow new ground if you can, or put a new spin on a perennial problem.
2. Find a mentor or a colleague interested in the same topics as you. If possible, join or form a support group of assistant professors who are writing and researching.
3. Familiarize yourself with the journals interested in your topic. (It does you no good to draft a dazzling manuscript if you don't have an appropriate journal in mind.)
4. Study articles in the journal you have selected for length, writing style, the audience, the number and type of references they tend to carry, and so on.

5. After you have written a rough draft, set it aside for two or three days and then revise the draft again.

6. Repeat this process (reading and revising) about six times, until you can make no further refinements.

7. Let a colleague with expertise in the area read your manuscript. If you don't have a mentor, then seek out a kindly soul from another department who writes well. If one is not available and you are particularly inexperienced or if English is your second language, you might even want to hire someone to do line-editing. Sometimes such a small investment pays large dividends in terms of learning how to write professionally. (*Note:* A mentor can be very helpful with many other issues besides editing and writing. They are sources of information [e.g., more suitable journals] as well as intellectual guides and sources of emotional support when things have taken a turn for the worst. See Bode [1999] for a discussion on mentoring and collegiality.)

8. Revise again.

9. Submit to the professional journal.

10. If the manuscript is rejected, carefully weigh each of the reviewers' comments and then revise again. Don't categorically reject or accept each recommendation. Try to read the reviewers' comments objectively; if the comments make you angry, put them aside until you can read them more dispassionately. Don't throw the manuscript in the mail the same day to another journal. Although reviewers don't always understand what you were trying to accomplish and reject your manuscript, oftentimes they have good suggestions for improving it and making the paper more appealing.

11. Revise the piece by making the modifications that seem to have the most merit.

12. Submit the revised manuscript to a different journal if you were flatly rejected the first time. If the journal receiving your initial manuscript encouraged you to resubmit, then, by all means, do so. Call or e-mail the editor if you need clarification about the extent of the revision necessary.

13. If rejected once again, study the comments, revise still again, and resubmit to a different journal.

14. Consult some of the guides to publishing and writing (e.g., Thyer, 1994; Henson, 1995; Beebe, 1993). Join a writing group; start a writing support group. Sign up for a writing workshop.

15. Salvage what you can of any manuscript rejected umpteen times. Slant it, if possible, in a slightly different direction. For instance, if it reported findings, consider making it a review of the literature piece only. If it reviewed the literature, think of a way to gather some data to put with it. Alternatively, downsize the article and make it a "brief note"—something less than a full-sized article—maybe you'll have better luck with that.

A useful rule of thumb is three submissions. If you submit to three different journals and not one is interested in the paper, then something may be seriously wrong with it—there also may be no problem other than you haven't sent it to the most appropriate journals. Before you give up, take it to a colleague who has had more success publishing and ask for a consultation. Even if a journal isn't interested in your manuscript, you might look around for a conference where it could be entered as a paper, part of a panel discussion, or poster session.

Meanwhile, don't sit around waiting for the letter of acceptance to arrive. As soon as you mail off one manuscript, start immediately working on another. Because projects move at different speeds (e.g., you may have to wait for a book to arrive from Interlibrary Loan before completing your literature review section, or you may have to wait on the Institutional Review Board to grant permission before you can start data collection on another), you may be able to handle two or three projects more or less simultaneously.

Political Mistakes

If you've gone to the trouble of getting into graduate school, making it through most of your classes, preparing for your qualifying exam and dissertation, and then finally securing a position teaching at the college or university level, it stands to reason that you wouldn't want to just throw it away. And yet, it is possible to start off on the wrong foot and you can do this quite unintentionally. Here is some practical advice that will help you stay out of trouble with your colleagues in the department:

1. *Do not criticize your colleagues or speak ill of them:* Although the chair of the department might be an arrogant and pompous blockhead, you do not want him or her to find out that is what you think. The more people who have heard you find fault with the chair, the more avenues that are created for this information to get back to him or her. Even a trusted colleague might, after a couple of glasses of wine at a party, let some comment slip about what you "really think about ol' Harley." Faculty members enjoy juicy gossip the same as anyone else. If you let it be known that some tenured faculty member is incompetent (even if he or she is), you should assume that sooner or later, that unflattering remark will get back to the individual. Similarly, when you are the "new kid on the block," it is not wise to be critical of the program as a whole, or of admission policies or practices that have well-entrenched faculty advocates. This is not to say that you should have no opinion—only that you should always be tactful and recognize that those who've been at the institution a long time are likely to have strong feelings about leaving things the way they are. Someone on the faculty for 30 years may feel quite a lot of ownership of the program, certain courses, and so forth. These individuals may take criticism of a program personally. Particularly in small colleges, also be cautious about criticizing administrators or faculty in other departments who, unbeknown to you, may be spouses or relatives of key persons that you do not want to offend.

2. *Do not engage in sexual activities with a student, staff member, or other faculty at the same institution* (unless you are married to him or her): When relationships break up, there's always the potential for the aggrieved party to want revenge in some way or another.

3. *Try to maintain a spirit of cooperativeness and helpfulness:* Although you may feel quite overwhelmed with duties and responsibilities, try to help your colleagues when they make a request. This doesn't mean you have to say yes to every new task group or ad hoc committee, but don't be known as someone who *isn't* a team-player, someone who automatically says no to every request. Try not to whine if you get an 8:00 A.M. class or if the spring schedule is not to your liking. Complaining about a real hardship is one matter; sounding off if you have three more students in your section than another faculty member or because your office wasn't dusted properly will really make it difficult for administrators to warm up to you.

4. *If there are pronounced factions within the faculty, try not to get caught up into the political fray your first year or two:* Gently deflect attempts to pull you into one camp or the other by saying something like, "I'm still pretty new here. I don't know all the issues or have enough information to decide one way or the other. Maybe we can have a conversation about this later." It is important that you listen and observe which players are on which teams. If you have a mentor on the faculty, find out what you can about the history of the split and about the nature of the most sensitive issues. Speak to everyone. Try not to show that you favor one faction over the other. Try to be on good terms with every faculty member, even if you must keep some conversations superficial and avoid certain topics.

5. *Take care of business:* Be well prepared for each class. Return papers promptly. Keep your office hours. Don't be the "office gossip" or spend much time with those who are. If others are going to discuss you, let them talk about what a fine job you are doing. In Sawyer, Prichard, and Hostetler's words, "Your most immediate priority on the job is teaching" (1992, p. 151). Abbott (1992) has expanded upon this somewhat:

> *Small liberal arts colleges are deep wells. They expect schol-arly achievement, excellent classroom teaching, loyalty to and love of the institution, good counseling skills, energy, imagination, collegiality, understanding of the values of the college and community, patience, hard work, personality, and tact. (p. 27)*

The good news in terms of the alliances and caucuses in aca-demia is that making it through a Ph.D. program has been a good preparation for the politics that you will encounter as a new faculty member. You already have acquired a lot of learning in this domain. You know, for instance, that there are faculty who swing a lot of clout and that there are faculty who are very territorial about their courses or programs. Faculty are not always open minded but some-times downright opinionated and inflexible when it comes to *their* courses and *their* students. In the years that it's taken you to obtain that Ph.D., you've already overcome a lot of obstacles and learned a great deal about handling sensitive issues and difficult people. This is valuable and irreplaceable learning that will serve you well in the years ahead. Don't forget your lessons.

The Rules for Surviving

New faculty often feel like they have to do everything well: They have to be popular with students, entertaining and yet informative in the classroom, productive scholars, hard-working committee members, stimulating conversationalists, and altruistic givers of their time to community service projects. There's a lot of truth to these broad expectations. However, in every institution there are also informal rules. Your department might not really care, for instance, whether you get good teaching evaluations as long as you have a strong publishing record or bring in a sizeable chunk of external funding. In the most competitive of academic environments, it is not just getting published, but publishing in the "right" journals that really matters. Sometimes there is the expectation that you should have a book published before tenure; in other locations, a book of readings might be viewed as being of less consequence than two peer-reviewed journal articles. Collaborative work with others may be encouraged or frowned upon. For example, if too much of your work is done with students, one criticism might be that you exploit students. If too much of your work is done with other faculty, you might be criticized for not being the lead author often enough.

No matter how much you accomplish, there may be faculty who will not like you or your work. Of course, you can't help the way you look, the fact that you were someone's else graduate student, or that your research contradicts that of a senior faculty member. There's nothing you can do about these things. What you *can* do is be unfailingly polite and respectful to those with whom you may not agree or care for. You should go about your business of teaching or researching and work diligently at these pursuits. Don't be the loner and avoid faculty social gatherings. Don't get the reputation as being one who is always stirring up trouble. In faculty meetings the first year, listen much more than you speak. Insofar as possible, be pleasant and positive—not moody and temperamental. Don't always insist on your own way. Find out what the informal rules are for grading: Don't give all As and don't fail everyone either.

Seeking or Hiding from Committee Assignments

Participating on committees within your academic unit and university is the proverbial double-edged sword. On one hand, it is often to your advantage as a new faculty member, because working together is a good way for you to learn more about your colleagues and for them to get to know you better. Some committees may meet only once or twice a year and require little work. On the other hand, some committees (e.g., admissions, curriculum revision, and possibly, faculty search committees) may meet frequently and can eat up several days a month when you can least afford the time (like right before the end of the semester).

Before you agree to serve on a particular committee, consider the following:

1. *The amount of your time this committee will need:*   Although at the beginning of the semester you may have the euphoric feeling that "all things are possible," by midterm, however—when you are frantically trying to prepare for the next lecture, grade a stack of papers, and send off an abstract with a deadline 48 hours away— you may come to resent two meetings scheduled for tomorrow that will demand substantial blocks of your time. This is not to say that it is in your best interest to refuse all committee work—it isn't. Faculty colleagues will expect you to be a team-player and to carry your fair share of committee work, too. The caution here is to be careful about agreeing to serve on so many committees that your own work and well-being suffers. This advice particularly applies to persons of color and women who are joining departments where they are clearly in the minority. You will need to learn, if you don't already know, how to say "no" nicely when overextended. Ultimately, your publications and productivity will be much more important in your quest for tenure than the number of committees on which you serve.

2. *Relative risk to untenured faculty:*   One of the great things about democracy and voting in committees is that everyone's vote counts the same, whether they are a full professor or a mere instructor. Your vote may be the one that breaks the tie or kills some ill-conceived proposal. The downside of this is that some issues before committees are politically charged and therefore place you in a position where you might have to vote against the pet proposal of a faculty member who is powerful and known to hold grudges. Before deciding to serve on a committee, it would be in your best interest to assess the possible political risk. Although it is not always possible to ascertain the potential for controversy that exists within each committee, those with chairs who are known for charging boldly ahead and those with members who have loudly professed their interest in making drastic changes to existing policies could be committees to avoid. There are usually safer committees, such as student recruitment, that won't get you into political hot water.

3. *Visibility:* Although they can consume your time, one advantage of serving on committees is that they may give you greater visibility within the department or larger university. This can be a real plus if you are a very large department (e.g., 50 faculty). And even if you aren't, serving with colleagues from various disciplines across the college or university will put you into contact with talented and creative colleagues who may become your friends or mentors. Your valuable contributions to one committee could lead to an appointment to an even more prestigious committee. At a minimum, colleagues from other areas are resources—individuals who may have knowledge or skills that could some day be useful to you or your students. Serving on a committee with prominent department heads or university officials can provide an informal access to them and can open doors later when you need help navigating through university bureaucracy. Volunteering to serve on committees associated with national associations and organizations can similarly work to your advantage, particularly if you want to make cross-institutional research connections (Sawyer, Prichard, & Hostetler, 1992).

4. *Personal contribution:* Given your background or personal experience, you may be a "natural" for some committees. For instance, if you are the only one in your department with a law degree, it is very likely you'll be recommended for or elected to the committee that deals with student terminations and appeals. You should probably accept this role, as to decline it might give the wrong impression to your colleagues. Along this line, knowing how you might contribute to a committee may make the prospect of your participation more enjoyable and fruitful than working on a committee with an unclear mission or charge.

Academic Advising

If you love teaching, you probably won't mind advising students. And if you are really good at it, students will pass the word and you will have even more students to advise because you'll hear these lines:

"My adviser is never in."

"My adviser forgot our appointment and I have to register today."

"My adviser doesn't know what he's talking about, and made me take a course last semester that I don't need."

"I don't know what to take, because I just transferred a bunch of credits in from Upper Frozen University."

Almost every faculty member gets students to advise. Depending on your institution, you may inherit a gaggle of students to advise your first semester or you may be given a period of grace (e.g., one semester or a year) in which to learn the curriculum first. The smaller your college or program, the more importance faculty advising will be given. In larger universities, there may be numerous advising resources; in small institutions, students will complain and word will travel if you don't do an adequate job.

If you are not provided an orientation about how to advise your students, then set one up for yourself by meeting with one of the more experienced faculty or staff who can tell you things such as which courses substitute for others, which courses must be taken in the fall semester because they aren't offered in spring, which courses every major must have to graduate, and so forth. Make yourself a file and write down the things you need to remember. Does your department have a checklist for graduating seniors or department majors? If so, get a copy and study it. If not, then create one for yourself.

Should you encounter a situation where you don't have an answer, then make a phone call and try to find the answer while the student is still there. Learning the answers to these questions early on will make for shorter advising sessions later. And even though advising may strike you as an odorous task, realize that students will be looking to you to be the expert and will be righteously indignant if you are not helpful. Being known as an uncaring, uninformed, or unhelpful adviser will not work to your advantage.

Some faculty try to minimize the amount of time required for advising by scheduling set appointment hours; others have "open-door" policies, allowing students to drop by at their convenience. Both of these approaches have strengths and weaknesses; decide which one works best for you. Particularly if you have a lot of advisees and a large enough office, you might try scheduling group advising sessions where four or five students can be advised simultaneously. If you plan well, say, by scheduling all the first-year students for one day, sophomores or juniors for different days, then there is some efficiency of effort in that your answering of one question will be applicable to others, as well.

You'll find it helpful to post some "rules" for your advisees. For instance, Rule 1, might be for them to verify that all the paperwork needed to establish them as a major in your department or graduate student in good standing has been completed.

Rule 2 might be for them to study the requirements needed for graduation (e.g., the number of English, math, and social science courses). Rule 3 could require that they examine the schedule of courses to be offered and do some prior planning before meeting with you. There's nothing wrong with expecting students to take a good deal of the responsibility here. The most time-consuming and frustrating advising sessions are always those where the student has not done any initial preparation and then discovers, in your office, that Math for Poets is offered only on Tuesdays and Thursdays, which conflicts with Chemistry for Chefs. When you point out an alternate schedule, the student doesn't want an 8:00 A.M. or a 4:00 P.M. class that meets the same time as her tennis lesson. You are quite within your rights to send these students out to the lounge, waiting area, or coffee shop to work out a schedule without wasting your time.

Harassment

We are living in an age where the rights of the individual are supreme. The particular danger for educators is that if we talk enough and give impromptu examples, it is not at all difficult to say something that may be experienced as offensive by someone in the class. Even as I am writing this, a local teacher has been suspended for 10 days from his high school because he used the word *penis*. His "crime" was preparing his class to view some classic works of art involving nudity (e.g., Michelangelo's *David*). In a human behavior course I once taught, a female student complained because I made mention of Desmond Morris's *(The Human Animal)* theorizing about the evolutionary value of female breasts as a mechanism to encourage pair-bonding. The point here is that even though you don't think of yourself as harassing students, there is no guarantee that one or more students won't take exception if you use sexual language, imagery, or examples.

As a new instructor, it is sometimes easy to fall into the trap of wanting to say something provocative or controversial to "stir up" the class, to bring the students to life, to generate some discussion. As a new educator, it might be tempting to want to show the class (particularly undergraduates) how "cool" you are by using street jargon or making humorous comments with an "edge" to them. Be careful. Although your intentions might be honorable and you didn't intend to single out any one individual or group, certain language (i.e., calling young adult women "girls," referring to "you people") can stir up a lot of trouble. Just remember that your job is not to be cool or to entertain, but to educate.

You may make a slip at some time and say something politically incorrect. When you do, simply say, "I'm sorry; I didn't mean to say that" or simply admit, "I spoke without thinking; I made a mistake." Most people forgive the contrite offender. Inadvertent misstatements do not usually end one's career. Most of us, at one time or another, have been guilty of this sort of thing—and such lapses are not generally considered harassment unless they are repetitive and severe.

Sexual harassment is often described in terms of being of two types: *quid pro quo,* which might involve something like trading grades for sexual favors, and *hostile environment,* which is conduct that intimidates or is so offensive that it interferes with an individual's work performance. Isolated incidents of misconduct generally will not create a "hostile work environment," although a single severe incident may give rise to a claim (e.g., the Paula Jones case) (Mallery, 1997; Fuertes, 1998).

Harassment consists of *unwanted* and *unwelcome* conduct of a sexual nature and can include jokes with suggestive themes, compliments of a personal or sexual nature, sexist slurs, visual images (e.g., sexually explicit posters, cartoons, or drawings), public humiliation, slander, pressuring someone for a date or sexual contact, sexual gestures, unwelcome notes, or such physical activities as brushing against someone, touching, unsolicited back rubs, or blocking a doorway with one's body. To support charges of harassment, courts are generally looking for "severe and pervasive" actions—behavior so offensive that any reasonable person would agree that it should be illegal (Risser, 1999). Victims of harassment feel threatened or assaulted—there is no reciprocity involved. An isolated joke or use of endearments generally would be viewed by courts as trivial—not harassment.

Faculty need to be especially careful in relationships with students, because one aspect of harassment is that the offender has a certain clout or power of position. In other words, students can argue that they felt pressured to comply with certain requests (e.g., repeated requests to go to dinner) due to the unequal power balance that existed—they didn't want to lose their grade of A or their research assistantship, for example.

Sexual harassment is also something you can experience from another faculty member or a peer, as well as from a student. Direct confrontation is often the best strategy: Tell the individual that you are not attracted to him or her, not interested in his or her notes or back rubs or whatever, and then instruct the person to respect your wishes. If this course of action does not work, then you need to go to your program chair or your dean and make a complaint. Do not be silent just because you are still a doctoral student or because you are new to the job. If you are being mistreated, there is a strong possibility that others have been, too. Courts are sympathetic to individuals who claim "hostile work environments" where it can be shown that pervasive and severe discrimination, intimidation, ridicule, or insult existed because of sexual orientation or gender, race, religion, national origin, age, disability, veteran status, pregnancy, or marital status. Most universities are concerned about discrimination in any form and will move relatively quickly to investigate and solve these situations.

Students as Research Subjects

In most, if not all, social science disciplines, it is quite acceptable to use one's students as research subjects—providing, of course, that it is voluntary on their part, that there is no harm or risk of harm, and that this activity does not detract from the educational instruction that ought to be occurring in the course. Always keep in mind that students (or their parents) generally do not pay tuition in order to advance your research.

The ethical principle of voluntary participation means that students cannot be coerced to complete survey forms, complete batteries of tests, reveal personal or sensitive information (e.g., about their experience with taking illegal drugs), or gather certain data against their will (particularly that from which you stand to benefit). Every student must have the right to decide whether to participate or not, without there being any penalty or repercussions for nonparticipation. Generally, this means providing (student) research participants with a written consent form that briefly explains the project, the extent of their involvement, and any benefits or risks. As a first step, you should discuss your research protocol with the Institutional Review Board (IRB) at your college or university. You will probably need to complete a form (e.g., Exemption Certification Form) identifying your research objectives and procedures to be used as well as how you plan to recruit your subjects. This somewhat formal process doesn't mean, however, that you shouldn't consider gathering data from or about your students. The classroom is a natural laboratory that has many advantages (convenience being perhaps the main one) to recommend it.

Sometimes instructors encourage students to participate in their research projects by awarding extra credit. This is generally well received in that students can look at what is being asked of them and then weigh whether they want to participate. Even when the research activity can be easily defended as a required assignment on pedagogical grounds, students should be given an option of working on another activity of similar importance or value if the student-produced data directly benefit the researcher. Students sometimes object to specific questions or sections of a questionnaire because of the fear that their data might not remain confidential or they may have religious objections to the project. In such cases, students who wish to receive extra credit without being research subjects should have other alternate projects or exercises available to them.

That engaging in a research project should not have any adverse effects on the participants seems straightforward enough. Ethically, your responsibility is to do no harm. The problem is that it is not always possible to anticipate how certain questions or activities may influence others. Interviewing students who have been victims of child abuse or domestic violence may provide much useful data but could, conceivably, impinge negatively on their self-esteem, leave them feeling depressed or in need of counseling to resolve painful issues that have been dredged up again. Studies where deception is used could leave participants feeling that they are naive or gullible, with a result that they become less likely to trust others. Punch (1986) has described a situation where a project designed to study the reactions of the police to reports of rape was scrapped because fabricated stories were going to be used and the fear was that the research might lead police to become skeptical of the real accounts of women who were sexually assaulted. Students might be willing to volunteer in such a project, particularly if there was a perception within a community that the police were insensitive to the claims of rape victims, but there would be legal repercussions for filing false police reports and the benefits might not outweigh the risks and potential harm that could result. Benefits should always clearly outweigh the potential for harm.

The third guideline is balance of the educational mission. It is one thing to take 15 minutes of class time to ask students to voluntarily fill out a questionnaire on their television viewing habits, but it is altogether another matter to ask students to give up every third class period to fill out questionnaires. If you are paid to be the instructor of a course, that must remain your paramount concern. The use of your students to supply data for your own research ought to be in a distant second or third place. In-class participation in research projects should not short-change or educationally impoverish your students. If you can't, with a clear conscience, easily defend what you are planning on having them do from an educational perspective, then you probably shouldn't involve them—even if it means you will have to conduct all of the interviews yourself or pay someone to help you.

Building a Professional Portfolio

One thing you can be sure of—you *will* need to present documentation of your competence and contributions at some point in your teaching career. Typically, these professional portfolios contain data such as:

1. Teaching evaluations from students, syllabi prepared, new courses created, workshops or special seminars conducted, invitational lectures given, and so on
2. Scholarship: publications authored, grants obtained, and the like
3. Professional service to the community, department, or college (e.g., committee appointments or elections, number of students advised)
4. Letters from reviewers of your portfolio
5. Unsolicited letters from students and former students

Create a filing system using the evaluation scheme or categories employed at your college university and begin it your first academic term. You might want to start one manilla folder for publications submitted, another for any unsolicited letters from students, a third for thank-you letters from organizations where you've provided consultation or volunteered, and so on. Update your vita whenever something significant occurs—keep track of all the different courses you've taught, the new courses you designed or created, the overloads you have carried, as well as any special honors or recognitions. Don't assume that you will remember everything four or five years in the future—it's better and easier to keep the vita current as things occur. If you have not been given a set of the guidelines that your department or college will use in determining your status relative to tenure, then by all means ask for a copy so that you can start preparing your portfolio.

Periodically browse through your materials. If your institution values teaching more highly than publishing, your teaching folder should be "fatter" than, say, your community service folder. Similarly, at a research university your scholarship folder would likely be thicker than your teaching folder. It may be useful to talk to colleagues to see what kinds of things they file and keep for their portfolios.

Promotion and Tenure

As alluded to previously, there is a tremendous amount of variation both in terms of the tenure review process, when it begins (e.g., the fourth year, fifth year, or sixth year), and what is expected and required of assistant professors in colleges and universities across the country. These expectations should be discussed during your job interview or soon afterwards, but, in any event, should be clear to you prior to signing your contract. Even so, it's a good idea early in your first year to confirm your understanding of the requirements with the head of your department or college. Ask colleagues who've recently been promoted about their experiences and for their advice. You may also want to read such books as those by Tierney and Bensimon (1996) and relevant chapters from Sawyer, Prichard, and Hostetler (1992) and Boice (1992).

A Model for Developing Teaching Assistants (by Linda Worley)

A colleague tells this story about the "training" he had before becoming a teaching assistant: "The composition director happened to see me on campus late in the summer and asked me to come to his office. This was in 1972. I was scheduled to begin graduate school in English in a month. 'How would you like to be a teaching assistant?' he asked. He told me I'd teach three sections of comp and told me the salary. 'Here's the text for the course,' he said, and handed me a copy. 'Good luck.'"

"Here's the text—good luck": That was the entire training program for a soon-to-be teaching assistant who would in a few weeks find himself under the spotlight in a classroom full of undergraduates. And for many of these undergraduates, this would be their first experience with university-level teaching and academic life.

Happily, things are changing. Teaching assistants around the country are increasingly being given thorough orientations and ongoing training for their instructional roles. This increased focus on the development of teaching assistants is linked to calls for improvement in undergraduate education, especially as it affects first-year students.

Teaching assistants play many roles in the life of undergraduates. In addition to interaction in the classroom, where the teaching assistant is the sole instructor for a section of a composition, communication, or foreign language course, an undergraduate's first-year course schedule may bring a teaching assistant into contact with the students as a tutor, grader, or recitation or lab instructor.

The teaching assistant may well be the most personal academic contact an undergraduate has with the institution and thus can help foster a sense of belonging to the academic enterprise and influence the success of the undergraduate's college career.

Besides their involvement in undergraduate education, it is vital to recognize the role that a teaching assistantship can play in the career of graduate students who wish to become members of the professoriate. The pedagogical knowledge base gained during the course of the teaching assistantship can become a solid foundation for the teaching functions all faculty members fulfill. In an increasingly competitive academic arena, the teaching assistant experience needs to be seen as an essential part of graduate education.

These factors underscore the necessity for a well thought-out, cohesive teaching assistant experience. How should this experience be structured? What kinds of activities should be included in a teaching assistant program? When and where should they occur? To answer these questions, we can turn to the literature on teaching assistant development. A particularly useful conceptual model sketches the changes in a novice teacher's concern vis-à-vis students over time (Sprague & Nyquist, 1991).

Preservice and first-year teaching assistants are likely concerned with issues that can best be described as interpersonal "self-concerns." Teaching assistants tend to hold "a highly engaged view toward students that is characterized by a sense of vulnerability or great ego-involvement on the TA's part" (Sprague & Nyquist, 1991, p. 309). The "self-concerns" of teaching assistants will often cause them to view their students as emotional allies/friends or, conversely, as sources of a threat to their authority. In a survey conducted in the summers of 1997 and 1998, the fear of losing control of the classroom and the fear of not being able to establish rapport dominated the worries of teaching assistants during university-wide orientations held at my institution. These apprehensions speak to a concern with basic survival in the classroom.

One strategy to help teaching assistants acquire more confidence in the classroom is initially to limit their duties to those that do not require high levels of complex interaction with students. Teaching assistants might first be asked to grade exams, set up experiments, work as tutors—literally, to assist a professor. If teaching assistants are asked to perform more extensive duties early in their graduate careers, then they need to be given very specific, even prescriptive, guidance.

Another highly effective activity at this stage is the micro-teach. A micro-teach allows the individual assistant to prepare and teach a short lesson to a small group in order to receive specific feedback from the group or facilitator in a safe, controlled environment before the teaching assistant has contact with many students. It is important that graduate students receive concrete help with their teaching duties from their home department or supervising professor in addition to an orientation that outlines more general roles and responsibilities.

A university-wide orientation can be the best place to focus on such issues as the rights and responsibilities of graduate students, on ways to establish rapport with students while keeping mutual respect alive in the classroom, and on the demographics of the student body at large. Case studies, simulations, and video clips are excellent ways to involve graduate students in these topics.

Departmental orientations build on the more general university-wide orientation, adding specificity. The department and individual supervising professor are the optimal sources for the detailed information a new teaching assistant needs in order to successfully complete the assigned tasks. Teaching assistants will learn about their specific duties, grading guidelines, as well as the resources and avenues of recourse available to them. They need to be prepared for their daily teaching assignments, whether these involve leading an effective discussion or demonstrating a lab technique. By the end of the orientation, teaching assistants should have the skills needed to be successful during the first weeks of the semester.

After gaining confidence and, indeed, "surviving" the first months, teaching assistants can begin to pay more attention to issues directly related to the craft of teaching. At this developmental stage, they become interested in acquiring and experimenting with a variety of teaching strategies. At a later point, a focus on students' learning may be added to the earlier concerns about interacting with students and instructional techniques. Changing the focus from "teaching" to "learning" produces monumental shifts in the teaching/learning enterprise—shifts that include attention to creating environments that recognize individual differences and that recognize the importance of learning outcomes (Barr & Tagg, 1995).

The supervising professor and graduate department need to be aware of and support this growth process. An optimal development plan has at least three components: knowledge and experience regarding pedagogy, data regarding performance, and feedback.

Which form these components take will vary with the expertise and maturity of the teaching assistant.

Teaching strategies can be learned in a formal graduate teaching seminar or in workshops. The teaching assistant meeting, with its emphasis on the daily needs of the course, will not in and of itself provide the depth or breadth needed to gain a solid foundation in teaching. The course supervisor, departmental faculty, or outside experts can all be involved in such formal instruction. Individual consultations between peers or the supervisor and the teaching assistant augment formal instruction. Topics may range from effective presentation techniques to issues of student motivation and classroom climate.

Data regarding performance should be gathered from various sources throughout the semester. Although teaching assistants probably know to use "minute papers" to assess how well students are learning content, such techniques can also provide valuable feedback in terms of instructor behavior and classroom procedures—indeed, what is working or not working well within the classroom. In addition to the standard end of semester evaluations, student input can be gathered through a class interview called the *small group instruction diagnosis*. In this process, faculty working with teaching assistants observe instruction directly through visiting or videotaping a class. A useful format for class visits is to arrange for a preobservation meeting during which time the teaching assistant and visitor can discuss the learning goals and plans for the particular class to be visited. It is helpful if the teaching assistant gives the observer several areas in which feedback is desired—for example, the pacing of the class, inclusion of all class members in a discussion, and so on. This way, the classroom observation becomes a process in which both the observer and observed are involved. The observer should take notes on both the teaching activities and the responses of the students, being sure to look for behaviors the teaching assistant had noted.

Gathering data on the performance of the teaching assistant is the first step. These data ought to be discussed with the TA and used for formative purposes—that is, to direct growth and change. As soon after a classroom visit as possible, the supervisor should meet with the teaching assistant. Feedback that is descriptive rather than personal will set the stage for the supervisor and teaching assistant to develop a joint plan of action designed to improve on strengths and weaknesses.

Teaching assistants nearing the end of their course of studies, especially those who wish to become faculty members, are best viewed as "junior colleagues." They might be given sole responsibility for a course. Along with such increased autonomy will come a new set of concerns. They need to know how to determine learning outcomes, construct a syllabus, tailor instruction so as to allow for various learning styles, assess student work fairly, and give informative feedback. The senior faculty member might be most useful at this point by encouraging the teaching assistant to become a reflective practitioner. This can be accomplished by sharing articles on teaching and learning as well as suggesting that the teaching assistant keep a teaching journal or begin to assemble artifacts for a teaching portfolio.

Graduate students who are considering pursuing an academic career need additional mentoring. They need to be introduced to the roles and responsibilities of college and university faculty. The national Preparing Future Faculty initiative[1] is designed to assist graduate students in understanding the variety of institutions in which faculty members work and the academic expectations, institutional identities, and particular policies and procedures that characterize different types of institutions of higher learning.

A recent survey I conducted asked new faculty at a wide range of postsecondary institutions to rate aspects of faculty life as to their importance for the individual's career advancement and to rank these same items with respect to graduate training received. The items that evidenced the largest numerical gap between the perceived importance to career and graduate training were:

1. Advising students
2. Creating a teaching portfolio
3. Working on department/university committees
4. Performing community service
5. Using multimedia effectively
6. Providing feedback designed to help students improve
7. Experimenting with innovative teaching strategies
8. Constructing a thoughtful syllabus
9. Understanding student abilities and preparation

The items on this list could readily become the basis of a departmental program designed to fill in some of the gaps for their future professionals.

A truly developmental view of graduate student professionalization recognizes that graduate students must gain the values, skills, and knowledge needed to be successful in their present teaching situations and to be engaged with the teaching/learning process throughout their careers.

References and Resources

Abbott, A. S. (1992). Teaching at a small liberal arts college. In R. M. Sawyer, K. W. Prichard, & K. D. Hostetler (Eds.), *The art and politics of college teaching*. New York: Peter Lang.

Barr, R. B., & Tagg, J. (1995). From teaching to learning: A new paradigm for undergraduate education. *Change, 27* (6), 12–25.

Beebe, L. (1993). *Professional writing for the human services*. Washington, DC: NASW Press.

Bedient, D. (1997–1998). Teaching assistant concerns and questions: What 252 TAs wanted to know and weren't afraid to ask. *The Journal of Graduate Assistant Development, 5* (3), 127–132.

Bode, R. (1999). Mentoring and collegiality. In R. K. Menges & Associates (Eds.), *Faculty in new jobs: A guide to settling in, becoming established, and building institutional support*. San Francisco: Jossey-Bass.

Boice, R. (1987). Is released-time an effective device for faculty development? *Research in Higher Education, 26,* 311–326.

Boice, R. (1992). *The new faculty member: Supporting and fostering professional development*. San Francisco: Jossey-Bass.

Dunn, D. S., & Zaremba, S. B. (1997). Thriving at liberal arts colleges: The more compleat academic. *Teaching of Psychology, 24,* 8–14.

Fuertes, M. (1998, November). Ruling out sexual harassment. *Techniques,* 42–43.

Henson, K. T. (1995). *The art of writing for publication*. Boston: Allyn and Bacon.

Mallery, M. (1997). The answers to your questions about sexual harassment. *Workforce, 76* (11), S7–S10.

McCrumb, S. (1998, May). Of time and the writer. *Writer's Digest, 78,* 18–20ff.

Parks, B. (1998). Taking care of teachers: 7 time-management sanity savers. *Instructor, 107* (5), 46.

Punch, M. (1986). *The politics and ethics of fieldwork*. Beverly Hills, CA: Sage.

Risser, R. (1999). Sexual harassment training: Truth and consequences. *Training & Development, 53,* 21–23.

Sandler, B., & Shoop, R. J. (1997). *Sexual harassment on campus: A guide for administrators, faculty, and students.* Boston: Allyn and Bacon.

Sawyer, R. M., Prichard, K. W., & Hostetler, K. D. (1992). *The art and politics of college teaching.* New York: Peter Lang.

Schoenfeld, A. C., & Magnan, R. (1992). *Mentor in a manual.* Madison, WI: Magna Publications.

Seldin, P. (1997). *The teaching portfolio: A practical guide to improved performance and promotion/tenure decisions.* Bolton, MA: Anker Publishing.

Sorcinelli, M. D. (1992). New and junior faculty stress: Research and responses. In M. D. Sorcinelli & A. E. Austin (Eds.), *Developing new and junior faculty* (pp. 27–37). San Francisco: Jossey-Bass.

Sprague, J., & Nyquist, J. D. (1991). A developmental perspective on the TA role. In J. D. Nyquist, R. D. Abbot, D. H. Wulff, & J. Sprague (Eds.), *Preparing the professoriate of tomorrow to teach: Selected readings in TA training.* Dubuque, IA: Kendall-Hunt.

Thyer, B. (1994). *Successful publishing in scholarly journals.* Thousand Oaks, CA: Sage.

Tierney, W. G., & Bensimon, E. M. (1996). *Promotion and tenure: Community and socialization in academe.* Albany: State University of New York Press.

Weaver, R. (1992). Building a future at "The Premiere Teaching University" in the Midwest. In R. M. Sawyer, K. W. Prichard, & K. D. Hostetler (Eds.), *The art and politics of college teaching.* New York: Peter Lang.

Endnote

1. The Preparing Future Faculty initiative is sponsored by the American Association of Colleges and Universities and the Council of Graduate Schools funded by the PEW foundation.

16

Values and Ethics

DINAH ANDERSON

Overview: What constitutes an ethical dilemma? Indeed, what kinds of ethical dilemmas might we face as faculty members? What is a process for resolving ethical problems? This chapter provides a succinct introduction to the topic of helping educators to develop a sensitivity to ethical issues and to formulate responses to them.

Ethical Dilemmas: Choosing the "Right Thing" to Do

Although students and their families, taxpayers, and others interested in higher education wouldn't suspect it, teaching is fraught with numerous ethical quandaries that require quick, on-the-spot decision making. And yet, most new college teachers have not considered nor been challenged in their doctoral studies to consider the ethical problems and conflicts inherent in the teaching profession.

We do, of course, make ethical decisions routinely, whether we are conscious of them or not, because our actions are often based on our values—even though we may not have clearly identified or enumerated them. And because not all faculty share the same values, it is very likely that even our well-meaning colleagues and loyal students will disagree at times with our decisions concerning the "right" course of action.

Accordingly, the purpose of this chapter is:

- To help you recognize and identify ethical dilemmas
- To review ethical principles to consider when confronting ethical issues
- To offer a way of thinking about ethical issues in teaching based on absolutist and relativist frameworks
- To alert new college teachers to a variety of ethical problems and dilemmas that may arise in the course of teaching
- To suggest a process for arriving at decisions

This brief chapter will not, however, attempt to suggest there are pat answers to ethical issues. There are no patented answers to most knotty problems. At best, all this chapter can offer are ways of thinking about ethical issues.

When Does an Ethical Issue Become an Ethical Dilemma?

Not all ethical issues are ethical dilemmas. Sometimes individuals engage in clearly illegal or unethical acts: They lie, steal, falsify documents, and so on. A faculty member who throws out negative student evaluations and presents only the positive ones to his or her chair has engaged in an unethical act. The dilemma may have occurred earlier, when the instructor pondered submitting negative evaluations or culling out the really bad ones in order to look better before the promotion and tenure committee. Thus, the instructor may have had to decide between the ethical course of action (submitting all the evaluations) or, as the breadwinner of the family, pulling out the negative comments in order to preserve a job that provided sole income for a spouse and three small children. In terms of the greatest good or the "right" thing to do, it would be easy to rationalize that feeding one's family could be as right, and possibly more right, than being ethical in this situation. After all, one could argue, no one would be harmed by failing to report some caustic comments from a few disgruntled students.

A *dilemma* implies a choice between two or more equally balanced alternative solutions to an ethical problem. For example, since the advent of high-tech medicine, bio-ethicists have been wrestling with the question of whether to prolong life if to do so also prolongs suffering. Usually, people would agree that prolonging life is better than ending or shortening life. But the decision to lengthen life by a few weeks or months is certainly complicated when those extra days are accompanied by intractable pain or a greatly diminished quality of life. One would like to argue for an increased number of days for oneself or for one's loved ones, but would one want those days if they couldn't be enjoyed? That's a tough decision to make, right? Dilemmas are characterized as being thorny problems—those where there is no clear path. Dilemmas can occur when the solutions are equally acceptable, when the alternatives are both unacceptable, or when the "right" thing to do has negative consequences and the "wrong" course of action has positive or beneficial effects.

For example, here are some typical grading dilemmas that you might encounter in your classroom:

- A talented freshman athlete in your class needs a grade of C to maintain his eligibility to play basketball. He currently has a D+ average. Should you raise his score a few points in the interest of assisting the school's athletic program and helping this poverty-born individual to achieve a possible multimillion-dollar professional contract?

- A courageous and persevering wheelchair-bound student is fighting depression brought on by further deterioration in her physical health and the recent departure of her campus caregiver. She failed her midterm exam. Although she doesn't talk much in class, she desperately wants to be the first in her family to graduate from college. Should you "fudge" her class participation score to close the gap between a passing and a failing grade in your course? She confides in you that if she fails your class, she is in danger of academic suspension, and that if she has to go home, she fears her parents won't support her return to college later.

- It is near the end of the semester and a small group of students invites you and several other faculty to dinner in a nice restaurant. Three of them are in your senior capstone course. Afterwards, they thank you for your help during their undergraduate careers and want to pay the bill. Can you accept such a gift?

Would it be permissible to accept the gift *after* but not before grades are turned in? What do you do if the other two faculty see no problem with the students buying dinner?

One logical approach to solving ethical dilemmas begins with the identification of our own values. What primary, cardinal value or values guide you as an educator? Thinking about this another way: Would violating certain values make you feel guilty or unhappy? Take a moment or two to consider what values you hold most important. You may even want to list them on a sheet of paper.

Basic Respect

If there is a single guiding principle that seems to be the basis for the majority of educators' ethical considerations, it is that of demonstrating respect for all students (Costanzo & Handelsman, 1998). New teachers are sometimes startled to discover that their students seldom conform to the "ideal"—that within the same classroom, they differ not only in age and developmental stage as well as in levels of intellect and hunger for knowledge but also in their honesty and integrity.

Sometimes it is easier for us to relate to some students than to others. We may also have misconceptions or stereotypes about who makes the "best" student; we can have preferences for working with certain types of students. Some faculty find it easier to relate to and respect the committed graduate student. Still others may prefer adolescents fresh out of high school, or middle-aged adults in their 40s and 50s planning midlife career changes, or even senior citizens going back for degrees they never finished. Which of the following students would be the most difficult for you to relate to? The 275-pound wide-end receiver hoping for an invitation to the NFL who never attends class; the 23-year-old Native American single mother of two preschoolers attempting to leave the welfare roles; or the 37-year-old foreign national with poor English? All these individuals deserve our respect and best effort.

Most of us have been acculturated in a predominantly racist society. We live in a culture still struggling to overcome institutional racism and white privilege. Examining our own biases and prejudices is a first step toward keeping discriminatory behavior in check while dealing with students. Research has shown that educators, both male and female, are more likely to call on men in their classes and to comment on their answers (Sandler & Hall, 1986). By simply not calling on a representative sample of *all* members of the class, even if it is unintentional, we may be communicating that we don't value the contributions of persons who are different from us.

Whatever our field of expertise, teaching provides us with an opportunity to model inclusiveness and sensitivity to human and cultural diversity. Discriminatory practices are almost always wrong. Approaching every student with an attitude of basic respect should be our beginning posture, but it alone is not sufficient to resolve our ethical dilemmas.

The Power Differential

As educators, we must always be aware of the power we have over the lives of others. Students have been socialized since their formative years to yield to the authority of the teacher. As the expert, the teacher defines the learning objectives in college courses and evaluates the extent to which the learners have mastered these. Grades are the widely accepted sign of mastery of the material and are also a tool of professional gatekeeping. Grades can have an enormous "make or break" influence on a student's future. Teachers can use grades to "punish" students they don't like and boost the GPAs of their favorites. Grades can encourage students to blossom and achieve their true potential or can be used to ruthlessly attack a student. The power imbalance between students and faculty is real and imposes a great responsibility on the instructor to be fair and just.

Five Ethical Principles

Beyond respecting students and constantly monitoring ourselves to make sure we don't abuse our power, there are at least five ethical principles that might apply when we're confronted with an ethical problem or dilemma.

The principle of *nonmaleficence* means that our actions should do no harm. Although our patience and our own self-esteem may be tested when students say unkind things or make terrible accusations, we must not deliberately lash out or attempt to "pay back" or hurt a student.

Related to this is the principle of *beneficence*. Wherever possible, our actions ought to do good. We need to lift up instead of tear down; constructive criticism is more helpful than destructive criticism. If caught in a dilemma where it is not always possible to do good, then this principle suggests that you choose the path of doing the least harm.

Justice, being fair and equitable, is also a vitally important principle—one that students quite rightly expect from us day in and day out. They don't want a classmate to get special consideration because her father is a member of the board of trustees; they don't want the student who doesn't carry his weight on a group project to get the same good grade as those who worked harder. Students expect "rules" to be administered consistently. If you state a policy in your syllabus (e.g., assessing a penalty on late papers), then you are obliged to enforce it. Don't just apply it to the shy student and then wimp out when the assertive student makes a case for special consideration. Students are very sensitive to inequity in all its various forms, and they talk to each other.

Autonomy refers to an individual's right to self-determination (Abramson, 1996). Where possible, allow choice. Don't be the petty tyrant forcing your views, values, or preferences on students. Be aware of your ability to subtly coerce. For instance, although you offer compelling arguments, your research assistant student may not want to write his or her thesis on the topic that most interests *you*—and he or she shouldn't have to.

Truthfulness is yet another essential principle. Without it, there is no hope that an educator could be viewed as an ethical individual. Although we all have various interpretations of what the "truth" actually is in just about any situation, it is one thing to report honestly what we have seen, thought, or believed and an altogether different matter to distort, misrepresent, or lie. Lying is a particularly insidious evil, because once an individual has been caught in a lie, then every subsequent statement of consequence that he or she makes is suspect. Promising what we can't deliver is also a close cousin to lying and therefore unethical. Honesty is the best policy, even if it is somewhat embarrassing or even painful.

Absolutists and Relativists

Having identified the ethical principles that will likely influence our decision making, it is still necessary to understand that our positions on ethical issues may vary depending on whether we think about rules in absolute or relative terms. Persons who think in absolute terms tend not to make exceptions. They are comfortable in stating and enforcing policies and rules without regard to the individual. Thus, if the syllabus reads, "Any paper submitted after the due date will be penalized," the professor who thinks in absolute terms will probably take points off even if John comes limping to the instructor's office the next day in a cast and explains that he had a bike wreck on the way to campus and his femur is broken in two places. The absolutist approach minimizes, in some ways, the number of tough decisions to be made as long as there are rules or policies that can be consulted. Absolutists would rather not make exceptions, because they so value the principle of fairness and equal treatment.

Relativists take a more person-centered or contextual approach to decision making. They weigh the individual's story. If John is credible (and wearing a cast certainly would strengthen his alibi), then the relativist may choose to "bend" the rules and make an exception, allowing John to turn in his paper a day or even several days late with no penalty because he had a valid excuse. In the relativist's eyes, the rest of the class is not being treated unfairly because an exception could have been granted to anyone with a similar stroke of bad luck. Thus, ethical principles may be applied according to two very different models about how the world is or ought to work.

Examples of Ethical Dilemmas

To illustrate the types of ethical dilemmas you might encounter in the classroom and to help you to think about your guiding principles, here are some additional examples of ethical problems where a number of potential alterative courses of action are possible.

A Problem of Religion

You announce in class that you intend to lead the students in an exercise to teach them progressive relaxation and visualization in a unit on stress management. This is a treatment technique that is widely employed by clinicians in the profession. A mature female student raises her hand and states, "Professor Jones, I can't stay for this exercise. It is against my religion." She is well aware that class attendance is required. Can she be excused? What are the principles that might apply?

To coerce her to stay by penalizing her for leaving puts you in direct conflict with her right to exercise her religious beliefs and challenges her autonomy. The principle of beneficence must be considered, because a future employer might expect her to know this technique, and if she doesn't, then her future clients will not benefit. The argument could also be made that these clients will suffer more if you allow the student to pass up learning this particular knowledge. Requiring the student to remain in class could also create an uncomfortable level of anxiety, and so the principle of doing no harm must be considered. Would it be fair to allow her to leave without penalty while other students are required to stay?

A possible compromise would be to provide an alternate assignment or make-up work for her absence. If, however, you see no area for compromise because this class is viewed as too important to miss, then the student always has the option of expressing his or her autonomy by taking the penalty associated with being absent.

A Problem of Basic Humanity

A female student needs a passing grade to graduate, but she falls a few points short. She calls you just before you turn in your grades and reveals that she just left her abusive husband of 16 years. When she learns she has not passed the course, she requests an extra-credit assignment in order to pass. Without the diploma, she will not be hired for a position promised to her. Without a job, she will not be able to support herself and her child.

The ethical relativist would want to consider the context of the situation as well as the consequences for the student, and may even decide that, on balance, the student deserves some slack. However, the principle of justice requires fairness to all. Is it fair to others to allow this student to do extra work at this late date to make the grade when her classmates do not have the same opportunity?

An ethical absolutist might take the position that a teacher should not extend privileges to one that aren't extended to all. Furthermore, changing the grading system for this one student could be considered a breach of the contract laid out in the syllabus. How many other students might have wanted to change their grades by doing extra-credit work? They, too, may have had unfortunate circumstances arise during the term but managed to cope effectively and still get a passing grade.

The principle of beneficence in the long term may also suggest that allowing this student to graduate without having passed your course is no favor to her. Employers, other professionals, friends, and relatives all hold expectations of her in the "real world" (i.e., outside the academic setting). Would the extra-credit work really teach her all that she did not learn in the class? This dilemma necessitates the violation of either the fairness principle (letting the student have a few extra points) or the principle of beneficence (possibly sending her back to an abusive husband because she doesn't have a diploma and therefore no job). There is no one best solution.

A Colleague's Malfeasance

You are teaching the second in a two-course sequence with 101 being a prerequisite for 102. Students consistently come to your class with an outdated explanation of a major concept in your discipline because the 101 professor is teaching old knowledge from yellowing lecture notes. In order to get the knowledge needed to make up for the deficits they present, you have to reteach the concept. In so doing, you have to cut some of the content of the 102 course. If you don't ensure that students gain competency in this foundation knowledge, they will fail your course and several to come.

What is fair or just in this situation? The principle of nonmaleficence suggests you cannot allow students to carry on with wrong foundation information. Conversely, is it fair to yourself to incur the extra burden of teaching your course and content assigned to the 101 course as well? If you don't do the remedial teaching for 101 (and let the chips fall where they may), will you have to defend a higher than expected failure rate in 102?

Confronting this senior colleague's malfeasance would seem to be the obvious solution. If so, will you do that yourself or will you go to the department chair or dean? Will complaining about a colleague put at risk the outcome of your own tenure application next year?

Although it is true that the principle of maleficence suggests you might be an accomplice to incompetence if you do not seek to remedy the situation, most untenured faculty will have to gauge the risk of potential political harm to themselves if they are too critical of a senior colleague. In some situations, the dilemma might boil down to: "Do I sacrifice myself for the good of the students?" This, of course, requires an individual response. One would have to weigh exactly how much damage is being done to students, whether there were other alternatives (e.g., additional readings that could be provided to students), and what might be the likely turn of events if an assistant professor went to the chair to complain.

Keeping Promises—Implied and Stated

Are instructors bound by their own course syllabi? Suppose that a terrific new book that sheds profound, new light on an important unit of material becomes available six weeks into your course. Is it fair to your students to ask them to do additional reading in a course already heavy in reading? The "add/drop" date for courses has passed. Would you be better off taking the issue to the students, making the decision to add the book yourself, or waiting until next semester to add the new reading?

On one hand, staying true to the syllabus could have some definite advantages. On the other hand, there may be times when you want to drop a reading or add a new one. If you want to drop a book that students have already bought so that they can buy a different one, then you have to decide if it is clearly better for them to have this new material than the old.

Additional ethical issues that may arise are presented below. (If that's not enough, even more are listed in Tabachnick, Keith-Spiegel, & Pope, 1991 and in Keith-Spiegel, Wittig et al., 1993). No set of solutions are provided for these problems. Their purpose in this chapter is to heighten your awareness of potential ethical dilemmas and, by helping you anticipate those that might come your way, to give you a jump-start on thinking about how you could or *should* respond.

Availability and Accessibility

Outside the classroom, what is your responsibility to be available and accessible to students? Are posted office hours sacred or is it okay to occasionally schedule a committee meeting during those times? Do such responsibilities "cheat" students of their time with you?

Dependability

You are routinely "a few minutes late" for classes. Is that a big deal, especially if your chronic tardiness is due to student advisees who seem to show up just as you are leaving for class?

Timely and Thoughtful Feedback

Work on your dissertation has been going so well that you failed to grade and return your students' midterm exams for three weeks. Does anyone really expect you to do a responsible job of teaching *and* to meet the deadline set by your chair for the third chapter? Timely and thoughtful feedback to students is for tenured professors, isn't it?

Self-Disclosure

One of your undergraduate students is intrigued about what you "really" think about a host of issues that come up in your social science class. Is it in your own or the students' best interest to reveal that you are homosexual and a Democrat who strongly opposes both the religious right and the Pope's position on abortion? Although you may take full responsibility for your political and personal choices, you are standing in the role of teacher. Will undergraduates be able to separate ideology from the person? Will some be offended? Should you give "equal time" for the expression of others' positions, opinions, and ideas? Will the less confident students speak their minds if doing so means opposing a teacher's lifestyle, politics, and religious beliefs? A teacher's personal disclosure carries ethical overtones, because, like so much else about teaching, it must take into account the possibility for influence and coercion—overt or covert.

Robert Audi (1994) has noted:

One is never just a teacher. One is always—even if not con-
sciously—an advocate of a point of view, a critic of certain
positions, an exemplar of someone trying to communicate, a
purveyor of images, a practitioner of behavioral standards, a
person dealing with, and indeed responsible for, others in
common tasks. (p. 35)

Teaching in Your Area of Competence

Your college/university department hasn't been staffed to teach all
the required courses, much less the electives, for years. It is simply
understood that faculty members and adjunct teachers may be
recruited to provide instruction outside their area of competence
(Congress, 1998). Refusing to teach a course outside of your area
will undoubtedly get you labeled as "not a team-player." Doing so
will mean delivering less than your best work to the consumers of
educational services (the students) and to the citizens they are
being educated/trained to serve. If you don't teach the class, someone even less qualified than you will be tapped. What is the ethical
thing to do?

Physical/Mental Fitness

You have been assigned to teach a course you've been honing for
years. But if you aren't physically fit and mentally alert when you
cross the classroom threshold, it is unlikely you can do your best
work. If you do not deliver your thoughtfully researched material in
a format that is pedagogically competent and consistent with students' learning styles, have you done an effective or even ethical job
of teaching?

Teaching to Student Evaluations

A junior faculty member facing application for tenure is in a somewhat precarious "political" position in the department and needs all
the help he can get. Although everyone agrees that student evalua-

tions of teachers are a lame measure of teaching competence, they have become the busy dean's shortcut to a more substantial evaluation of teaching competence. Should the teacher cut back on homework or lighten up on the midterm and final exams in order to evoke more favorable student evaluations of one's teaching?

Nonacademic Counseling

In an advisement session, a student confides that he is having suicidal thoughts. Does *in loco parentis* still apply? What is your professional and ethical duty? What do you do if one of your third-year medical students confides that another student is stealing narcotic drugs from patients' supplies and wants you to help his friend without busting her out of the program? Student A lets it slip that her roommate, Student B, purchased her excellent term paper from a source on the Internet. You know the instructor involved. Should you inform your colleague?

Perhaps the core problem of accepting information deleterious to others is that you, the teacher, are put in the position of colluding if you don't take action and of breaking confidence if you do. Or as one colleague recently put it, how can you maintain objectivity and fairness when you know more than you ought (or want) to know?

Confidentiality

A student's parent phones to ask about his child's grades, unaware of the legislation protecting students' right to privacy. Maintaining confidentiality about students' grades means that we may not discuss a student's grades with parents or guardians. For the same reasons, we don't post grades on exams or papers in public places. Can you make an exception because the student's father was a fraternity brother?

A Process for Ethical Decision Making

Whether you see yourself as a relative absolutist or an absolute relativist, ethical decision making requires looking at these dilemmas from many perspectives and looking deeply. What follows is not the "answer" to ethical issues or dilemmas, but a framework to help arrive at a decision, realizing that any resolution may be only the best of two or more poor choices. Many times, however, the solution becomes apparent when a deliberate process of considering basic ethical principles is begun.

1. Determine if the issue is one subject to professional ethics. It probably is if (a) there is an imbalance of power between the people involved; (b) choosing one set of responses over another would give even the appearance of a conflict of interests; or (c) choosing one set of behaviors over another would create an unstated or burdensome obligation on anyone's part, or if questions about fairness arise.
2. List and consider possible alternatives and the ramifications of each response.
3. Consult with other respected and experienced teachers whom you trust as mentors.
4. Consult your professional Code of Ethics if you're teaching in a professional school. If your discipline has no professional code, consult those of the American Association of University Professors or the American Psychological Association.
5. Consider your basic contractual obligations as an employee.
6. Consult the college/university academic ombud or attorney.
7. Consider whether your behavior would stand public scrutiny, remembering there are few "secrets" in the academic community.
8. Try to take the perspective of the other person, the student's point of view. How does the situation change when viewed from that perspective?
9. Don't make an impulsive decision, but give yourself some time to reflect on your alternatives.

Opportunities for growth and development as a human being and a professional may be enhanced by the nature of these challenges. Through privately and collectively wrestling with these hard questions for which there may be no best answers, we have the chance of becoming ethical role models for our students. This would be no small accomplishment!

References and Resources

AAUP Statement of Professional Ethics. (1987). *Academe, 73* (4), 49.

Abramson, M. (1996). Reflections on knowing oneself ethically: Toward a working framework for social work practice. *Families in Society: The Journal of Contemporary Human Services, 77* (2), 195–202.

Audi, R. (1994). On the ethics of teaching and the ideals of learning. *Academe, 80* (5), 27–36.

Beabout, G. R., & Wennemann, D. J. (1994). *Applied professional ethics: A developmental approach for use with case studies.* Frederick, MD: University Press of America.

Congress, E. (1998). *Social work ethics for educators: Navigating ethical change in the field and in the classroom.* Paper presented at the Annual Program Meeting of the Council on Social Work Education, Orlando, FL.

Costanzo, M., & Handelsman, M. M. (1998). Teaching aspiring professors to be ethical teachers: Doing justice to the case study method. *Teaching of Psychology, 25* (2), 97–102.

Fisch, L. (1996). Ethical dimensions of college and university teaching: Understand and honoring the special relationship between teachers and students. *New Directions for Teaching and Learning,* 66. San Francisco: Jossey-Bass.

Keith-Spiegel, P., Taachnick, B. G., & Allen, M. (1993). Ethics in academia: Students' views of professors' actions. *Ethics & Behavior, 3,* 149–162.

Keith-Spiegel, P., Wittig, A. F., Perkins, D. V., Balogh, D. W., & Whitley, B. E. (1993). *The ethics of teaching: A casebook.* Muncie, IN: Ball State University.

Lane, A. J. (1998). "Consensual" relations in the academy: Gender, power, and sexuality. *Academe, 84* (5), 24–31.

Markie, P. J. (1994). *A professor's duties: Ethical issues in college teaching.* Lanham, MD: Rowman & Littlefield.

Matthews, J. R. (1991). The teaching of ethics and the ethics of teaching. *Teaching of Psychology, 18* (2), 80–85.

Sandler, B. R., & Hall, R. M. (1986). *The campus revisited: Chilly for women faculty, administrators, and graduate students.* Washington, DC: Project on the Status and Education of Women, Association of American Colleges.

Tabachnick, B. G., Keith-Spiegel, P., & Pope, K. S. (1991). Ethics of teaching: Beliefs and behaviors of psychologists as educators. *American Psychologist, 46* (5), 506–515.

17

Have You Chosen the Right Career?

Overview: Not everyone is suited to be a surgeon, a television talk-show host, or a professional golfer. And it follows that being highly intelligent or having the gift of facile speech does not ensure that a given individual will be a good teacher. When things are not going well, how is a novice educator to know whether he or she has chosen the right career? This chapter is written for new faculty who are having severe doubts about their careers and who need guidance in thinking through negative feedback or unhappiness with teaching at the college level.

Being Realistic

Teaching is enormously satisfying when things are going well—especially when you have bright, inquisitive minds hungry for instruction; when you are able to see the progress that an individual student or a whole class is making; when penetrating questions are asked and no one jumps up to leave after the bell rings; when students come by your office and ask for advice; and when, in preparing a lecture, you discover a little known fact or case that will become the basis for a paper that you want to write.

When you get back a good set of teaching evaluations or a colleague tells you that he or she has heard from students what a super job you are doing in the classroom, there will be no doubt in your mind that teaching is the right career for you. And the former students who unexpectedly drop by to thank you, to say that you were their favorite teacher, will give you a dose of euphoria better than a box of chocolates on Valentine's Day. Treasure these memories.

Life, however, is composed of both ups and downs. There are going to be low spots in your career as a faculty member—go ahead and recognize that—prepare yourself for these. You can expect, for instance, that someday a hostile student will charge into your office and argue some minor point until you become angry yourself and don't handle the situation well; when a student will try to cheat on a test and then accuse you of lying; when it is Sunday and you will have a bad case of the flu and three piles of term papers to grade before you have to turn in final grades on Monday morning; when you've spent four hours preparing an exam only to have it stolen right off the secretary's desk; and when a student or a class evaluates you unfairly and says hurtful things.

There may be territorial and political battles within the department where you feel that you are torn between two powerful adversaries and must steer a course that allows you to walk down the middle without stepping into the minefields to the left or right. You will also be saddened when close friends do not get tenure despite the fact that they are excellent teachers or have a better publishing record than most of the individual members of the promotion and tenure committee. In short, you will experience a mixture of both highs and lows. There will be times when you feel that your destiny, your calling, is to be a damn good educator. And there will be occasions when you are sorely tempted to tell the department head what you *really* think of him or her and when all you want to do is to walk out of the classroom, throw the students' papers away, and apply for a job stocking shelves at Wal-Mart. Fortunately, these days will be relatively rare.

Teaching is a great vocation. Seldom is anyone looking over your shoulder telling you what to do or how to do it. There's no clock punching and there's few emergencies to handle. Best of all, teaching is not a singular craft, but is a profession composed of very different and discrete pursuits involving such pleasurable activities as reading (now tell the truth, isn't this one of your favorite things to do?); organizing, creating, and locating interesting material for lectures; preparing instructional materials (e.g., transparencies, handouts, homework assignments); delivering the lecture; serving as a discussion facilitator, a cheerleader, a motivational speaker, and an entertainer; and advising not only in the academic area but also in the realm of roommates, lovers, parents, and vocational choices. And in many universities, that is only half the job. There's also writing professional articles, data analysis, doing lab work, and tracking down that elusive reference to complete a literature review. In short, there's something almost for everyone who is interested in intellectual matters.

Those who strongly favor one portion of the job more than another—for instance, who like conducting research better than classroom teaching—tend to gravitate toward niches where they can do just that. Even the worst part of being a faculty member—the drudgery of grading—typically doesn't consume all that much time, and instructors often find creative solutions to minimize the amount of time that it does take. There is an enormous amount of freedom within academe. With the right amount of self-discipline, you can get the onerous parts of the job done and out of the way, and still have the bulk of the time you want to work left over for activities that you find more enjoyable. So, when tasks that aren't fun or enjoyable are getting to you, just remember that usually these sorts of things don't constitute most of your job. Consider the things that you do like to do—and then try to find more time to do what's enjoyable.

Have You Chosen the Right Career?

When your jokes and lectures fall flat and students are sleeping in your classroom, even the most enthusiastic educator can become discouraged. A bit of advice here: Don't generalize from a single negative experience, an unmotivated class, or even a single semester and conclude that you aren't cut out to be an educator. There are classes which, for whatever reasons, are more unruly or denser or less amenable to your form of instruction than others. Expect to run into some of these. Just one just class can make you feel that you are having a terrible semester. When things aren't going well, don't make hasty decisions. Don't resign on the spot, set your office on fire, or slap the student who has been trying to look down your blouse all semester.

To gain perspective, it might be helpful to talk with a friend or colleague you can trust. Explain the event or situation. Ask for advice. Sometimes experienced faculty have wonderful suggestions for how to improve difficult situations. You may even want to invite a more experienced instructor to sit in with your class to observe the dynamics. Or you might wish to observe more seasoned instructors.

Negative experiences can also originate from a bad match of your skills and talents with what the department or college wants. If all you want to do is to teach Chaucer, but the dean wants you writing federal grants for money to combat adult illiteracy in the Aleutian islands, then there's a problem. In a situation like this, it's often helpful to try to estimate how long an unpleasant task might last. Your course of action will likely depend on whether the distasteful project is time limited to three or four weeks or if it is presented as your *major* responsibility for the foreseeable future.

It's possible to be unhappy in an academic setting for a lot of different reasons. For instance, you could feel dejected because of (1) separation from a loved one or family members, (2) physical isolation (e.g., an individual from the city takes a job in a small college located in a rural area), (3) problems with teaching assignments or course load, (4) inadequate pay or educational resources, or (5) the academic milieu (e.g., the department head is an absolute tyrant and an ignoramus to boot). Try to identify the source of your unhappiness. The solutions are very different if you are separated from a loved one because of appointments to different universities than if you are having a personality clash with a single student in your English 101 class.

If your unhappiness is not a temporary thing—that is, if it doesn't go away after several weeks—then this is one that can't be ignored. However, it doesn't necessarily mean that you should think about leaving the profession; instead, your dispiritedness might be directly attributable to the *place* where you are employed. In another college or university you may once again feel that you were destined to be an educator. And, if you discover that you aren't cut out to be a researcher, then you might want to consider moving from a research university to a smaller college or junior college.

Even the best teacher may have an "off" semester, but if you have received several semesters of bad teaching evaluations, then it is clear you are doing something incorrectly. It doesn't mean that you are not well suited for a career in teaching, but it is pointing to the need for you to get some help from someone more experienced.

If you get back student evaluations that are personally devastating, immediately get consultation from someone you trust. Get your mentor or department chair actively involved. Have an experienced faculty member sit in with your classes and make observations. Sawyer, Prichard, and Hostetler (1992) stated, "It is almost impossible to cover up poor teaching. Poor research can be destroyed, and few will know about it. No so for the public performance that teaching entails" (p. 151).

In a set of essays entitled *The Chalk Dust Collection*, Fisch (1996) has listed a set of key questions that he says teachers should reflect on because they will result in better teaching. But these questions can also be used to help those struggling with a decision about whether to leave teaching. An abbreviated listing of some of his pertinent questions are as follows:

1. *What activities in teaching give me the greatest satisfaction? What causes me to come away from a class feeling really high?*
2. *What do I do that seems to produce good response in students—not just positive comments but eager attention, intelligent questions, and desire to engage the material?*
3. *What modifications can I make in my teaching in order to increase the frequency of the wonderful moments referred to above?*
4. *Why did I decide to go into teaching? How can I work to enhance the attainment of the goals implied in that choice?*
5. *If I had the freedom to spend the next day doing exactly what I want (without regard to schedule, commitments, and responsibilities), what would I do?*
6. *In what personal and professional activities would I like to be engaged five years from now? (pp. 158–159)*

Only you know what you want to accomplish in life. If you have worked hard to get where you are but now are ready to quit in disgust, give yourself some time to gather additional information, to consult with others, to reflect and examine your options, as well as to look at what you can do and what you can do *differently*. You are not alone. A wonderful thing about being in academia is that there are so many resources available to us, ranging from the library and the instructional development center, to supportive colleagues, to talented students. If you are having difficulty with your teaching, take advantage of the intellectual riches around you; tackle it as though it were a dissertation topic—do the necessary research to get to the source of the problem.

Teaching is a fine and noble profession, and if you are dedicated to the notion of teaching, there *is* a place for you. Your particular venue may, however, reside in a different place than where you currently are; perhaps you are better suited to be an instructor in a community college instead of a Research 1 institute. Only you know the depth of your desire to teach. This was how Palmer (1998) phrased it: "I am a teacher at heart, and there are moments in the classroom when I can hardly hold the joy. When my students and I discover uncharted territory to explore, when the pathway out of a thicket opens up before us, when our experience is illumined by the lightning-life of the mind—then teaching is the finest work I know" (p. 1). If this is how you feel, then you should follow your passion, even though there may be small setbacks and obstacles in your path.

Interestingly, this is what Palmer (1998) wrote just one paragraph later:

> *But at other moments, the classroom is so lifeless or painful or confused—and I am so powerless to do anything about it— that my claim to be a teacher seems a transparent sham. Then the enemy is everywhere: in those students from some alien planet, in that subject I thought I knew, and in the personal pathology that keeps me earning my living this way. What a fool I was to imagine that I had mastered this occult art—harder to divine than tea leaves and impossible for mortals to do even passably well! (p. 1)*

Experienced faculty know that the sailing is not always smooth, that there will be good days and bad days, and even good classes and good semesters as well as bad ones. Don't capitulate too soon. As Parker's book on the craft of teaching describes time and again, even those who know what they are doing are often uncertain and anxious and don't have a clue at the beginning if it is going to all work out.

Some actual data may be of assistance in helping you to evaluate any unhappiness with teaching. According to a poll of 1,500 full-time faculty members both at two- and four-year institutions conducted by the National Opinion Research Center, over 90 percent expressed a clear satisfaction with their career choice; 87 percent would definitely (63 percent) or probably (24 percent) pursue a career in higher education again if they were to begin their professional careers anew. Although the percentage of educators who would choose careers in education fluctuates somewhat, it does so narrowly across age, gender, race/ethnicity, academic rank, and institution type. However, about 40 percent of faculty respondents reported that they had considered a career change. Sources of dissatisfaction mentioned most frequently were displeasure with the financial compensation; personal issues, such as new opportunities in outside fields, family considerations, and feeling burned out or wanting a new challenge; and frustration with the "system" <www.norc.uchicago.edu/online/tiaa-fin.pdf>.

As you were inspired by the excellent teachers whom you encountered, so you, too, will encourage and stimulate students to become future educators. You probably won't get a gaggle of students waiting for you after the final exam, bubbling and gushing eager adorations. Don't be disappointed; you can't really expect that. You may, however, find that a student or two have penned petite little notes, "Thanks, Dr. Miller—I really enjoyed this course!" on the bottom of their exams or course evaluation forms. Maybe a former student will stop by someday and want to chat. Or perhaps a student might bake you some cookies or send a small gift over when your new son is born. Teachers often don't get a lot more dramatic evidence than that of a job well done. Students seldom go out of their way to show appreciation to their instructors. But at some point in your career, you'll develop a quiet confidence that you *are* a good teacher, despite the fact that students don't push and shove to get into your classes; eventually, you'll come to terms with your shortcomings as well.

To paraphrase the British educator and Greek scholar Benjamin Jowett, to teach someone how to learn to think independently is perhaps the greatest service that one can ever do for another. Excellent teachers have always been and will always be needed by society. If you have a particular craving to teach, then you will likely have a very rich and interesting life. Congratulations on having made the right vocational decision!

References and Resources

Fisch, L. (1996). *The chalk dust collection: Thoughts and reflections on teaching in colleges and universities*. Stillwater, OK: New Forums Press.

Palmer, P. J. (1998). *The courage to teach: Exploring the inner landscape of a teacher's life*. San Francisco: Jossey-Bass.

Sawyer, R. M., Prichard, K. W., & Hostetler, K. D. (1992). *The art and politics of college teaching*. New York: Peter Lang.

Index